Recent Advances in Neo-Schumpeterian Economics

Recent Advances in Neo-Schumpeterian Economics

Essays in Honour of Horst Hanusch

Edited by

Andreas Pyka

Professor of Economics, University of Hohenheim, Germany

Uwe Cantner

Professor of Economics, Friedrich Schiller University of Jena, Germany

Alfred Greiner

Professor of Economics, Bielefeld University, Germany

Thomas Kuhn

Professor of Economics, Chemnitz University of Technology, Germany

Edward Elgar

Cheltenham, UK • Northampton, MA, USA

Published by
Edward Elgar Publishing Limited
The Lypiatts
15 Lansdown Road
Cheltenham
Glos GL50 2JA
UK

Edward Elgar Publishing, Inc.
William Pratt House
9 Dewey Court
Northampton
Massachusetts 01060
USA

A catalogue record for this book is available from the British Library

Library of Congress Control Number: 2009922758

Mixed Sources
Product group from well-managed
forests and other controlled sources
www.fsc.org Cert no. SA-COC-1565
© 1996 Forest Stewardship Council
FSC

ISBN 978 1 84720 663 3

Printed and bound by MPG Books Group, UK

Contents

PART III   THE PUBLIC SECTOR AND THE FUTURE
OF THE WELFARE STATE

Contributors

Alain Alcouffe, Professor, LIRHE, University of Toulouse 1, France

Christiane Alcouffe, Professor Emeritus LIRHE, University of Toulouse 1, France

Uwe Cantner, Professor of Economics, Friedrich Schiller University of Jena, Germany

Giovanni Dosi, Sant' Anna School of Advanced Studies, Pisa, Italy

Burkhard Drees, IMF Institute, International Monetary Fund, Washington, DC, USA

Bernhard Eckwert, Department of Economics, Bielefeld University, Germany

Peter Flaschel, Centre for Empirical Macroeconomics, Bielefeld University, Germany

Marco Grazzi, Sant'Anna School of Advanced Studies, Pisa, Italy

Alfred Greiner, Professor of Economics, Bielefeld University, Germany

Arnold Heertje, Professor Emeritus, University of Amsterdam, the Netherlands

Friedrich Kugler, Fachhochschule Schmalkalden, Germany

Thomas Kuhn, Professor of Economics, Chemnitz University of Technology, Germany

Stanley Metcalfe, Stanley Jevons Professor of Political Economy, Cobden Lecturer and Co-Director, ESRC Centre for Research on Innovation and Competition (CRIC), University of Manchester, UK

Michael Pickhardt, Institut für Finanzwissenschaft, University of Münster, Germany

Andreas Pyka, Professor of Economics, University of Hohenheim, Germany

Andreas Röthig, Institute of Economics, Darmstadt University of Technology and Centre for Empirical Macroeconomics, Bielefeld University, Germany

Pier Paolo Saviotti, UMR GAEL, Université Pierre Mendès France, Grenoble and CNRS GREDEG, Sophia Antipolis, France

Norbert Schütt, Bielefeld University, Germany

Willi Semmler, New School University, New York and Centre for Empirical Macroeconomics, Bielefeld University, Germany

Introduction

Uwe Cantner, Alfred Greiner, Thomas Kuhn and Andreas Pyka

This Festschrift attempts to cover the scientific work that Horst Hanusch has been accomplishing during the past 40 years or so. Looking at his publication record, one can easily identify several periods of research interest, starting with public finance in the 1970s, then branching out into neo-Schumpeterian and evolutionary economics from the second half of the 1980s on, and finally diversifying into financial markets starting in the mid-1990s. Only recently have these various research interests merged into the so-called comprehensive neo-Schumpeterian approach (CNSA) built on just three pillars: the industrial sector, the state, and the financial sphere. In the following we want to track briefly the research path taken by Horst Hanusch, leading finally to the CNSA.

THE RESEARCH PATH TAKEN

Public Finance and Public Economics

Horst Hanusch's work in public finance started when he was a university assistant under Horst-Claus Recktenwald at the University of Nuremberg in the 1970s. His primary interests were in the theory of public goods (Hanusch, 1972) and studies on tax incidence (Hanusch, 1976). When he was a professor at the University of Augsburg his research focus shifted towards productivity and efficiency in the state sector (Hanusch, 1982, 1983, 1984). The work that followed included that with Karl-Heinz Weiss on tax policy in rationing frameworks (Hanusch and Weiss, 1988), with Gerhard Rauscher on communal policy issues (Hanusch and Rauscher, 1981), with Klaus-Norbert Münch on unemployment compensation and distribution (Hanusch and Münch, 1982), with Peter Biene on voting behaviour (Hanusch and Biene, 1985), with Manfred Schlumberger on cost–benefit analysis (Hanusch and Schlumberger, 1989), with Günther Jänsch (Hanusch and Jänsch, 1988) and Uwe Cantner on efficiency in the public sector (Hanusch and Cantner, 1991; Cantner et al., 1995), with Alfred Greiner on tax policy in a framework of endogenous growth (Greiner and Hanusch, 1998), and with Thomas Kuhn on tax revenue equalization at the regional level (Hanusch and Kuhn, 1985, 1991), on environmental issues, and on cost–benefit analysis (Hanusch, 1994). The research results achieved finally received international attention, leading to Horst Hanusch's presidency of the International Institute of Public Finance (IIPF) from 1994 to 1997. He then was responsible for outstanding international IIPF conferences: 'The Changing Role of the Public Sector: Transitions in the 1990s' (Lisbon, 1995), 'Globalization of Economic and Financial Activities' (Tel Aviv, 1996) and 'Public Investment and Public Finance' (Kyoto, 1997).

Neo-Schumpeterian and Evolutionary Economics

The branching out into neo-Schumpeterian and evolutionary economics was fuelled by Hanusch's friendship with Wolfgang Stolper, one of Schumpeter's close disciples. During the early 1980s both discussed the possibility of an international society devoted to Schumpeterian economics. This was a time when a wide range of economists started to take note once more of Joseph Alois Schumpeter, who had been more or less forgotten for around three decades. The situation in the early 1980s was characterized by abundant scientific opportunities for Schumpeterian and later neo-Schumpeterian economics. Both approaches were considered extremely broad, in a period when traditional economic approaches were increasingly criticized for addressing issues seen as of minor relevance to the economic problems arising after the difficult decade of the 1970s, affected by two oil crises. The economic mainstream concentrated on analysing market-based allocations, as well as the prerequisites for the working of the price mechanism, and on short-run effects and market efficiency. In contrast, the modern Schumpeterian approach took the long-run perspective by focusing on the drivers of change. Leaving behind the tight corset of mechanical equilibrium-oriented analysis, homogeneous actors and technologies, as well as perfect rationality, this approach opened up possibilities for analysing innovation processes as collective learning processes, including volatile growth and uneven development paths accompanied by structural changes.

In this period, the combined initiatives of Wolfgang Stolper and Horst Hanusch finally led to the foundation of the International Joseph A. Schumpeter Society (ISS) in Augsburg, Germany in September 1986. The Society's statutes were signed by Mark Perlman, Horst-Claus Recktenwald, Michio Morishima, Ernst Helmstädter, Wolfgang Stolper and Horst

Hanusch. The Society developed quite quickly, not least because Horst Hanusch was very successful at institutionalizing a world congress of the Society in alternate years. Scholars of high repute served as ISS president, starting with Wolfgang Stolper, followed by Arnold Heertje (Siena, 1988), F.M. Scherer (Airliehouse, VA, 1990), Yuichi Shionoya (Kyoto, 1992), Ernst Helmstädter (Münster, 1994), Gunnar Eliasson (Stockholm, 1996), Dennis Mueller (Vienna, 1998), Stan Metcalfe (Manchester, 2000), Robert Lanzilotti (Gainesville, FL, 2002), Franco Malerba (Milan, 2004), Jean-Luc Gaffard (Nice, 2006), and recently Maria Fonseca Derengowski (Rio de Janiero, 2008).

With the foundation of the ISS, Horst Hanusch and his collaborators set up research projects devoted to innovation and evolutionary dynamics: Markus Hierl with work on the relationship between innovation on the one hand and productivity and profitability on the other (Hanusch and Hierl, 1992), Alfred Greiner with models on the dynamics of the Schumpeterian firm (Hanusch and Greiner, 1993), Georg Westermann on an empirical approach towards localized technological change (Cantner et al., 1998b), Christian Boucke with work on innovation systems (Boucke et al., 1994), Jens Krüger with work on international growth and productivity development (Krüger et al., 2000), and Uwe Cantner with methodological considerations on heterogeneity and evolutionary change (Cantner and Hanusch, 2001), formal and empirical approaches to localized technological change, innovation and international trade (Cantner and Hanusch, 1990), international productivity dynamics (Cantner et al., 2003), innovation systems and technology flow analysis (Cantner and Hanusch, 1999), Schumpeterian growth policy (Hanusch and Cantner, 1997), innovation strategies (Cantner et al., 1998), and industry dynamics and industry evolution (Cantner and Hanusch, 1998a). These made up the research agenda until about 2000. After that another generation of collaborators took over: Markus Balzat on national innovation systems (Balzat and Hanusch, 2004), Thomas Grebel on entrepreneurship (Grebel et al., 2003), Michael Menhart on industry dynamics in service industries (Menhart et al., 2004), Bernd Ebersberger on energy issues (Pyka et al., 2004), and Andreas Pyka on innovation strategies (Cantner et al., 2000), entrepreneurship, energy and environmental issues, and industry dynamics and evolution. Currently a third generation of innovation-interested collaborators is working under Horst Hanusch. The research interests of Nicole Bieber, Torben Karl, Florian Wackermann and Gerhard Ilg continue the projects started earlier and are devoted to high technology and the financial sector, knowledge diffusion, efficiency and productivity, and co-evolutionary processes.

Of additional importance to research in Schumpeterian and evolutionary economics has been the founding of the *Journal of Evolutionary*

Economics in 1991. Together with Mark Perlman, already the founder of the *Journal of Economic Literature*, Horst Hanusch set up an international forum for research in evolutionary economics which is ranked in the top two in the field of innovation and evolutionary economics, and among the top 80 in economics in general. The journal has, over time, been edited by Steven Klepper, Elias Dinopoulos, Luigi Orsenigo and Uwe Cantner.

Financial Markets

In the mid-1990s, probably triggered by tremendous problems in the national and international financial markets, Horst Hanusch felt that financial markets also needed a non-neoclassical theoretical foundation, probably an evolutionary and/or a Schumpeterian one. The resulting line of research has been accomplished with Friedrich Kugler on a quartic modal approach as an alternative to rational expectations (Hanusch and Kugler, 1995), with Jörg Sommer applying neural networks to analyse the formation of expectations (Kugler et al., 1996), and with Ester Merey and Thomas Grebel (Grebel et al., 2004) on Schumpeterian dynamics and financial market anomalies.

The Comprehensive Neo-Schumpeterian Approach

At around the millennium Horst Hanusch started thinking about combining various fields of research interest into one approach. Inspired by the principal idea of national innovation systems as being more comprehensive, but searching for a more individualistic and agent-based approach, he suggested not only looking at industry dynamics driven mainly by innovation but, in order to understand the long-run development of economies, also the public sector and the financial sphere. The new approach has been labelled the comprehensive neo-Schumpeterian approach and comprises the research fields that have been central to the work of Horst Hanusch. To accomplish this task, an analytical broad basis and the ability to combine the various aspects in a logical way are required. Work with Andreas Pyka paved the way. First there is the *Elgar Companion to Neo-Schumpeterian Economics*, edited by Horst Hanusch and Andreas Pyka (Hanusch and Pyka, 2007a). This volume shows that modern Schumpeterian economics has reached a certain maturity in the analysis of industrial innovation processes and their impact on economic growth and development. Other work, such as *Technical Change and Economic Theory* (Dosi et al., 1988), *Evolutionary Economics and Creative Destruction* (Metcalfe, 1998) or the *Oxford Handbook of Innovation* (Nelson et al., 2005), clearly evidence the tremendous advances made in neo-Schumpeterian, innovation and evolutionary economics.

Such progress has not been without influence on the policy side. Within the last 25 years policy actors have increasingly acknowledged the achievements of modern Schumpeterian approaches. Starting with recommendations of the OECD in the early 1990s to its member countries to foster innovation and promote the prerequisites for technical change, more and more countries started to apply Schumpeterian designs to their innovation and growth policies. This development has peaked most prominently in the passage of the Lisbon Agenda by the EU Heads of States and Governments in the year 2000 with the ambitious Schumpeterian aim 'to make Europe the most competitive and dynamic knowledge-driven economy by 2010'.

However, despite these successes, one may wonder what an innovation- and future-oriented economic theory can say about the role of the state as well as of financial markets. These important domains have not been addressed in detail by neo-Schumpeterian, innovation and evolutionary economics during the last 25 years. Consequently one has to confess that modern Schumpeterian economics is still far from offering an overarching economic theory, as is done by the orthodox neoclassical approaches.

In order to close this gap, Horst Hanusch and Andreas Pyka (2007b, 2007c) introduced an outline for developing a broad theoretical approach under the heading of comprehensive neo-Schumpeterian economics (CNSE). The general idea is that innovation and strong uncertainty are the common denominators of a Schumpeterian economic theory covering the future orientation of industry, of the public domain and of financial markets – the three pillars in the CNSE approach. Deficiencies in the future orientation of a single pillar might hamper the development of an economic system or even lead to a breakdown of economic growth.

THE STRUCTURE OF THIS VOLUME

The contributions in this Festschrift for Professor Hanusch aim to indicate how one may be able to bring together approaches analysing the future orientation of the various economic realms, especially the three pillars of CNSE. The book is organized in three parts: Part I, Industry and Innovation; Part II, Finance in Modern Economics; and Part III, The Public Sector and the Future of the Welfare State.

Uwe Cantner, in his contribution 'Competition and innovation', tackles a question that is at the heart of modern Schumpeterian reasoning on innovation, namely the relationship between economic and innovative performance of firms. The explicit consideration of intra-industry heterogeneity in his replicator dynamics leads to meso-level dynamics in the area of conflict between turbulence and change, as well as persistence and regularities. The contribution of Giovanni Dosi and Marco Grazzi lies between the industry and the public pillar. The authors address the issue of technological developments in the energy sector, driven by new knowledge as well as increasing environmental bottlenecks. In order to cope with the fundamental challenges for human life on earth, the authors revitalize the concept of mission-oriented policy design (Ergas, 1992; Cantner and Pyka, 2001) and transfer it to an international level: the solution to the climatic catastrophe can be found in major technological breakthroughs that integrate a broad set of different knowledge fields and overburden the financial possibilities of single economies. In his chapter, 'Marshall and Schumpeter: evolution and the institutions of capitalism', Stanley Metcalfe outlines the rich contribution of Schumpeter concerning capitalism as an engine of progress by connecting Schumpeter's theory to the approach of Alfred Marshall. He shows the important complementarities and the synergies that can be gained for the understanding of innovation-driven economic development by the intellectual amalgamation of these two great thinkers.

The second part of the book, focusing on the financial pillar of CNSE starts with a contribution by Pier Paolo Saviotti and Andreas Pyka entitled 'The co-evolution of technologies and financial institutions'. The authors stress the subtle relationship between innovation-driven qualitative economic development and the availability of finance necessary for the implementation of innovations. The interactions between the real and monetary realms turn out to be on a fine line between prosperous development and chaotic stagnation. The contribution by Burkhard Drees and Bernhard Eckwert, 'The role of information and risk sharing for R&D investment, technological change and economic welfare', tackles a related topic – the role of risk sharing in financial sectors in shaping technological development. What is the causality between the financial sector and technological development? Is the financial structure determined by technological developments or vice versa? Within their general-equilibrium framework approach the authors work out the co-evolutionary relationships between the two domains in an economy. Friedrich Kugler, in his contribution 'Bubbles, crashes and the psycho-economic forces behind them' has in mind the pathological case of speculative exaggeration and collapse. Due to strong non-linearities between individual decision making and complex market processes, speculative bubbles on markets for financial assets can drag down the whole economic development for a while. The last contribution to Part II, by Andreas Röthig, Willi Semmler and Peter Flaschel, entitled 'Corporate currency hedging and currency crises', extends the challenging economic analysis of the relationship between the real and monetary realms by including the currency markets. As a strategy to improve protection against financial crisis stemming from turbulence on currency markets, the authors suggest improving hedging instruments and lowering hedging costs basically by increasing transparency and improving information flows on international financial markets.

Part III of the book, 'The Public Sector and the Future of the Welfare State', is devoted to the future orientation of the public pillar in CNSE. Alfred Greiner and Norbert Schütt focus on the impact of increasing public debt on the future state of economies. They show that a transitorily increasing public debt to GDP ratio can be compatible with sustainability of public finance. However, they also outline the severe limitations to this, as an upper bound for the primary surplus–GDP ratio exists beyond which the surplus cannot be increased further; instead the debt ratio in this situation must become constant or even decline sooner or later. The chapter by Thomas Kuhn and Michael Pickhardt, 'Biofuels, innovations and endogenous growth', deals with the prominent role of biofuels for sustainable growth and lies like the contribution of Dosi and Grazzi, to the edge of the CNSE approach between the public and private pillars. A conventional Romer-type endogenous growth model is extended by incorporating a non-renewable and a renewable resource sector which can both serve to produce transport fuels. In addition, transport fuel produced from the renewable resource is taken to cause less environmental damage than fuel produced from non-renewable fossil resources. Innovations that enhance the energy efficiency of transport are necessary to move along the optimal growth path of the economy. Moreover, it can be shown that the growing stock of knowledge must be accompanied by an ongoing process of factor substitution in the production of transport commodities where biofuels must replace fossil fuels over time. In the given framework, this is the only means to ensure sustainability of growth in terms of non-degrading environmental quality.

The last two chapters in Part III clearly have policy objectives in mind. Arnold Heertje discusses 'Paretian welfare theory and European competition policy' from a theoretical angle. Without doubt the need of a welfare-oriented theoretical approach within the CNSE approach cannot be neglected. Alain Alcouffe and Christiane Alcouffe, in their contribution on 'French industrial policy', have chosen a pragmatic perspective and give a detailed overview on the changing prerequisites and designs of French policy. This also sheds light on the important co-evolutionary relationships between the political, industrial and financial domains in France.

In summary, all contributions to this Festschrift show the high stage of development of dynamic Schumpeterian research methodologies for the three pillars of CNSE. Although one has to state that within each pillar modern Schumpeterian economic reasoning has left its infancy and now offers important insights, one also has to share Hanusch's mission: there is still a long way to go to connect the seemingly unrelated sub-disciplines and connect them to a comprehensive alternative approach in economic theory. This Festschrift is devoted to Horst Hanusch's part in this endeavour, characterized by work already done in the 1970s and developing over the last 40 years, and it offers a first step in this direction.

REFERENCES

Balzat, M. and H. Hanusch (2004), 'Recent trends in the research on national innovation systems', *Journal of Evolutionary Economics*, **14** (2), 197–210.
Boucke, C., U. Cantner and H. Hanusch (1994), 'Technopolises as a policy goal: a morphological study of the Wissenschaftsstadt Ulm', *Technovation*, **14** (6), 407–18.
Canter, U. and H. Hanusch (1990), 'Internationale Wettbewerbsfähigkeit und technischer Fortschritt', *Jahrbuch für neue politische Ökonomie*, **1990**, 71–90.
Cantner, U. and H. Hanusch (1998), 'Industrie-Evolution', in U. Schweitzer and G. Silverberg (eds), *Selbstorganisation*, Jahrb. Bd 9, *Evolution und Selbstorganisation in der Ökonomie*, Berlin: Duncker & Humblot, pp. 265–93.
Cantner, U. and H. Hanusch (1999), 'Technologiestromanalyse', in A. Maußner and K.G. Binder (eds), *Ökonomie und Ökologie*, Berlin: Duncker & Humblot, pp. 15–42.
Cantner, U. and H. Hanusch (2001), 'Heterogeneity and evolutionary change – empirical conception, findings and unresolved issues', in J. Foster and J.S. Metcalfe (eds), *Frontiers of Evolutionary Economics: Competition, Self-Organization and Innovation Policy*, Cheltenham, UK and Northampton, MA: Edward Elgar, pp. 228–69.
Cantner, U. and A. Pyka (2001), 'Classifying technology policy from an evolutionary perspective', *Research Policy*, **30**, 759–75.
Cantner, U., H. Hanusch and A. Pyka (1998a), 'Routinized innovations: dynamic capabilities in a simulation study', in G. Eliasson, C. Green and C. McCann (eds), *Microfoundations of Economic Growth: A Schumpeterian Perspective*, Ann Arbor, MI: University of Michigan Press, pp. 131–55.
Cantner, U., H. Hanusch and A. Pyka (2000), 'Horizontal heterogeneity, technological progress and sectoral development', in U. Cantner, H. Hanusch and S. Klepper (eds), *Economic Evolution, Learning, and Complexity*, Heidelberg: Physica (Springer), pp. 73–96.
Cantner, U., H. Hanusch and G. Westermann (1995), 'Effizienz, öffentlicher Auftrag und Deregulierung. Die Berücksichtigung nicht-marktfähiger Outputs mit Hilfe der DEA', in *Jahrbücher für Nationalökonomie und Statistik*, **214** (3), pp. 257–74.
Cantner, U., H. Hanusch and G. Westermann (1998b), 'Technological performance and variety – the case of the German electronics industry', in K. Nielsen and B. Johnson (eds), *Institutions and Economic Change. New Perspectives on Markets, Firms and Technology*, Cheltenham, UK and Northampton, MA, USA: Edward Elgar Publishing, pp. 109–30.
Cantner, U., J. Krüger and H. Hanusch (2003), 'Explaining International Productivity Differences', (Erklärung internationaler Produktivitätsunterschiede), in *Jahrbücher für Nationalökonomie und Statistik*, **223** (6), 659–79.

Dosi, G., C. Freeman, R.R. Nelson, G. Silverberg and L. Soete (eds) (1988), *Technical Change and Economic Theory*, London: Pinter Publishers.

Ergas, H. (1992), 'A future for mission-oriented industrial policies? A critical review of developments in Europe', OECD Working Paper, Paris.

Grebel, T, A. Pyka and H. Hanusch (2003), 'An evolutionary approach to the theory of the entrepreneur', *Industry and Innovation*, **10**, 493–514.

Grebel, T., H. Hanusch and E. Merey (2004), 'Schumpeterian dynamics and financial market anomalies', Institut für Volkswirtschaftslehre der Universität Augsburg, Volkswirtschaftliche Diskussionsreihe, No. 264, May.

Greiner, A. and H. Hanusch (1998), 'Growth and welfare effects of fiscal policy in an endogenous growth model with public investment', *International Tax and Public Finance*, **5**, 249–61.

Hanusch, H. (1972), *Theorie des öffentlichen Gutes: allokative und distributive Aspekte*, Göttingen: Vandenhoeck & Rupprecht.

Hanusch, H. (1976), *Verteilung öffentlichen Leistungen: eine Studie zur personalen Inzidenz*, Göttingen: Vandenhoeck & Rupprecht.

Hanusch, H. (1982), 'Determinants of public productivity, in R. Haveman (ed.), *Public Finance and Public Employment: Proceedings of the 36th Congress of the International Institute of Public Finance, Jerusalem 1980*, Detroit, MI: Wayne State University Press, pp. 275–88.

Hanusch, H. (1983), 'Inefficiencies in the public sector: aspects of demand and supply', in H. Hanusch (ed.), *Anatomy of Government Deficiencies*, Berlin–Heidelberg: Springer, pp. 1–14.

Hanusch, H. (1984), 'Public finance and the quest for efficiency', in H. Hanusch (ed.), *Public Finance and the Quest for Efficiency. Proceedings of the 38th Congress of the International Institute of Public Finance, Copenhagen, 1982*, Detroit, MI: Wayne State University Press, pp. 1–9.

Hanusch, H. (1994), unter Mitarbeit von T. Kuhn and U. Cantner, 'Nutzen-Kosten-Analyse, 2.', überarb. Aufl. Verlag F. Vahlen, München.

Hanusch, H. and P. Biene (1985), 'Distributive and allocative effects of individual voting behaviour', in R. Pethig (ed.), *Public Goods and Public Allocation Policy*, Staatliche Allokations-politik im Marktwirtschaftlichen System, Bd 14, Frankfurt am Main: Peter Lang, pp. 117–40.

Hanusch, H. and U. Cantner (1991), 'Produktion öffentlicher Leistungen: Effizienz und Technischer Fortschritt', *Jahrbuch für Nationalökonomie und Statistik*, **208** (4), 369–84.

Hanusch, H. and U. Cantner (1997), 'Ansätze zu einer Schumpeterianischen Wachstumspolitik', in *Fortschritte in Theorie, Empirie, Politik? Wissenschaftliches Symposium anlässl. d. 65. Geburtstages von Prof. Karl Heinrich Oppenländer*, ifo-Studien, 43. Jg. 2, pp. 287–308.

Hanusch, H. and A. Greiner (1993), 'A dynamic model of the firm including Keynesian and Schumpeterian elements', *Journal of Institutional and Theoretical Economics*, **149** (3), 516–30.

Hanusch, H. and M. Hierl (1992), 'Productivity, profitability and innovative behaviour in West German industries, in F.M. Scherer and M. Perlman (eds), *Entrepreneurship, Technological Innovation, and Economic Growth* (Schumpeter Conference Proceedings, Airlie House, 1990), Ann Arbor, MI: Michigan University Press, pp. 237–50.

Hanusch, H. and G. Jänsch (1988), 'Produktivität im Öffentlichen Sektor, Endbericht zu einem von der DFG geförderten Forschungsprojekt', Augsburg.

Hanusch, H. and F. Kugler (1995), 'Subjektive Kurserwartungsbildung auf Aktienmärkten. Rationaler Erwartungsansatz versus Ansatz der Quartischen-Modalwert-Erwartungen', *Jahrbücher für Nationalökonomie und Statistik*, **214** (2), 195–208.
Hanusch, H. and T. Kuhn (1985), 'Messung des kommunalen Finanzbedarfs. Ein alternativer Ansatz für die Schlüsselzuweisungen', in Akademie für Raumforschung und Landesplanung (ed.), *Räumliche Aspekte des Finanzausgleichs*, FuS 159, Hannover, pp. 55–74.
Hanusch, H. and T. Kuhn (1991), 'Vertical and horizontal equity and the grants to communities in the FRG', in R. Prud'homme (ed.), *Public Finance with Several Levels of Government: Proceedings of the 46th Congress of the IIPF Brussels 1990*, The Hague: Foundation Journal Public Finance, pp. 211–22.
Hanusch, H. and K.-N. Münch (1982), 'Arbeitslosenunterstützung: Ungewollte Überzahlungen und Verteilungswirkungen', in Ph. Herder-Dorneich (ed.), *Arbeitsmarkt und Arbeitsmarktpolitik, Schriften des Vereins für Socialpolitik, N.F.*, Bd. 127, Berlin, pp. 29–59.
Hanusch, H. and A. Pyka (eds) (2007a), *The Elgar Companion to Neo-Schumpeterian Economics*, Cheltenham, UK and Northampton, MA, USA: Edward Elgar.
Hanusch, H. and A. Pyka (2007b), 'Manifesto for comprehensive neo-Schumpeterian economics', *History of Economic Ideas*, **15**, 11–29.
Hanusch, H. and A. Pyka (2007c), 'The principles of neo-Schumpeterian economics', *Cambridge Journal of Economics*, **31** (2), 275–89.
Hanusch, H. and G. Rauscher (1981), 'Kommunale Wirtschafts- und Sozialpolitik', in W. Albers et al. (eds), *Handwörterbuch der Wirtschaftswissenschaften*, Bd 3, Stuttgart etc., pp. 495–508.
Hanusch, H. and M. Schlumberger (1989), 'Nutzen-Kosten-Analysen', in P. Eichhorn and K. Chmielewicz (eds), *Handwörterbuch der Öffentlichen Betriebswirtschaft*, Stuttgart: C.E. Poeschel, pp. 993–1002.
Hanusch, H. and K.-H. Weiss (1988), 'Tax reform in a revised Keynesian framework', *Atlantic Economic Journal*, 16 (1), 72.
Krüger J., U. Cantner and H. Hanusch (2000), 'Total factor productivity, the East Asian miracle and the world production frontier', *Weltwirtschaftliches Archiv*, **136** (1), 111–36.
Kugler, F., H. Sommer and H. Hanusch (1996), 'Captital markets from an evolutionary perspective: the state preference model reconsidered', Institut für Volkswirtschaftslehre der Universität Augsburg, Volkswirtschaftliche Diskussionsreihe, No. 155.
Menhart, M., A. Pyka, B. Ebersberger and H. Hanusch (2004), 'Product innovation and population dynamics in the German insurance market', *Zeitschrift für die gesamte Versicherungswirtschaft*, **3**, 478–519.
Metcalfe, S.J. (1998), *Evolutionary Economics and Creative Destruction*, London: Routledge.
Nelson, R.R., D. Mowery and J. Fagerberg (eds) (2005), *The Oxford Handbook of Innovation*, Oxford: Oxford University Press.
Pyka, A., B. Ebersberger and H. Hanusch (2004), 'A conceptual framework to model long-run qualitative change in the energy system', in J.S. Metcalfe and J. Foster (eds) *Evolution and Economic Complexity*, Cheltenham, UK and Northampton, MA, USA: Edward Elgar, pp. 191–213.

PART I

Industry and Innovation

1. Competition in innovation

Uwe Cantner

December 5, 1985, 11 am, University of Augsburg, Memmingerstrasse 14, 5th floor

> *P(rofessor):* Organizing our conference next year, we need to have a list of economists related to the research field of Joseph Alois Schumpeter!
>
> *S(tudent):* Schumpeter? Never heard of him!
>
> *P:* Never heard of him? He was one of the most interesting economists ever.
>
> *S:* Never heard about him in my classes – not even in my classes on the history of economic thought.
>
> *P:* Innovation as the major force in market competition and economic dynamics, that's the topic Schumpeter pushed – a field with high potential for further research. Schumpeter's era is to come – you'll see.

(Professor: Horst Hanusch; Student: Uwe Cantner)

1. INTRODUCTION

Joseph Alois Schumpeter made prominent the notion of competition in innovation by highlighting the fact that entrepreneurs introduce new combinations into the economic system (Schumpeter, 1912) and thereby destroy old structures. The notion of 'creative destruction' (Schumpeter, 1942) quite nicely describes this relationship of competition between the new and the old. With this approach in mind, market competition can be seen as a mechanism that drives this competition. Thus markets can be interpreted as a mechanism that continuously evaluates different, competing solutions to a problem (new products, new ways of production and consumption etc.) and this comparative evaluation leads to differential rewards (in the sense of profits, market shares etc.). Thus, if the market process works sufficiently well, firms with above-average performance levels (high productivity growth rates) are expected to grow, firms with below-average performance levels (low productivity growth rates) are expected to shrink and better-performing firms will replace less well-performing exiting firms. Schumpeter describes this as the process of creative destruction (Schumpeter, 1942).

This relationship between innovations, their market success and the

13

resulting structural development is at the core of an evolutionary interpretation of economic development as introduced by Schumpeter and
as developed during the last nearly six decades. Those endeavours also
comprise formal modelling, initiated prominently in the work of Nelson
and Winter in the 1970s and 1980s, which applies the concept of replicator dynamics, a concept that has been present in the literature of mathematical biology since the work of Fisher (1930). This dynamics applies a
formal approach for understanding in the easiest way how the relationship
between differential performances of actors (maybe due to their differential abilities to apply or generate different technologies) translates into
differential market success – even possibly leading to market exit. This
approach can be enhanced quite readily by an endogenous dynamics for
innovative success, leading to the rather simple model relating innovative
success and market selection. This kind of modelling has been very prominent in various simulation models of an evolutionary type. These aspects
are also present in the more recent evolutionary models of Metcalfe (1994,
1998) and Winter et al. (2000, 2003).

Besides these formal approaches, empirical analyses focus on the
question of whether this market selection operates in the way suggested
by theory. Such an endeavour has been shown to be rather difficult, and
a direct test through regression analysis has not as yet led to a confirma-
tion of replicator dynamics. As an exception, the paper by Metcalfe and
Calderini (1998) must be mentioned, where the parameter β is tested for
constancy over time and thus for the constancy of the selection to work.
The literature on industry life cycles quite nicely shows how market
exit of firms can be related to a relatively weak technological or innovative performance (Klepper and Simmons, 2005). It also shows, for
firms entering a market, that a subsequent high probability to survive
is higher, the more innovative an entrant (Cantner et al., 2005, 2006,
2009).

In addition to this literature, empirical work developed exploring the
patterns of plant entry, growth and exit in four-digit US manufacturing
industries (see Dunne et al., 1988, 1989) and also among UK manufacturing establishments (Disney et al., 2003a). Other work, such as Nickell
(1996) and Nickell et al. (1997), concentrates on the generation of firm-
level evidence on the positive relation of product market competition and
total factor productivity growth. These results are thoroughly surveyed by
Caves (1998) and by Bartelsman and Doms (2000), with special focus on
the relation to productivity. For the investigation of the relation of market
turbulence and technological (i.e. productivity) change, decompositions
of productivity measures into several components that shed light on the
sources of aggregate productivity change at the micro-level and therefore

provide an explanation for aggregate productivity change have been developed. These decomposition formulae allow in particular for the separation of the contributions of structural change and firm entry and exit to aggregate productivity development from the contribution of within-firm productivity growth. Those decomposition formulae have been proposed by Baily et al. (1992, 1996) and Foster et al. (1998), together with applications to productivity change of US manufacturing establishments. Disney et al. (2003b) provide related results for the UK. A notable and to date unnoticed precursor for the development of productivity decompositions is Salter (1960).[1]

This chapter extends these analyses to Germany. The decomposition of productivity changes is here used to get an account of the working of the replicator dynamics mechanism. Changes in firms' market shares and the relation to their respective relative technological performance and their innovative performance are investigated, with productivity levels as a proxy for technological performance and productivity changes as a proxy for innovative performance.

The chapter proceeds as follows. The theoretical section (2) introduces replicator dynamics as a mechanism able to cope with the relationship between innovativeness, market selection and structural change. The empirically oriented section (3) attempts to investigate whether the mechanism of replicator dynamics – as discussed in section 2 – holds for selected industrial sectors in Germany between 1981 and 1998. Section 4 concludes.

2. THE RELATIONSHIP BETWEEN INNOVATIVENESS AND COMPETITION – A FORMAL EVOLUTIONARY APPROACH[2]

Within the evolutionary approach, the relationship between innovativeness and competition is a central one for the explanation of structure, structural development and structural change. In order to provide a formal analysis, we refer to the so-called 'replicator dynamics'. This principle goes back to Fisher (1930) and allows the formal representation of the Darwinian principle of 'survival of the fittest'. The dynamic competition among heterogeneous agents can be dealt with here.

In a number of models, replicator dynamics are applied to explain the dynamic development of certain sectors or whole economies. In general, the high complexity of these models does not enable analytical solutions, and therefore it is necessary to run simulation experiments (see, e.g., Kwasnicki and Kwasnicka, 1992; Kwasnicki, 1996; Saviotti and Mani,

1995). This holds especially when innovative activities are modelled as a search, and experimental behaviour (see, e.g., Nelson and Winter, 1982; Silverberg and Lehnert, 1994, 1996; Silverberg and Verspagen, 1994; Kwasnicki and Kwasnicka, 1992; Metcalfe, 1994, 1998; Winter et al., 2000, 2003) and stochastic effects are taken into account. In the following, we want to present the basic mechanisms within a quite simple deterministic model of an industry.

Replicator dynamics is formally given as follows: we consider N constant magnitudes or replicators, i, $i \in N$, the relative frequency of which (share within total population N), s_i, changes over time. This change is dependent on the fitness, f_i, with respect to the average weighted fitness, $\bar{f}$, of the whole population. Fitness in general is dependent on a vector $\mathbf{s}$, which contains the relative frequency of all replicators.[3] The respective dynamics is given by the following differential equation, where β is a parameter governing the speed of the selection dynamics:

$$\dot{s}_i = \beta \cdot s_i \cdot (f_i(\mathbf{s}) - \bar{f}(\mathbf{s})) , \qquad \bar{f}(\mathbf{s}) = \sum_N s_i \cdot f_i(\mathbf{s}) \qquad (1.1)$$

For the analysis of industry evolution, this dynamic is interpreted as follows: replicators i are considered as different firms within a sector which have a respective market share of s_i. Fitness, f_i, can be measured looking at the level of unit costs, productivity or some other measures (see, e.g., Metcalfe, 1994, 1998; Mazzucato and Semmler, 1998; Cantner, 2002). The replicator dynamics now states, for a constant fitness function f_i, that a firm i will increase (reduce) its market share whenever its fitness is above (below) the average weighted fitness within the sector. Then, by competitive selection, those firms with comparatively low fitness are driven out of the market. In the end, the firm with the highest fitness gains a monopoly position.[4]

At this point, it has to be stated that, in formulation (1.1), single firms have no impact on the selection dynamics, that is, the routine of producing with fitness f_i will not be changed.[5] At least for real actors with a selection disadvantage ($f_i < \bar{f}$), a reaction is to be expected.

Let us assume that the only kind of reaction to be expected is that firms attempt to innovate. How can this be introduced into this formal model? Our discussion of empirical studies has shown that there are different feedback effects from the economic to the technological–innovative sphere. Quite generally, this can be taken into account by a dependence of fitness f_i on economic success e_i and within the context of innovative activities by way of 'dynamic scale effects'. These imply that the 'change of fitness' depends on the success of the firm. In principle, the following formulation holds:

$$\dot{s}_i = \beta \cdot s_i \cdot (f_i(e_i) - \overline{f}), \qquad \overline{f} = \sum_N s_i \cdot f_i(e_i) \qquad (1.2)$$

$$\dot{f}_i = g(e_i)$$

Translating this into a sectoral model, it can be asked how the economic success of a firm might be represented there. In quite a simple formulation, it could be assumed that the market share, s_i, accounts for economic success. This market share can then represent economic as well as technological aspects relevant for further innovative success. With respect to the former, (relative) firm size is related to the ability of appropriating profits and of financing R&D projects. With respect to technological abilities and know-how, a large market share and, thus, a large firm size imply that know-how can be accumulated quite easily, and a broad range of technological possibilities and directions can be covered. This case implies a model formulated with 'positive dynamic scale effects' and oriented on the principle of 'success breeds success'. Then the formulation fits along the regime of 'Schumpeter II', where relatively large firms are innovatively more successful.

However, contrary to this, it could also be argued that small firms are more flexible and therefore more innovative. This flexibility refers to the fact that small firms do not have large R&D laboratories that can be directed only with high product costs; and in a technological context, large R&D laboratories apply very standardized routines in order to be innovative; these routines are not easily changeable. This problem should not be too difficult for small firms to solve. Therefore an interpretation according to the regime of 'Schumpeter I' seems appropriate here, and the model formulation contains 'negative dynamic scale effects' (see Malerba and Orsenigo, 1993, 1997).

Both alternatives are discussed in Mazzucato and Semmler (1998) and in Cantner (2002). For the competition among firms, and for the innovations that improve the production process and therefore imply higher fitness, the following model holds:

$$\dot{s}_i = \beta \cdot s_i \cdot (f_i - \overline{f}), \qquad \overline{f} = \sum_N s_i \cdot f_i. \qquad (1.3)$$

$$\dot{f}_i = v \cdot g(s_i)$$

The function $g(s_i)$ represents the relationship between technological improvement $\dot{f}_i$ and market success: as stated, we can distinguish positive and negative dynamic scale effects where the rate and not the direction of technological improvement is influenced; the latter will always be increased. We assume that there is an upper level of technological fitness

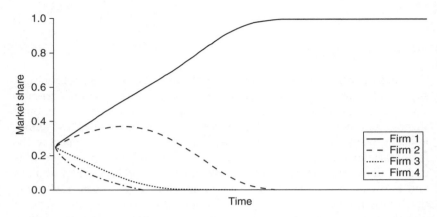

*Figure 1.1   Development of market shares with increasing dynamic returns
to scale*

(f_{max}) that cannot be exceeded, representing the maximum technological
opportunities that can be exploited. ν is a parameter that represents the
intensity of the economic feedback.

Analysing first the case of 'Schumpeter II', the process of 'success
breeds success' is modelled. Comparative selection as well as scale and
size-dependent innovative success lead to increasing economic and technological dominance of the technology leaders and, consequently, to
monopolization (see Mazzucato and Semmler, 1998; Cantner, 2002).
Simulations show this result, as is seen in the example of Figure 1.1, where
four technologically different firms 1–4 compete, where the ranking in
technological fitness in $t = 0$ is $f_1 > f_2 > f_3 > f_4$.

In period 0, all firms have an equal market share, $s_1 = s_2 = s_3 = s_4 = 0.25$.
The technological leader 1 then increases its market share s_1 due to a selective advantage and, based on this, on 'scale advantages'. The other firms
will, one after the other, be driven out of the market; firm 2 with the lowest
initial technological fitness first, then firm 3 and finally firm 4. Innovation
$\dot{f}_i$ and competition dynamics $\dot{s}_i$ act here in the same direction of monopo-
lizing the market.

Let us contrast this result with the constellation of 'Schumpeter I',
which is characterized by decreasing returns to scale in innovative activities. Consequently, driven by selection dynamics, the market share of
the firms with the lowest technological fitness will increase because the
innovation dynamics of firms with a small market share is quite intensive.
Thus competitive selection $\dot{s}_i$ and innovation dynamics $\dot{f}_i$ are counteract-
ing forces. There are many cases where one or the other force dominates,

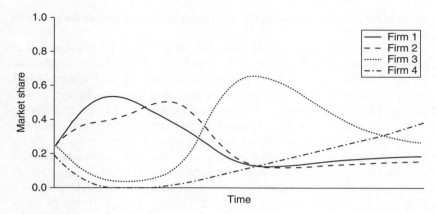

*Figure 1.2   Development of market shares with decreasing dynamic
returns to scale*

and a smooth development to coexistence[6] or monopoly[7] is observed. For
appropriate parameters, it can be shown that both forces are in a changing
balance and the development of market shares is characterized by turbulence. Figure 1.2 exemplifies this case again for the four firms.

In period 0, the technologically different firms again share the market
equally. Innovation and competitive selection dynamics start and the technological leader 1 gains market shares. However, as a result, its innovation
dynamics slows down and the backward firms 2–4 are able to catch up and
finally even to overtake firm 1. This applies to the technological level as
well as to the economic success measured in market shares. With reversed
signs, this process can be repeated over and over again.[8] By the degree,
however, to which technological opportunities become exploited (f_{max})
and further technological advances diminish, these turbulences will slow
down, the intensity of innovation $\dot{f_i}$ and selection dynamics $\dot{s_i}$ will decrease
and, finally, a technologically homogeneous structure, that is, identical
technological levels with different market shares, will come about.[9]

3.   INNOVATION COMPETITION AND
REPLICATOR DYNAMICS: AN EMPIRICAL
ANALYSIS USING THE DECOMPOSITION OF
PRODUCTIVITY CHANGE[10]

Having outlined the model of competition in innovation, we devote this
section to testing whether the mechanism described holds empirically. In

more general terms, a test of the mechanism of replicator dynamics is to be undertaken.

In this chapter, the following route is taken. First, it is assumed that technological fitness of a firm can be expressed by total factor productivity, a_i.[11] Second, we consider certain sectors and assume that firms assigned to this sector (with their main activity) compete in the same market. Third, we consider the development of total sector productivity of each sector over time and look, by decomposing the respective productivity changes, at the role of market competition and innovation for the productivity development of the sector. This implies, as we shall see, an investigation as to what degree replicator or selection dynamics holds.

Productivity change is here decomposed using the formula proposed in Foster et al. (1998), which is a modification of the formula of Baily et al. (1992) that also accounts for the contributions of entering and exiting firms. This formula is here preferred to the alternative decomposition formula of Griliches and Regev (1995), which is deemed to be more robust to measurement errors but is straightforward to interpret. Denote the share-weighted aggregate productivity levels of periods t and $t - k$ $(k > 0)$ by $\overline{a}_t^s = \Sigma_{i=1}^n s_{it} a_{it}$ and $\overline{a}_{t-k}^s = \Sigma_{i=1}^n s_{it-k} a_{it-k}$, respectively. Then the average change of share-weighted aggregate productivity can be denoted by $\Delta \overline{a}_t^s = \overline{a}_t^s - \overline{a}_{t-k}^s = \Sigma_{i \in C \cup N} s_{it} a_{it} - \Sigma_{i \in C \cup X} s_{it-k} a_{it-k}$, where C denotes the set of continuing firms, N denotes the set of entering firms and X denotes the set of exiting firms. Clearly, these sets are disjoint and $C \cup N \cup X = \{1,\ldots,n\}$, taking account of the fact that $s_{it-k} = 0$ (and $a_{it-k} = 0$) in the case of the entering, and $s_{it} = 0$ (and $a_{it} = 0$) in the case of the exiting, firms.

With this notation, the annual percentage average growth rate of the share-weighted aggregate productivity over the period t to $t - k$ can be written as $\frac{100}{k} \cdot \Delta \overline{a}_t^s / \overline{a}_{t-k}^s$. The part $\Delta \overline{a}_t^s$ of this expression can be decomposed into

$$\Delta \overline{a}_t^s = \sum_{i \in C} s_{it-k} \Delta a_{it} + \sum_{i \in C} \Delta s_{it}(a_{it-k} - \overline{a}_{t-k}^s) + \sum_{i \in C} \Delta s_{it} \Delta a_{it}$$

$$+ \sum_{i \in N} s_{it}(a_{it} - \overline{a}_{t-k}^s) - \sum_{i \in X} s_{it-k}(a_{it-k} - \overline{a}_{t-k}^s),$$

where Δa_{it} and Δs_{it} are understood to denote $a_{it} - a_{it-k}$ and $s_{it} - s_{it-k}$, respectively.

The interpretation of this formula is straightforward: for the continuing firms, the growth rate of share-weighted average industry productivity is expressed as the sum of the share-weighted productivity change within industries (the within component), the share cross-term which is positive if firms with above-average productivity increase their shares (the between component), and a covariance-type term which is positive if firms with increasing productivity tend to gain in terms of their shares (the covariance component). The latter two terms summarize the effect of the structural change on aggregate productivity growth among the continuing firms of the industry under consideration.

In the final two terms of the formula, the contributions of the entering and the exiting firms to aggregate productivity growth are stated. They are called the entry and exit components in the following. The contribution of an entering firm to aggregate productivity change is positive if it has a productivity level above the initial average, and the contribution of an exiting firm to aggregate productivity growth is positive if its productivity level is below the initial average. The entry and exit effects summarize these contributions, weighted by s_{it} in the case of the entry component and by s_{it-1} in the case of the exit component.

Particularly appealing from an evolutionary point of view is that the between component is positive if the share development follows a discrete-time version of the familiar replicator dynamics mechanism. In that case, above-average productivity levels in period $t - k$ tend to be associated with positive share growth between periods t and $t - k$ and below-average productivity levels tend to be associated with negative share growth. On the other hand, if below-average productivity firms tend to grow in terms of shares and above-average-productivity firms tend to shrink in terms of shares, the between component will be negative, thereby contradicting the replicator mechanism. Admittedly, in a heterogeneous sample of firms, this mechanism will be confirmed by a certain part of the sample and contradicted by another part of the sample, and positive and negative contributions may cancel out to some extent. Thus one has to bear in mind that a positive between-component may just be the result of an excess of firms with positive contributions over firms with negative contributions.

Similarly, a positive covariance component indicates that selection is faster than predicted by the replicator dynamics mechanism alone, while a negative covariance component is associated with a slower selection compared to the replicator dynamics mechanism. Both between and covariance components can be added, resulting in the combined component $\sum_{i \in C} \Delta s_{it}(a_{it} - \bar{a}_{t-k}^s)$, which is distinguished from the discrete-time replicator dynamics mechanism by the fact that the productivity levels of period t are compared with the average productivity level of period $t - k$.

Turning to the results in Table 1.1, the average percentage growth rate of the aggregate productivity levels during 1981–98, again with employment shares used as weighting factors, is reported, together with the five terms of the decomposition formula. It should be stressed that only in the long run do the components other than the within component show

Table 1.1   Foster–Haltiwanger–Krizan decomposition, 1981–98 (employment shares)

	Change	Within	Between	Cov.	Entry	Exit
Total sample	0.7428	0.2654	0.0563	0.2066	0.1731	−0.0413
Construction	−0.1469	−0.0712	0.0298	−0.1902	0.0961	0.0114
Food and beverages	0.1491	0.1195	−0.0344	0.1458	−0.0846	−0.0027
Textiles and apparel	0.9975	0.5734	0.1571	−0.1970	0.3290	−0.1349
Paper and printing	1.9066	0.3195	0.0649	−0.1263	1.7800	0.1314
Chemicals and petroleum	0.9614	0.0705	0.2525	0.1770	0.3967	−0.0646
Rubber and plastics	0.7528	0.5179	0.0099	0.3536	−0.0599	0.0688
Metal products	0.2751	0.2112	0.0621	−0.0165	0.0717	0.0534
Machinery and equipment	2.1975	0.5637	0.0790	0.9111	0.4631	−0.1805
Electronics	0.1253	−0.0322	0.2898	−0.1971	0.0190	−0.0458
Transportation equipment	1.1350	0.5667	0.3450	0.0331	0.2198	0.0296
Instruments	0.9027	0.3495	0.0428	0.2455	0.2981	0.0333

Note: Reports average percentage growth rate of the aggregate productivity levels in the column 'Change' and the terms of the decomposition formula in the subsequent columns, each divided by the initial share-weighted average productivity level and multiplied by 100/ (1998–81).

up with considerable magnitude, so that time spans of several years are necessary to achieve meaningful results. Note that each single term of the above-stated decomposition formula for $\Delta \bar{a}_t^s$ appears in the table as divided by $\bar{a}_{t-k}^s$ and multiplied by $100/k$.

First of all, the results show a positive aggregate productivity development for the total sample, as well as for most industries considered (the sole exception being construction). A certain part of this outcome can be attributed to productivity growth within the industries, as is evident from the positive within component. Concerning the effects of entry, we observe that entering firms are more productive than the average of the starting period, with the exception of food and rubber. Exiting firms tend to have below-average productivity levels in the total sample and in five individual industries, thus contributing positively to aggregate productivity growth. In the remaining six industries, exiting firms contribute negatively to aggregate productivity growth. Generally, net entry provides a positive contribution, except for rubber. Thus, on average, more productive entering firms replace less productive exiting firms.

Structural change takes place not only in the form of entry and exit of firms, but also within the group of continuing firms. This shows up in the between and covariance components that relate employment share changes either to the deviations from the average productivity level or to productivity changes. Assuming a positive relation of the number of employees of a firm to its size, these two effects reflect the intensity of competition within an industry driven by micro-heterogeneity in productivity levels and growth. For the between component, we generally observe positive effects (except for food). This indicates a development pattern as expected to be generated by the replicator dynamics mechanism, which postulates that firms with above-average productivity levels tend to grow in terms of shares, and vice versa. The actual strength can be seen from the relative contribution of the between component to aggregate productivity change. This contribution is rather low in most industries, except chemicals, electronics and transportation.

This between component can be enforced or weakened by the covariance component. For the total sample, the positive but small between component is reinforced by a covariance component that is positive and of considerable magnitude. Thus productivity growth (or decline) of the individual firms in the total sample tends to be associated with share growth (or decline). The selection represented by a positive between effect is accelerated in a similar fashion by a positive covariance component in the case of chemicals, rubber, machinery, transportation and instruments. In most of these cases, the covariance component represents a quantitatively important contribution to aggregate productivity growth (except for transportation). In construction, textiles, paper, metal and electronics, the covariance component is negative and therefore reduces or even outweighs the positive between components. As shown in Table 1A.2 in the Appendix, the between component becomes negative in a larger number of industries if sales shares are used for the aggregation instead of employment shares. The other results are analogous to those discussed here.

The combined effect of the between component and the covariance component is characteristic of the structural development of an industry. If both components are positive, the heterogeneity of firms with respect to both productivity differentials and size differentials is increasing. Eventually, a bimodal structure emerges as a result of the working of replicator dynamics, and reinforcement effects between market share changes and productivity changes (as a kind of positive dynamic economies of scale). In the case of a positive between component, a negative covariance component and a positive combined effect represent a replicator dynamics effect which, however, is damped by a negative feedback between changes in productivity and employment shares. If the combination of the between and the covariance term is negative, replicator dynamics effects do not show up as expected but are superimposed by a tendency towards a more homogeneous structure of firms as a kind of negative dynamic economies of scale. Relating these results to results found in previous work, by Cantner and Krüger (2004a, b, c), for example, for the chemicals and rubber sector shows that not only a rather simple success-breeds-success dynamics with respect to productivity leadership shows up; in addition, a coupled success-breeds-success process is detected where economic and technological successes reinforce each other (see especially Cantner and Krüger, 2004c).

The results just discussed for the total sample of German manufacturing firms are quite similar to those of studies for US manufacturing establishments, which are succinctly surveyed by Bartelsman and Doms (2000) and Haltiwanger (2000). In most of these studies, establishments are sampled together, irrespective of the industry of origin. Although the results vary considerably across time periods, data frequency, the specification of the shares in terms of labour or output, and the choice of labour productivity or total factor productivity, the within component usually represents the largest contribution to aggregate productivity growth. The between component is sometimes found to be quite small in absolute magnitude, while the covariance component is frequently positive and of considerable magnitude. Net entry contributes positively to aggregate productivity growth. An analogous investigation of UK manufacturing establishments by Disney et al. (2003b) reaches qualitatively the same results.

Dividing the sample period into two parts, one before the German reunification (1981–89) and the other after (1990–98), reveals some interesting developments. Comparison of Tables 1.2 and 1.3 reveals that aggregate productivity growth is much stronger for the total sample and in most industries in the period since reunification compared to the period before (with the sole exception of the transportation equipment industry).

To a large extent, these productivity improvements since 1990 can be explained by the components of the productivity decomposition that are related to structural change either in the form of selection among continuing firms (the between and covariance components) or in the form of entry and exit (the entry and exit components). These components play a much larger role after German reunification than before. Only in the case of construction and of food does the within component dominate. The covariance component is positive in all industries except construction and textiles, and is often large. In all other industries, the within component deviates substantially from the aggregate productivity change, leaving a large role for the productivity improving forces of structural change. The

*Table 1.2   Foster–Haltiwanger–Krizan decomposition, 1981–89
            (employment shares)*

	Change	Within	Between	Cov.	Entry	Exit
Total sample	0.3399	0.4745	0.0837	−0.2614	0.0389	−0.0042
Construction	−0.9622	−1.0047	0.0038	−0.0892	0.0884	−0.0396
Food and beverages	−0.3507	−0.4331	−0.0314	0.4809	−0.3675	−0.0005
Textiles and apparel	0.4587	0.5780	−0.0423	−0.1390	0.0863	0.0243
Paper and printing	1.5269	0.8984	0.0715	−0.4199	1.0445	0.0675
Chemicals and petroleum	1.0408	0.8358	0.0824	−0.1219	0.2440	−0.0006
Rubber and plastics	1.4102	1.4566	−0.0635	0.0423	0.0000	0.0251
Metal products	0.2985	0.1567	0.1022	−0.0007	0.0407	0.0005
Machinery and equipment	1.5150	1.8655	0.2125	−0.9474	0.4121	0.0277
Electronics	−1.1056	−0.8829	0.1673	−0.3105	−0.0930	−0.0136
Transportation equipment	1.7890	2.0476	0.1417	−0.3848	−0.0154	0.0000
Instruments	−0.0068	−0.0209	0.0564	−0.0570	0.1156	0.1008

Note: Reports average percentage growth rates of the aggregate productivity levels in the column 'Change' and the terms of the decomposition formula in the subsequent columns, each divided by the initial share-weighted average productivity level and multiplied by 100/(1989–81).

same holds for the total sample. Thus the widespread acceleration of productivity since 1990 is mainly driven by the exceptional growth of firms with above-average productivity levels which are also growing in terms of productivity, and by the entry of firms with above-average productivity levels combined with the exit of firms with below-average productivity levels. Again, the same pattern can be discerned from the results in the Appendix when the sales shares are used.

In sum, the results reported in this section show that structural change and net entry can explain an important part of aggregate productivity growth. This outcome appears to be much weaker before German reunification, and to be particularly pronounced in the period since that then. The general pattern of results holds for the whole sample in which all firms are sampled together, irrespective of their industry of origin. It also holds in most cases if the firms are assigned to industries at the two-digit (SIC) level. Thus support for the replicator dynamics mechanism can be given, although we have to be cautious at the present stage of our analysis. Importantly, the overall pattern of results is rather robust to the specification of the shares in terms of employment or sales.[12]

Table 1.3   Foster–Haltiwanger–Krizan decomposition, 1990–98 (employment shares)

	Change	Within	Between	Cov.	Entry	Exit
Total sample	1.9661	0.5198	0.2942	0.6775	0.2447	−0.2299
Construction	0.8701	0.7424	−0.0108	−0.1390	0.3904	0.1129
Food and beverages	0.5767	0.4619	−0.1770	−0.0008	0.3883	0.0955
Textiles and apparel	1.6705	0.8385	0.6945	−0.3214	0.0245	−0.4344
Paper and printing	2.3926	1.2999	0.0289	0.3472	0.5759	−0.1408
Chemicals and petroleum	4.7091	0.2012	2.1206	0.6732	1.1409	−0.5731
Rubber and plastics	2.2103	0.5495	0.7244	0.1984	−0.0502	−0.7882
Metal products	0.7526	0.1877	0.4008	0.0521	0.0512	−0.0608
Machinery and equipment	2.9296	1.4835	−0.0259	1.2685	0.2299	0.0264
Electronics	1.6838	0.3520	0.3743	0.6113	0.2648	−0.0815
Transportation equipment	1.1477	0.5257	0.1340	0.4416	−0.0206	−0.0671
Instruments	1.9845	0.5559	0.0738	0.8190	0.4861	−0.0497

Note: Reports average percentage growth rates of the aggregate productivity levels in the column 'Change' and the terms of the decomposition formula in the subsequent columns, each divided by the initial share-weighted average productivity level and multiplied by 100/ (1998–90).

4.   CONCLUSION

The analysis performed in this chapter is concerned with the heterogeneous micro-dynamics at the intra-sectoral, firm level and the aggregate development of sectors. The theoretical basis of the analysis first serves replicator dynamics, which governs the selective competition, and, second, specific innovation dynamics, which is modelled as endogenously driven. This simple model is tested for industrial sectors in Germany from 1981 to 1998. Firm-level total factor productivity is used as a proxy for technological performance of a firm, whereas the change in total factor productivity serves as a proxy for innovative performance. The main results can be summarized as follows.

First, we find that within-firm productivity growth accounts for much of the performance at the aggregate level, especially in the period before German reunification. Second, we also find that entering firms tend to have productivity levels above the average, whereas exiting firms are mainly characterized by productivity levels below the average. Both results confirm the results of other studies for US and UK manufacturing establishments. Third and most important, in the period since German reunification, we can identify the impact of success-breeds-success dynamics coupling economic and technological improvements for the majority of sectors. The accompanying structural change can explain a non-negligible part of the aggregate productivity performance, and can be interpreted in terms of the replicator dynamics mechanism, where well-performing firms (in terms of productivity) are selected in favour of badly performing firms. Our results give an indication of the forces of structural change that, together with entry–exit dynamics, seem to shape a substantial part of aggregate productivity development and are much more difficult to uncover by an investigation of short-run (year-by-year) changes.

Our findings additionally support the rather general and stylized observation of quite smooth developments at the aggregate level as the result of fairly turbulent micro-dynamics discussed in Dosi et al. (1997, p. 12):

> In general, what is particularly intriguing is the *coexistence* of turbulence and change on the one hand, with persistence and regularities at different levels of observation – from individual firms' characteristics to industrial aggregates – on the other. Industrial dynamics and evolution appear neither to be simply characterized by random disorder nor by perfectly self-regulating, equilibrium processes that quickly wipe away differences across firms. Rather, the evidence accumulated so far seems to suggest a subtle and intricate blend of these two elements.

NOTES

1. See Salter (1960, pp. 184ff.) for the derivation of his decomposition and his chapters XI and XIII for the application to UK and US industry data, respectively.
2. This section draws on Cantner (2002).
3. This broad formulation already contains the possibility of frequency-dependent fitness.
4. It can be shown that average fitness, here unit costs, decrease proportionally to the variance of unit costs:

$$\frac{\partial \bar{f}}{\partial t} = \mathrm{var}(f_i) \leq 0.$$

5. When the level of fitness is affected, static economies of scale are at work (Metcalfe, 1994, 1998).
6. The rate of exploiting technological opportunities is fast compared to the rate of competitive selection.
7. Here, compared to innovation dynamics, selection dynamics is fast.
8. The number of takeovers depends on the chosen parameters for innovation and selection dynamics.
9. For a further discussion of this issue, see Mazzucato (1998), Mazzucato and Semmler (1998) and Cantner (2002).
10. This section draws on Cantner and Krüger (2006).
11. See Cantner and Hanusch (2005) for a discussion of this issue.
12. See Appendix.

REFERENCES

Baily, M.N., C. Hulten and D. Campbell (1992), 'Productivity dynamics in manufacturing plants', *Brookings Papers on Economic Activity: Microeconomics*, pp. 187–267.

Baily, M.N., E.J. Bartelsman and J.C. Haltiwanger (1996), 'Downsizing and productivity growth: myth or reality?', *Small Business Economics*, **8**, 259–78.

Bartelsman, E.J. and M. Doms (2000), 'Understanding productivity: lessons from longitudinal microdata', *Journal of Economic Literature*, **38**, 569–94.

Cantner, U. (2002), 'Heterogenität, Technologischer Fortschritt und Spillover-Effekte', in M. Lehmann-Waffenschmidt (ed.), *Studien zur Evolutorischen Ökonomik V*, Berlin: Duncker & Humblot, pp. 15–40.

Cantner, U. and H. Hanusch (2005), 'Empirical issues in evolutionary economics: heterogeneity and evolutionary change – concepts and measurement (with H. Hanusch), in K. Dopfer (ed.), *Economics, Evolution and the State: The Governance of Complexity*, Cheltenham, UK and Northampton, MA, USA: Edward Elgar, pp. 13–42.

Cantner, U. and J. Krüger (2004a), 'Geroski's stylized facts and mobility of large German manufacturing firms', *Review of Industrial Organization*, **24**, 267–83.

Cantner, U. and J. Krüger (2004b), 'Technological and economic mobility in large German manufacturing firms', in J.S. Metcalfe and J. Foster (eds), *Evolution and Economic Complexity*, Cheltenham, UK and Northampton, MA, USA: Edward Elgar, pp. 172–90.

Cantner, U. and J. Krüger (2004c), 'Innovation, imitation and structural development within industries – on technological heterogeneity and beyond-the-mean-dynamics', mimeo, Friedrich Schiller University of Jena.

Cantner, U. and J. Krüger (2006), 'Micro-heterogeneity and aggregate productivity development in the German manufacturing sector: results from a decomposition exercise', *Jenaer Schriften zur Wirtschaftswissenschaft*, **2**.

Cantner, U., K. Dressler and J. Krüger (2005), 'Knowledge compensation in the German automobile industry', *Jenaer Schriften zur Wirtschaftswissenschaft*, **11**.

Cantner, U., J. Krüger and K. von Rhein (2006), 'Firm survival in the German automobile industry', *Empirica*, **33**, 49–60.

Cantner, U., J. Krüger and K. von Rhein (2009), 'Knowledge and creative destruction over the industry life cycle: the case of the German automobile industry', *Economica*, **76** (301), February, 132–48.

Caves, R.E. (1998), 'Industrial organization and new findings on the turnover and mobility of firms', *Journal of Economic Literature*, **36**, 1947–82.

Disney, R., J. Haskel and Y. Heden (2003a), 'Exit, entry and establishment survival in UK manufacturing', *Journal of Industrial Economics*, **51**, 93–115.

Disney, R., J. Haskel and Y. Heden (2003b), 'Restructuring and productivity growth in UK manufacturing', *Economic Journal*, **103**, 666–94.

Dosi, G., F. Malerba, O. Marsili and L. Orsenigo (1997), 'Industrial structures and dynamics: evidence, interpretations and puzzles', *Industrial and Corporate Change*, **6**, 3–24.

Dunne, T., M.J. Roberts and L. Samuelson (1988), 'Patterns of firm entry and exit in U.S. manufacturing industries', *RAND Journal of Economics*, **19**, 495–515.

Dunne, T., M.J. Roberts and L. Samuelson (1989), 'The growth and failure of U.S. manufacturing plants', *Quarterly Journal of Economics*, **104**, 671–98.

Fisher, R.A. (1930), *The Genetical Theory of Natural Selection*, Oxford: Clarendon Press.

Foster, L., J. Haltiwanger and C.J. Krizan (1998), 'Aggregate productivity growth: lessons from microeconomic evidence', NBER Working Paper No. 6803.

Griliches, Z. and H. Regev (1995), 'Productivity and firm turnover in Israeli industry: 1979–1988', *Journal of Econometrics*, **65**, 175–203.

Haltiwanger, J.C. (2000), 'Aggregate growth: what have we learned from microeconomic evidence?', OECD Economics Department Working Paper No. 267.

Klepper, S. and K.L. Simmons (2005). 'Industry shakeouts and technological change', *International Journal of Industrial Organization*, **23**, 23–43.

Kwasnicki, W. (1996), *Knowledge, Innovation and Economy: An Evolutionary Exploration*, Cheltenham, UK and Brookfield, USA: Edward Elgar.

Kwasnicki, W. and H. Kwasnicka (1992), 'Market, innovation, competition: an evolutionary model of industrial dynamics', *Journal of Economic Behaviour and Organization*, **19**, 343–68.

Malerba, F. and L. Orsenigo (1993), 'Technological regimes and firm behaviour', *Industrial and Corporate Change*, **2** (1), 45–72.

Malerba, F. and L. Orsenigo (1997), 'Technological regimes and sectoral patterns of innovative activities', *Industrial and Corporate Change*, **6** (1), 83–118.

Mazzucato, M. (1998), 'A computational model of economies of scale and market share instability', *Structural Change and Economic Dynamics*, **9** (1), 55–84.

Mazzucato, M. and W. Semmler (1998), 'Market share instability and financial dynamics during the industry life cycle: the U.S. automobile industry', Special Issue, *Journal of Evolutionary Economics*, **9** (1).

Metcalfe, J.S. (1994), 'Competition, Fisher's principle and increasing returns in the selection process', *Journal of Evolutionary Economics*, **4** (4), 321–46.

Metcalfe, J.S. (1998), *Evolutionary Economics and Creative Destruction*, London: Routledge.

Metcalfe, J.S. and M. Calderini (1998), 'Chance, necessity and competitive dynamics in the Italian steel industry, in U. Cantner, H. Hanusch and S. Klepper (eds), *Economic Evolution, Learning, and Complexity*, Heidelberg and New York: Physica-Verlag, pp. 139–58.

Nelson, R.R. and S.G. Winter (1982), *An Evolutionary Theory of Economic Change*, Cambridge, MA: Harvard University Press.

Nickell, S.J. (1996), 'Competition and corporate performance', *Journal of Political Economy*, **104**, 724–46.

Nickell, S.J., D. Nicolitsas and N. Dryden (1997), 'What makes firms perform well?', *European Economic Review*, **41**, 783–96.

Salter, W.E.G. (1960), *Productivity and Technical Change*, Cambridge, MA: Cambridge University Press.

Saviotti, P. and G.S. Mani (1995), 'Competition, variety and technological evolution: a replicator dynamics model', *Journal of Evolutionary Economics*, **5** (4), 369–92.

Schumpeter, J.A. (1912), *Theorie der wirtschaftlichen Entwicklung* (*Theory of Economic Development*), Berlin: Duncker & Humblot, 5th edn 1935.

Schumpeter, J.A. (1942), *Capitalism, Socialism, and Democracy*, London: Unwin, reprinted 1987.

Silverberg, G. and D. Lehnert (1994), 'Growth fluctuations in an evolutionary model of creative destruction', in G. Silverberg and L. Soete (eds), *The Economics of Growth and Technical Change*, Aldershot, UK and Brookfield, USA: Edward Elgar, pp. 74–108.

Silverberg, G. and D. Lehnert (1996), 'Evolutionary chaos: growth fluctuations in a Schumpeterian model of creative destruction', in W.A. Barnett, A. Kirman and M. Salmon (eds), *Nonlinear Dynamics in Economics*, Cambridge: Cambridge University Press, pp. 45–74.

Silverberg, G. and B. Verspagen (1994), 'Learning, innovation and economic growth: a long-run model of industrial dynamics', *Industrial and Corporate Change*, **3**, 199–223.

Winter, S.G., Y.M. Kaniovski and G. Dosi (2000), 'Modeling industrial dynamics with innovative entrants', *Structural Change and Economic Dynamics*, **11**, 255–93.

Winter, S.G., Y.M. Kaniovski and G. Dosi (2003), 'A baseline model of industry evolution', *Journal of Evolutionary Economics*, **13**, 355–83.

APPENDIX: RESULTS FOR SALES SHARES

Table 1A.1 *Foster–Haltiwanger–Krizan decomposition, 1981–98 (sales shares)*

	Change	Within	Between	Cov.	Entry	Exit
Total sample	0.4242	0.0077	−0.3624	0.3762	0.1861	−0.2166
Construction	−0.1459	−0.2087	−0.0710	0.0523	0.0729	−0.0086
Food and beverages	0.5543	0.1402	−0.0358	0.1314	0.2990	−0.0195
Textiles and apparel	0.9827	0.4469	0.0418	−0.2321	0.7212	−0.0049
Paper and printing	1.9786	0.2573	0.0460	−0.0613	1.8754	0.1389
Chemicals and petroleum	0.1002	−0.4441	−0.0909	0.0858	−0.1431	−0.6925
Rubber and plastics	0.9707	0.5868	−0.1430	0.6738	−0.0287	0.1183
Metal products	0.2273	0.1226	−0.1138	0.1622	0.1382	0.0819
Machinery and equipment	2.7359	0.5971	0.0248	0.2745	1.7324	−0.1071
Electronics	0.2049	−0.0593	0.2367	−0.1950	0.1573	−0.0653
Transportation equipment	1.2799	0.4476	0.0915	0.5019	0.2504	0.0114
Instruments	0.8944	0.3198	−0.0157	0.3652	0.2640	0.0390

Note: Reports average percentage growth rates of the aggregate productivity levels in the column 'Change' and the terms of the decomposition formula in the subsequent columns, each divided by the initial share-weighted average productivity level and multiplied by 100/(1998–81).

Table 1A.2   Foster–Haltiwanger–Krizan decomposition, 1981–89 (sales shares)

	Change	Within	Between	Cov.	Entry	Exit
Total sample	−0.3524	−0.1722	−0.7090	0.4598	0.0596	−0.0095
Construction	−0.9907	−1.1952	−0.1816	0.1691	0.1535	−0.0636
Food and beverages	0.3231	−0.1439	−0.0367	0.3701	0.1327	−0.0009
Textiles and apparel	0.4043	0.1898	−0.1823	0.0330	0.3651	0.0013
Paper and printing	1.3043	0.9606	0.0154	−0.4476	0.8827	0.1068
Chemicals and petroleum	−1.3370	−0.8422	−1.3092	0.8636	−0.0507	−0.0016
Rubber and plastics	1.4493	1.4322	−0.0728	0.1099	0.0000	0.0200
Metal products	0.3049	−0.1722	0.0863	0.4486	−0.0575	0.0003
Machinery and equipment	1.9471	1.0750	−0.1859	0.0014	1.0589	0.0023
Electronics	−1.0775	−1.0322	0.1056	−0.1609	−0.0047	−0.0147
Transportation equipment	1.8481	1.7794	−0.0274	−0.0306	0.1267	0.0000
Instruments	0.2041	−0.0366	−0.0227	0.0456	0.3222	0.1044

Note: Reports average percentage growth rates of the aggregate productivity levels in the column 'Change' and the terms of the decomposition formula in the subsequent columns, each divided by the initial share-weighted average productivity level and multiplied by 100/ (1989–81).

Table 1A.3   Foster–Haltiwanger–Krizan decomposition, 1990–98 (sales shares)

	Change	Within	Between	Cov.	Entry	Exit
Total sample	1.3977	0.2994	−0.0942	0.7369	0.2199	−0.2356
Construction	0.6105	0.6953	−0.1101	−0.0371	0.2770	0.2146
Food and beverages	0.0540	−0.6667	−0.9268	1.1724	0.1160	−0.3592
Textiles and apparel	1.9147	0.6646	0.6663	0.0612	0.0266	−0.4960
Paper and printing	2.5929	1.1534	0.0439	0.3914	0.8807	−0.1235
Chemicals and petroleum	1.8318	0.1583	0.6406	0.5621	−0.0167	−0.4875
Rubber and plastics	3.2429	0.3816	0.4454	1.2233	0.1020	−1.0906
Metal products	0.6771	0.1198	0.1177	0.4305	−0.0375	−0.0466
Machinery and equipment	3.3852	1.2552	0.2219	0.8625	1.0118	−0.0337
Electronics	1.7989	0.2900	0.1425	0.6435	0.5843	−0.1386
Transportation equipment	0.9123	0.2653	−0.2884	0.6808	−0.0302	−0.2847
Instruments	1.8058	0.5639	−0.0924	0.9052	0.4478	0.0187

Note: Reports average percentage growth rates of the aggregate productivity levels in the column 'Change' and the terms of the decomposition formula in the subsequent columns, each divided by the initial share-weighted average productivity level and multiplied by 100/(1998–90).

2. Energy, development and the environment: an appraisal three decades after the 'limits to growth' debate*

Giovanni Dosi and Marco Grazzi

1. INTRODUCTION

This work builds upon some long-term secular regularities concerning the relation between consumption of energy, technological progress and economic growth, and reassesses the old question raised around 40 years ago in the 'limits to growth' discussion (Meadows et al., 1972), namely, are the current patterns of development, and in particular the current patterns of energy use, environmentally sustainable?

Without the ambition to offer any conclusive answer, in this work we try to identify some critical interpretative issues and suggest some (admittedly controversial) policy conclusions.

Departing points are: (a) the long-term substitution of inanimate sources of energy for animate, starting at least with the English Industrial Revolution, (b) a slowly decreasing – on a shorter time scale – trend of energy intensity per unit of output, at least in developed countries, as the joint outcome of total energy consumption which continues to increase (IEA, 2005), and at the same time more efficient exploitation of energy itself (Grüber and Nakićenović, 1996, see also Figure 2.3).

The topics we shall address are the following:

1. The environmental sustainability of patterns of energy consumption that for so long have implied the notion of the environment as a free good, without any negative social externalities and even less so any environmental threat.
2. The importance – and limits – of relative price changes with respect to the dynamics of consumption of energy.
3. The role of fundamental discontinuities between different 'technological paradigms'.

Given the observed trends, we propose some interpretative and normative conjectures:

1. The proposition that 'growth takes care of itself' in terms of the environmental consequences is analytically largely ungrounded and normatively reckless.
2. The higher the price for fossil fuels, the better it is in the long run for the world economy and for humankind in general.
3. Even sky-rocketing prices of fossil fuels alone might not be enough to induce endogenously a sustainable pattern of consumption.
4. Major research projects involving massive public investments in basic research are needed if we want to maintain (or regain?) long-term environmental sustainability.

2. THE LONG TERM PATTERNS OF ENERGY CONSUMPTION AND THEIR SUSTAINABILITY

Let us begin with the patterns identified by Landes (1969), who provides a careful history of the diffusion of various energy sources during and after the Industrial Revolution.

Before the eighteenth century, the only non-animal source of chemical work was heat from charcoal-fired furnaces. Coal had entirely replaced charcoal in England before 1800 due to prior deforestation. In the USA, the process took longer. Inanimate sources of work exceeded animal work in the USA for the first time in 1870. However, it was not until the twentieth century that the contribution of fossil fuel combustion and heat engines using fossil fuels overcame the contribution of biomass, and this has been the case only for industrialized countries; see Ayres (2004). Figure 2.1 offers an appraisal of the trends in energy[1] consumption in the USA.

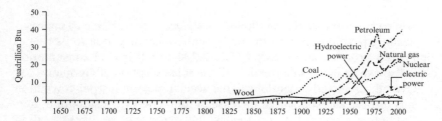

Source: DOE/EIA (2004).

Figure 2.1 Energy consumption by source, USA, 1635–2004

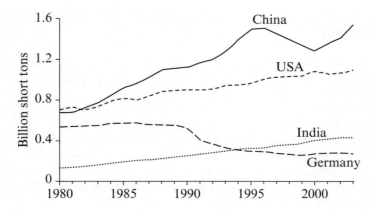

Source: DOE/EIA (2004).

Figure 2.2   World coal consumption, 1950–2004

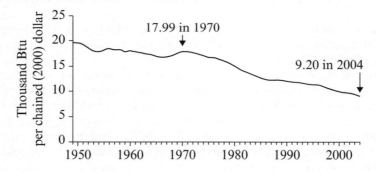

Source: DOE/EIA (2004).

Figure 2.3   Energy use per dollar of GDP

Somewhat surprisingly, as Figure 2.1 shows, coal was able to maintain its leading position up until the mid-twentieth century, due to its role in industrial production: indeed, Figure 2.2 shows that coal consumption still displays an increasing trend, with the sole exception of Germany.

Overall, as already mentioned, the secular post-industrial revolution trends display an exponential increase in total energy consumption, notwithstanding a slowdown over the last half-century or so due to a fall in energy intensity per unit of GDP (at least above some levels of GDP per capita): see Figure 2.3 for the USA. We see similar patterns in CO_2 emissions, since the bulk of the increase in energy use has involved fossil fuels.

Are such patterns sustainable in the long run?

As many recall, the first spur in such debate occurred in the early 1970s around the 'Club of Rome' manifesto, in turn grounded in forecasts of the simulation exercise by Forrester and his colleagues at MIT (Meadows et al., 1972).

Within that discussion, the major emphasis was on the limit to growth related to 'resource availability', coupled with rapid population growth and, after 1973, by the rising trend in oil prices and declining growth in output in many industrialized countries (see also Nordhaus, 1992).

Those who stood on the pessimists' side argued that, on the basis of the MIT models, disaster could be avoided only by zero population growth and zero economic growth from the year 2000 on. Optimists – which at the time included Chris Freeman and collaborators at the Science Policy Research Unit at Sussex University – argued that growth could continue, provided that the two following conditions were met: (a) a combination of institutional changes that led to a different path of world development (with emphasis on sustainability) and (b) a reorientation of world R&D so that environmental objectives could be given higher priority (see Freeman, 1992).

The scenario drawn by the Club of Rome turned out be overpessimistic in assessing the importance of natural resource shortages in constraining economic growth. At the same time, the scenario was heavily optimistically biased in relation to the environmental impact of pollutant emissions into the environment in general and the impact of energy use on climate in particular. As Brock and Taylor (2004) vividly put it: 'Recently it has become clear that limits to growth may not only arise from nature's finite source of raw materials, but instead from nature's limited ability to act as a sink for human wastes.' A much more reasonable setting to assess the interactions of human activities and the ecosystem is to frame it in terms of the twofold role of 'source and sink' played by the environment, with the sink role and its long-term effect at the forefront. In fact, in our view, the Club of Rome warnings massively underestimated the powers of technological progress with respect to the access to/exploitation of natural resources. Knowledge accumulation has worked wonders in disproving dismal predictions dating back in economics at least to Ricardo and Malthus. Contrary to the Ricardian intuition on scarce factors of production, very little by way of decreasing returns to resource availability (including energy) has played out over the last two centuries. Rather, technology-driven dynamic increasing returns exerted their powerful influence also in agricultural, mining and energy extraction.

Conversely, the crucial long-term sustainability issue regards, we suggest, the compatibility between current patterns of resources use – and in particular energy use – and environmental dynamics. The latter include of course greenhouse effects, by now abundantly documented. Hence, even granted the ability of nature partly to fulfil its 'sink role', what are the limits of its recycling capacity? And on the other side, what is the relationship between rates of environmental waste and development?

Environmental Kuznets Curve

The statistical features of the relationship between energy consumption and levels of development are often summarized by means of the so-called 'Kuznets curve'.

As Dasgupta et al. (2002, p. 147) put it:

> The Environmental Kuznets Curve (EKC) posits an inverted-U relationship between pollution and economic developments. Kuznets's name was apparently attached to the curve by Grossman and Krueger (1994), who noted its resemblance to Kuznets's inverted-U relationship between income inequality and development.

Different versions of the EKC characterized by different degrees of optimism are illustrated in Figure 2.4. Dasgupta et al. (2002) and Stern (2004a) offer two quite comprehensive reviews of the literature on the subject.

Their most optimistic interpretations have been popularized, not too surprisingly, by the World Bank's *World Development Report 1992*, which argued:

> The view that greater economic activity inevitably hurts the environment is based on static assumptions about technology, tastes and environmental investment. (IBRD, 1992, p. 38)

Should the EKC be verified, the take-away message would be: grow first, then clean up: i.e. the so-called 'too poor to be green' hypothesis (Martinez-Alier, 1995).

Clearly, if supported by the data, the EKC, especially in its most optimistic versions (the two lower curves in Figure 2.4), would apparently suggest that, first, a path to environmentally sustainable growth is available for developing countries, given existing techniques and, second, developed countries are already following it. Emerging economies would only need to 'replicate' the growth path already set by more advanced economies.

The most robust evidence supporting EKC is for developed countries, as, for these countries, more data on emissions and longer time series are available.

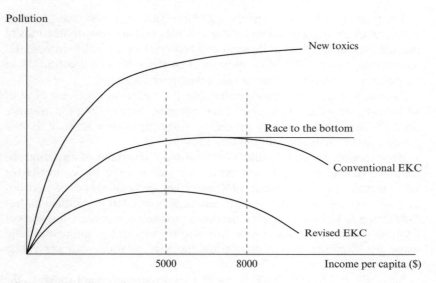

Source: Dasgupta et al. (2002).

Figure 2.4 Environmental Kuznets curve

De Bruyn et al. (1998) spell out some possible drivers of EKC (at least for local air pollutants): first, one tends to observe positive income elasticities for environmental quality; second, structural change in production and consumption towards 'good' environmentally friendly directions tend to be associated with higher per capita income; third, information on environmental consequences of economic activities increases with income levels.

Granted that, what is the evidence supporting the EKC and what does it imply?

Some statistical evidence on EKC
Let us consider the following basic 'reduced form' model, largely tested in the literature (de Bruyn et al., 1998, pp. 163 and 164):

$$E_{i,t} = \alpha_{i,t} + \beta_1 Y_{i,t} + \beta_2 Y_{i,t}^2 + \beta_3 Y_{i,t}^3 + \beta_4 t + \beta_5 V_{i,t} \qquad (2.1)$$

where E is 'environmental pressure' (however defined), Y is per capita income, i stands for a country index, t is a time index and V_t reflects other variables that influence the relation between Y and E. Clearly, the picture would be coherent with the traditional EKC for $\beta_1 > 0$, $\beta_2 < 0$ and $\beta_3 = 0$.

The typical approach to test the EKC has been to regress cross-country measures of environmental and water qualities on various specifications of income per capita. Most of these studies rely on the Global Environmental Monitoring System (GEMS), sponsored by the UN, which collects data on pollution, in both developed and developing countries.

Researchers are far from agreement on the empirical goodness of fit of an EKC type model. For example, according to Stern (1998), the evidence on a U-shaped relation only applies to some air pollutants such as suspended particulates and sulphur dioxide.

Bandyopadhyay and Shafik (1992) correlate ten types of environmental pressure with per capita income for a panel of up to 149 countries for various time intervals between 1960 and 1990. Only two types of environmental pressure, urban air concentrations of suspended particulate matter (SPM) and SO_2, follow an EKC according to their estimates. Emissions of CO_2, an indicator for water pollution and the amount of municipal solid waste per capita, satisfy a monotonic, positive relation with per capita income.

Bertinelli and Strobl (2005) propose a semi-parametric approach to the EKC with the consequent advantage of allowing for higher flexibility in accounting for the relation between income per capita and some measure of pollution. They find a linear relation, with pollution increasing with country wealth for low levels of GDP/capita and becoming flat thereafter. The only exception to linearity is for very high GDP/capita ratios, with the disclaimer that, due to very few observations in the higher tail, the curve is poorly estimated.[2]

Stern (2004a) suggests that structural factors on both the input and output side do play a role in modifying the gross scale effect, although they are mostly less influential than time-related effects. The income elasticities of emissions are likely to be less than one – but not negative in wealthy countries as proposed by the EKC hypothesis. Further, the author also notes that most of the studies supporting the EKC might exaggerate any apparent decline in pollution intensity with rising income. Indeed, in our finite world, the poor countries of today would be unable to find other countries from which to import resource-intensive products as they become richer. As a result, future research on this issue has to account for the effects of pollution regulations on trade. With this in mind, Levinson and Taylor (2004) find – very reasonably – that those industries whose abatement costs increased most have seen the largest relative increases in net imports.

Moreover, thousands of potentially toxic materials remain untested and unregulated. Such an issue also affects the analysis of the effects of environmental regulation, in both developed and developing countries.

There is nearly a paradox here in that, when the evidence of a damage is beyond any reasonable doubt, it might also be too late to reverse the course of events. Further, some scholars suggest that, even if some EKC relationship existed in the past, it is unlikely to persist in the future because of the pressures that global competition places on environmental regulations – the so-called 'race to the bottom' (Dasgupta et al., 2002:[3] see Figure 2.4).

Decomposing the determinants of energy use and environmental pressure

Given the highly controversial empirical evidence on the EKC, further insights might be drawn from dynamic frameworks explicitly disentangling the diverse underlying relations between growth, energy consumption and pollution.[4]

Grossman (2005) and de Bruyn (1997) propose the following decomposition:

$$E_t = \sum_{j=1}^{n} Y_t I_{jt} S_{jt} \tag{2.2}$$

where E_t is emissions in year t for a given country, Y is GDP, I_j is the emission intensity of sector j and S_j is the share of that sector in the country's economy. Such a representation allows us to analyse emissions accounting for scale, (sectoral) composition and technique effects. Equation (2.2) is in fact an identity, since $I_{jt} = E_{jt}/Y_{jt}$ and $S_{jt} = Y_{jt}/Y_t$, and can be used to distinguish various factors that influence emissions. Differentiating both sides with respect to time, we can write:

$$\hat{E} = \hat{Y} + \sum_{j=1}^{n} e_j \hat{S}_j + \sum_{j=1}^{n} e_j \hat{I}_j \tag{2.3}$$

where $e_j = E_j/E$ is the share of emissions of sector j in total emissions and $\hat{X} = (dX/dt)/X$.

The first term on the right-hand side of equation (2.3), $\hat{Y}$, accounts for the effects on emissions directly related to scale, i.e. to the growth of the size of the economy, holding constant the composition of the economy and, broadly speaking, the technology as proxied by the intensity of emissions, while the two other terms on the right-hand side precisely account for the latter.[5]

Stern (2002) adopts a similar procedure to decompose sulphur emissions in 64 countries during 1979–90:

$$\frac{S_{it}}{P_{it}} = \gamma_i \frac{Y_{it}}{P_{it}} A_t \frac{E_{it}}{Y_{it}} \prod_{j=1}^{n} \left(\frac{y_{it}}{Y_{it}}\right)^{\alpha_j} \sum_{k=1}^{K} \frac{e_{kit}}{E_{it}} \varepsilon_{it} \tag{2.4}$$

Table 2.1   Contributions to total change in global sulphur emissions

	Weighted logarithmic percent change (%)
Total change	
Actual emissions	28.77
Predicted emissions	27.37
Unexplained fraction	1.40
Decomposition	
Scale effect	53.78
Emissions-related technical change	−19.86
Energy intensity	−10.20
Output mix	3.77
Input mix	−0.13

Source: Stern (2002).

where S is sulphur emissions; P population; Y_{it}/P_{it} is scale as proxied by GDPcapita; A_t is a common global time effect representing emissions-specific technical progress over years t; E_{it}/Y_{it} is energy intensity; y_{1it}/Y_{it}, ..., y_{nit}/Y_{it} represent the composition effect and e_{1it}/E_{it}, ..., e_{kit}/E_{it} is the input mix given by the share of different energy sources e in total energy use, E. Additionally, γ_i is the relative efficiency of country i compared to best practice, and ε_{it} is a random error term.

The results of the empirical analysis, which we report in Table 2.1, show that input and composition effects globally contributed very little, even though they might be important for certain countries. The two components accounting for technological change (A_t and E_{it}/Y_{it}) limit the increase in emissions to half, but are unable to prevent them from increasing.

Wing and Eckaus (2004) carefully review the existing empirical works and identify the following 'stylized facts':

- declining aggregate energy intensity (notwithstanding an upward trend in its total use);
- evidence of induced energy-saving innovations at the micro level, associated with significant energy-saving technological change in a number of energy-intensive manufacturing industries;
- indications of the embodiment of energy-saving innovations in durable goods;
- (somewhat at odds with the evidence mentioned above) structural change as a significant source of reduction in aggregate energy intensity.

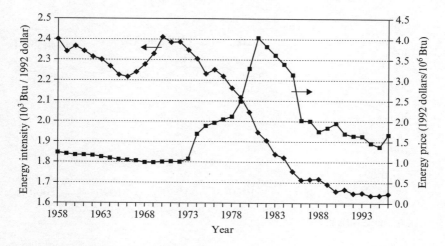

Source: Wing and Eckaus (2004).

Figure 2.5 US energy intensity and energy prices, 1958–96

These authors suggest that, in the most recent period, innovations embodying information technology in electrical capital goods played an important role in energy intensity decline (see Figure 2.5). The issue of reductions in energy intensity is not a simple one.

> There have been a number of energy-saving influences: changes in the sectoral composition of the economy, changes in the scale of its constituent sectors, as well as substitution due to shifts in the relative prices of energy and other variable inputs. [. . .] In particular, a significant portion of the energy-saving technical changes we observe may have been the coincidental result of innovations which were intended to accelerate production, reduce both labor and capital costs, or make use of alternative materials. (Wing and Eckaus, 2004, p. 19)

The bottom line is that technical progress – possibly together with structural change – has barely succeeded in stabilizing or even marginally reducing energy consumption per capita in high-income countries (see Figure 2.6 for the USA). However, demography plays heavily against any stabilization, let alone reduction of total energy consumption and of emissions in the environment.

Demography, Energy Consumption and Emissions

Indeed, the evidence on the past and the most likely projections for the future suggest a massive overall growth of energy consumption (see Figure

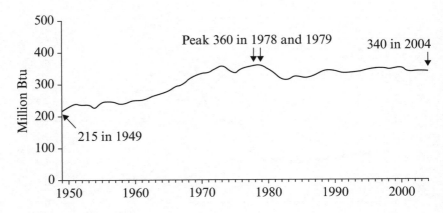

Source: DOE/EIA (2004).

Figure 2.6   Energy consumption per person, USA

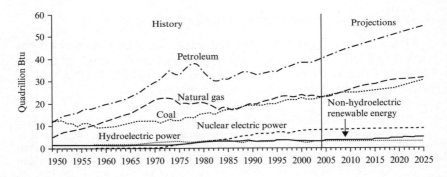

Source: DOE/EIA (2004)

*Figure 2.7   Energy consumption by source, history and projections, USA,
1949–2025*

2.7) and of emissions, with some increases even in high-income countries:
see Figure 2.8.

The picture is even bleaker for other sources of emissions (see Figure 2.9
on projections concerning total sulphur emissions).

In order to be more precise in identifying the importance of demographic factors in shaping such patterns, one has to identify the elasticity
– i.e. the percentage change – in energy use or emissions resulting from a
corresponding change in the population. In this respect, when considering per capita emissions, the EKC approach – discussed above – often

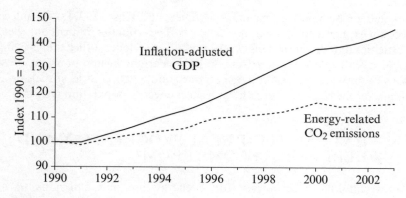

Source: DOE/EIA (2004).

Figure 2.8 GDP growth and CO₂ emissions, USA

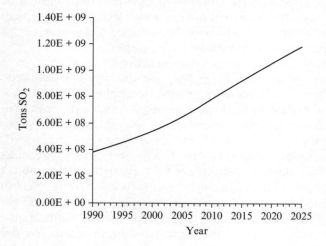

Source: Stern et al. (1996).

Figure 2.9 Projected sulphur emissions

implicitly assumes an elasticity of population of one. Note that, while this is not necessarily the most accurate estimate, it would spell doom for any hope of emissions reduction, given the current and projected growth of world population.

Some – including the so-called IPAT (Impact Population Affluence per capita Technology) model (see Ehrlich and Holdren, 1971) and others (see

Shi, 2003; Cole and Neumayer, 2004; Dietz and Rosa, 1997) – do indeed account explicitly for demographics effects. The estimates, it turns out, yield elasticities that are in the neighbourhood of one. Hence, other things being equal, even neglecting the effects on both energy consumption and emissions of growing per capita incomes, one should expect at least their doubling over the next three decades as a sheer effect of population growth.

3.   WHAT CAN TECHNICAL PROGRESS DO? AND WHERE DOES IT COME FROM?

Can technological advances reduce energy use and emissions so as to compensate for the effect of both per capita income growth and demographics?

We have already seen that energy-saving changes in production techniques appeared to have contributed significantly to the fall of energy intensity of GDP – at least at relatively high levels of development. Could the rate of technological progress be increased to the extent of providing full compensation for growth and demography?

The answer, we suggest, is largely negative.

In order to see that, we employ the distinction introduced a while ago in Dosi (1982) between 'normal' technological progress occurring within established technological paradigms and 'extraordinary' discontinuities associated with the emergence of new ones. For the purpose of this discussion, diverse paradigms – with their distinct knowledge bases and 'trajectories' of advance – tend to be associated with distinct energy sources and modes of generation of heat, electricity and motion. Thus the generation of electricity through fossil fuels and through nuclear fission is associated with two distinct technological paradigms. Similarly, the use of systems of locomotion based on the internal combustion engine is at the core of the current dominant paradigm of automobile design and production, etc.

In turn, it happens that market prices and other forms of 'inducement' are indeed able to 'tune up' or slow down the rates of technological change, but this happens within the relatively narrow boundaries set by the nature of the incumbent knowledge bases (the incumbent paradigm). So, for example, the price of energy may have some effect on energy use in steel production, but only within the rather strict limits set by the procedures we currently know for transforming the iron oxide input. And these constraints on price-induced input savings appear to be the general case in contemporary production paradigms.

A good case in point is precisely the effect of the 'oil shocks' (consider

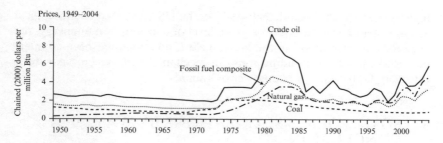

Source: DOE/EIA (2004).

Figure 2.10   Fossil fuel production prices, USA, 1950–2004

together Figures 2.10, 2.5 and 2.7), which did indeed significantly influence the time series of petroleum consumption. Nevertheless, soon thereafter, consumption resumed to its path of almost steady growth.

Still, under the 'inducement' rubric, public regulations have turned out to be a rather effective means of influencing the patterns of energy use and of emissions.[6] In a curious paradox in the literature and in a good deal of policy debate, the environmental impact of the negative externalities stemming from production and locomotion has been underestimated, at the same time as the cost of regulation has been overestimated.

In fact, as Porter and van der Linde (1995) argue, regulatory constraints may not be as costly as one could expect because of the possibility that regulation itself might spur innovative activities and lead to the discovery of 'new ways of doing things'.[7]

There is a general lesson here: imported price shocks might exert an important influence on the energy intensity of particular energy sources, but dramatic changes in their use can only be made possible by the emergence and diffusion of new technological paradigms. In the case of electricity generation, these are plausibly nuclear power and, eventually, photovoltaic and nuclear fusion; and, in the domain of locomotion, hydrogen-based means of transportation.

Conversely, despite the theoretical inclinations of the economists, the notion that changes in relative prices may induce substitution among inputs – in particular between energy and capital – tend to be a far-fetched idea with little empirical support. The general case is, on the contrary, that of a complementary relation between energy resources and manufactured capital (Stern, (2004b); Smulders, (2005); Landes, 1969; Cleveland, 2004; see also the special issue of *Ecological Economics*, Vol. 22, No. 3, 1997: Daly, 1997). Frank (1959) reports that the correlation coefficient between consumption of energy and manufactured capital is surprisingly high: 0.9995 for the period 1880–1948 in the USA.[8] Indeed, technological advancement has reduced, for a given level of consumption of energy, the need for manufactured capital. Nevertheless, this trend has been counter-balanced by a corresponding trend in mechanization, which has substituted capital to work of manpower or animals.

4. SOME POLICY SUGGESTIONS BY WAY OF A CONCLUSION

The diffusion of different sources and forms of energy as well as the environmental problems to which they are closely related provide an excellent example of the 'evolutionary' nature of processes of growth and development. As Kemp and Soete (1990, p. 245) point out, the

> current environmental problems stem from the accumulation of small effects, which at some point in time appear to exceed the critical boundaries of the ecosystem or at least the public perception of those boundaries. They represent a typical example of an *evolutionary* process in which apparently small events, developing in a certain direction during a long period of time, lead to considerable change.

What is certain, in our view, is that the cumulative effect of such big and small evolutionary changes will not take care of itself, as the most optimistic proponents of the environmental Kuznets curve appear to suggest. Most likely an explosive demography left running until a new 'steady state' forecast somewhere between 12 and 20 billion inhabitants would be sufficient to lead beyond a disaster threshold, which in fact some analysts believe we have already passed (see Ehrlich and Ehrlich, 1990).

At the same time, it is hard to see how, on the grounds of current technological paradigms, one could reach zero net emissions of CO_2 – not to mention the negative net emissions required in order to reverse the current greenhouse effect.

Hence unsustainability is looming not for reasons of scarcity, as was claimed three decades ago, but in a sense for lack of scarcity – at least with respect to energy availability and consumption.

What to do, then? Here are some proposals, from the modest to the nearly impossible.

First, prices and regulatory measures, we have argued, have limited 'inducement effects' but *do* have some. Hence it is urgent to revive the regulatory side which nowadays tends to be neglected in favour of more incentive-centred, supposedly 'market-friendly' measures, such as the development of markets for pollution permits.

As Nelson and Winter (1982, p. 368) put it:

> The processes of change are continually tossing up new 'externalities' that must be dealt with in some manner or other. In a regime in which technical advance is occurring and organizational structure is evolving in response to changing patterns of demand and supply, new nonmarket interactions that are not contained adequately by prevailing laws and policies are almost certain to appear, and old ones may disappear. Long-lasting chemical insecticides were not a problem eighty years ago. Horse manure polluted the cities but automotive emissions did not. The canonical 'externalities' problem of evolutionary theory is the generation by new technologies of benefits and costs that old institutional structures ignore.

Indeed, a much greater *bona fide* effort ought to go in the early identification of 'negative externalities' and the development of institutions and (generally international) policy measures able to cope with them.

Second, one should consider high prices of fossil fuels as a blessing rather than a curse. Of course there is, associated with this, a serious distributive problem which it is not possible to discuss here. However, one should worry even more if some fossil fuels – especially the most polluting one, coal – remains relatively cheap.

Third, it is unfair and impractical to demand that emerging economies pay the full cost of 'greener' patterns of production: only a mix of (i) mechanisms of preferential treatment of 'greener' commodities and (ii) international transfer of less polluting technologies is likely to lower the peaks of EKCs, if they exist at all.

Fourth, we have mentioned above that massive reductions in the levels of net emissions – to repeat, as such, a necessary condition for long-term environmental sustainability – are likely to come only with the development of new technological paradigms.

On the grounds of what we know now, the photovoltaic paradigm appears to be the most promising one, with, maybe, fusion, in a future further away. The emergence of new paradigms, however, generally demands major advances in basic and applied research, sponsored to a good extent by public agencies. Massive 'mission-oriented' projects in this area by the ensemble of developed countries are an urgent must.

Finally, possibly the most difficult issue: introduce measures aimed at the fast stabilization of population levels well before the 'natural asymptotic levels' from current forecasts.

The alternative is probably the 'evolution toward collapse' brilliantly described by Diamond (2005) in several occurrences of 'suicidal civilization' from the past.

NOTES

*   Prepared for the Conference 'Structural Dynamics and Economic Growth: the Central Role of the Energy Paradigm' jointly organized by the Accademia Nazionale dei Lincei and EniTecnologie, Rome, 27–28 March, 2006.
1. The term 'energy' as used in everyday discussion – economics included – is technically incorrect (see Ayres et al., 2003) as it means conserved quantity. Therefore it cannot be 'used up' but only converted from available to unavailable forms. The correct term in this context is 'exergy', which is, roughly speaking, 'available energy' or 'potentially useful' energy. Having said that, we conform to the existing terminology adopted in economics and we reiterate the misuse of the expression 'energy consumption'.
2. They also note that a source of bias could be in the unit root of the time series for pollutant emissions. Thus they proceed to first-difference the series. Nonetheless, their estimates for both sulphur and carbon dioxide emissions suggest that the relationship still appears to be linear.
3. Moreover, the 'new toxics' scenario claims that, while some traditional pollutants might have an inverted U-shaped curve, the new pollutants that are replacing them do not.
4. Needless to say, such a decomposition is only possible when detailed data about the economy and its sectoral composition are available for fuel use, output, emissions etc.
5. Clearly, equation (2.3) requires a discretization for empirical applications.
6. For more on the factors influencing the so-called 'environmental' innovations, see Mazzanti and Zoboli (2006).
7. The authors support this interpretation, providing a series of successful case studies.
8. Incidentally, Landes (1969) wonders if it really makes sense to bear all troubles related to capital measurement, when energy use provides such a good proxy.

REFERENCES

Ayres, R.U. (2004), 'Thermodynamics and economics, overview'. in *Encyclopedia of Energy*, vol. 6, San Diego, CA: Elsevier, pp. 91–7.

Ayres, R.U., L.W. Ayres and B. Warr (2003), 'Exergy, power and work in the U.S. economy 1900–1998', *Energy, The International Journal*, **28** (3), 219–73.

Bandyopadhyay, S. and N. Shafik (1992), Economic growth and environmental quality: time series and cross-country evidence', Policy Research Working Paper Series 904, The World Bank, June.

Bertinelli, L. and E. Strobl (2005), 'The environmental Kuznets curve semi-parametrically revisited', *Economics Letters*, **88**, 350–57.

Brock, W.A. and M. S. Taylor (2004), 'Economic growth and the environment: a review of theory and empirics', NBER Working Papers 10854, October.

Cleveland, C.J. (2004), 'Biophysical constraints to economic growth', in D.A. Gobaisi (ed.), *Encyclopedia of Life Support Systems*, Oxford: EOLSS.

Cole, M.A. and E. Neumayer (2004), 'Examining the impact of demographic factors on air pollution', *Population and Environment*, **26** (1), 5–21.

Daly, H. (ed.) (1997), *Ecological Economics*, **22**, Special Issue.

Dasgupta, S., B. Laplante, H. Wang and D. Wheeler (2002), 'Confronting the environmental Kuznets curve', *Journal of Economic Perspectives*, **16** (1), 147–68.

de Bruyn, S.M. (1997), 'Explaining the environmental Kuznets curve: structural change and international agreements in reducing sulphur emissions', *Environment and Development Economics*, **2**, 485–503.

de Bruyn, S., J. van den Bergh and J. Opschoor (1998), 'Economic growth and emissions: reconsidering the empirical basis of environmental Kuznets curves', *Ecological Economics*, **25**, 161–75.

Diamond, J.M. (2005), *Collapse: How Societies Choose to Fail or Succeed*, New York: Penguin.

Dietz, T. and E.A. Rosa (1997), 'Effects of population and affluence on CO_2 emissions', *Proceedings of the National Academy of Sciences, USA*, **94**, 175–9.

DOE/EIA (2004), *Annual Energy Review 2004*.

Dosi, G. (1982), 'Technological paradigms and technological trajectories', *Research Policy*, **26**, 147–62.

Ehrlich, P.R. and A.H. Ehrlich (1990), *The Population Explosion*, New York: Simon and Schuster.

Ehrlich, P.R. and J. P. Holdren (1971), 'Impact of population growth', *Science*, **171**, 1212–17.

Frank, A.G. (1959), 'Industrial capital stocks and energy consumption', *The Economic Journal*, **69** (273), 170–74.

Freeman, C. (1992), 'A green techno-economic paradigm for the world economy', in *The Economy of Hope*, London: Pinter, pp. 190–211.

Grossman, G.M. (2005), 'Pollution and growth: what do we know?', in *Sustainable Economic Development*, Cambridge: Cambridge University Press, pp. 19–47.

Grossman, G. and A.B. Krueger (1994), 'Environmental impacts of a North American Free Trade Agreement', in P.M. Garber (ed.), *Mexico–U.S. Free Trade Agreement*, Cambridge, MA: MIT Press, pp. 13–56.

Grüber, A. and N. Nakićenović (1996), 'Decarbonizing the global energy system', *Technological Forecasting and Social Change*, **53**, 97–110.

IBRD (1992), *World Development Report 1992. Development and the Environment*, New York: Oxford University Press.

IEA (2005), *Key World Energy Statistics. Annual Report*, International Energy Agency.

Kemp, R. and L. Soete (1990), 'Inside the "green box": on the economics of technological change and the environment', in C. Freeman and L. Soete (eds), *New Explorations in the Economics of Technical Change*, London: Pinter, pp. 245–57.

Landes, D.S. (1969), *The Unbound Prometheus: Technological Change and Industrial Development in Western Europe from 1750 to the Present*, Cambridge: Cambridge University Press.

Levinson, A. and M. S. Taylor (2004), 'Unmasking the pollution haven effect', NBER Working Papers 10629, July.

Martinez-Alier, J. (1995), 'The environment as a luxury good or "too poor to be green"', *Ecological Economics*, **13**, 1–10.

Mazzanti, M. and R. Zoboli (2006), 'Examining the factors influencing environmental innovations', Working Paper 20.2006, Fondazione Eni-Enrico Matti.

Meadows, D.H., D.L. Meadows, J. Randers and W.W. Behrens (1972), *The Limits to Growth*, New York: Universe Books.

Nelson, R.R. and S.G. Winter (1982), *An Evolutionary Theory of Economic Change*, Cambridge, MA: The Belknap Press of Harvard University Press.

Nordhaus, W.D. (1992), 'Lethal model II: the limits to growth revisited', *Brookings Papers on Economic Activity*, **2**, 1–59.

Porter, M.E. and C. van der Linde (1995), 'Toward a new conception of the environment–competitiveness relationship', *Journal of Economic Perspectives*, **9** (4), 97–118.

Shi, A. (2003), 'The impact of population pressure on global carbon dioxide emissions, 1975–1996: evidence from pooled cross-country data', *Ecological Economics*, **44**, 29–42.

Smulders, S. (2005), 'Endogenous technological change, natural resources, and growth', in R.D. Simpson, M.A. Toman and R.U. Ayres (eds), *Scarcity and Growth Revisited: Natural Resources and the Environment in the New Millennium*, Baltimore, MD: The Johns Hopkins University Press for Resources for the Future.

Stern, D.I. (1998), 'Progress on the environmental Kuznets curve', *Environmental and Development Economics*, **3** (2), 175–98.

Stern, D.I. (2002), 'Explaining changes in global sulfur emissions: an econometric decomposition approach', *Ecological Economics*, **42** (1–2), 201–20.

Stern, D.I. (2004a), 'The rise and fall of the environmental Kuznets curve', *World Development*, **32** (8), 1419–39.

Stern, D.I. (2004b), 'Economic growth and energy', in *Encyclopedia of Energy*, vol. 2, New York: Elsevier, pp. 35–51.

Stern, D.I., M.S. Common and E.B. Barbier (1996), 'Economic growth and environmental degradation: the environmental Kuznets curve and sustainable development', *World Development*, **24**, 1151–60.

Wing, I.S. and R.S. Eckaus (2004), 'Explaining long-run changes in the energy intensity of the US economy', Working Paper 116, MIT, Science and Policy of Global Change, September.

3. Marshall and Schumpeter: evolution and the institutions of capitalism

Stanley Metcalfe

PREFACE

It is a pleasure and an honour to contribute to this Festschrift in celebration of the scholarly life and contributions of Prof. Dr Horst Hanusch. As a founding member and ongoing secretary of the International J.A. Schumpeter Society, he has stimulated countless scholars and students to think long, hard and productively about the contribution that a Schumpeterian vision and analysis makes to our understanding of modern economic life. For this alone we owe him a great deal, and this contribution is a token of my own deep appreciation of all that Prof. Hanusch has contributed to this field of endeavour. It is no diminution of the importance of Schumpeter's work that I have chosen to base this chapter on a comparison of his writing with that of Alfred Marshall, for both are evolutionary economists in the modern meaning of that term. Were they alive today, I have not the slightest doubt that they would be active contributors to the *Journal of Evolutionary Economics*, on which Prof. Hanusch continues to exert a great, guiding influence. Marshall would surely have been a member of the Society too, and Schumpeter as well: how grand to be a member of one's own society – he would certainly have enjoyed that.

INTRODUCTION[1]

Joseph Schumpeter stands, without question, as one of the great social scientists of the twentieth century, an intellectual giant whose work not only inspired research into the role of innovation in the development of capitalist economies, but also provided the foundations for renewed interest in the economic sociology of creative destruction and economic development. His contributions to these themes also inspired the development of a specific evolutionary approach to the role of enterprise and innovation in the functioning of modern capitalism, but here he is not alone. Another great economist, Alfred Marshall, also understood the deep evolutionary nature of the economic development of capitalism, even going so far as to claim that the higher branches of economic analysis, when developed, would find their roots in biological, that is to say evolutionary reasoning. Yet outside the group of modern evolutionary economists, Schumpeter is routinely criticized for his poor theoretical (read non-mathematical) skills, while Marshall's evolutionism is all but consigned to the margins of the history of thought. My purpose here is to address the relation between the economic thought of Schumpeter and Marshall, recognizing very important differences that divide them but insisting on the common threads that bind their approaches to innovation-led competition and economic development. Much is to be learnt from a comparison of the two bodies of writing on this complex theme. They differ greatly in style and theoretical structure but they are at one in seeking to understand the sources and consequences of economic variation and change. The force of their respective writing is greatly strengthened by a deep knowledge of economic and technological history, evidence of which is distributed widely throughout their work. Both scholars lived through a period of great transformation in the economic performance of capitalism, and both were deeply aware of the link between developments in energy supply and new materials for the economies of Europe and North America. Their writings overlap to a degree in time, but Marshall was past the height of his powers when Schumpeter was emerging as a precocious talent in the first two decades of the twentieth century. Schumpeter too had the advantage of witnessing how trustified capitalism could generate new dimensions to the innovation process, a privilege denied to Marshall, although he was certainly aware of the emergence of industrial R&D laboratories.

JOSEPH A. SCHUMPETER

It is appropriate to begin with Schumpeter, and the central role of innovation in economic development. His vision of capitalism as an inherently dynamic system was set out in the *Theory of Economic Development* (1912 [1934]) and remained substantially, though not entirely, intact through *Business Cycles* (1939) and the postwar articles that provide such a convenient summary of his mature position (1947a, 1947b). In *Capitalism, Socialism and Democracy* (1943), the vision took on a subtly different hue, a sharper statement of the restless nature of capitalism more attuned to big-business-driven competition than the competitive capitalism that is more central to the earlier work. The essential feature of the vision is the necessarily uneven nature of the development process in capitalism, which follows in turn from the uneven distribution of innovation opportunities and imitative responses at any one time. Disharmony, explosions rather than gentle persistent transformation, is inherent to the *modus operandi* of the system, and so the idea emerges that a model of a stationary or regularly expanding capitalism is tantamount to being a contradiction in terms. Schumpeter offers a theory of the self-transformation of economic systems operating within the instituted frames of capitalism in which the associated dynamic processes continually redraw the contours of economic evolution between as well as within economies and industries. This is where the comparison with Marshall is most instructive, for Marshall's approach was gradualist not saltationist, and emphasized the continuity of the invention and economic development process. As is well understood, the three pillars of Schumpeter's theory are innovation, enterprise and credit. Innovation, the novelty that defines economic variation, is not to be equated with invention precisely because innovation is an embedded economic phenomenon, and the market process conditions the particular way in which the system stimulates innovation and responds to innovation: stimuli and responses that would follow a quite different mechanism under non-capitalist institutional arrangements.

Thus it is somewhat surprising that, like Marshall, although with a different intent, Schumpeter begins by separating the reality of capitalist development from a model of a stationary or even a regularly expanding economy, the circular flow, which in his case is grounded in the writing of Menger and the Austrians as well as of Walras.[2] In fact the model of the circular flow plays an ambiguous role in Schumpeter's hands. From one point of view, it is a model of capitalism without its *primum mobile*: it is a set of arrangements that could not be reproduced in a world defined by the particular instituted processes of capitalism as they had developed historically. From a second point of view, a concept of economic coherence is an essential statement of the nature of an economic order in which goods and services can be valued and activities evaluated and tested for their viability. The use of the word equilibrium to characterize the circular flow is perhaps unfortunate, as we shall explore further below, but the essential point is that a substrate of economic and social order is essential for evolution. Economic evolution is not a random process in Schumpeter's work; it operates on an existing structure and the logic of evolution cannot be separated from the logic that establishes that structure. In this sense Schumpeter's statics and dynamics are part of the same problem, namely the nature of development from within. By this Schumpeter means that innovation does not occur in a vacuum: economic factors stimulate innovation although innovation cannot be explained by economic factors alone and no formal explanation of economic creativity may be possible (the within always needs its companion, the without). Furthermore, economic factors also explain the adaptive response to innovation, the famous role of imitation in response to the profit differentials created by a novelty. Moreover, this process is path dependent in the sense that the innovations that are currently viable are contingent on the prevailing order: 'Every process of development creates the prerequisites for the following' and 'finally rests on preceding development' (*TED*, p. 64). Thus it was merely an expositional device, a clearing of the decks on Schumpeter's part, to start the analysis of development from the circular flow as *tabula rasa*. However, this is a method that begs the question of how development from within could ever arise if the conditions for the circular flow were in place. It is no answer to say that the circular flow is the state that would be returned to without innovation, because Schumpeter's model of capitalism does not exist without innovation; it cannot be understood by studying it from the perspective of a perennial lull (*CSD*, p. 84), for to do so is to commit the error of being concerned only with the way a system administers its existing structures rather than engaging with how those structures are created and destroyed. Thus we do not counterpoise statics and dynamics in a Schumpeterian analysis; rather we counterpoise order and evolution. Indeed, the whole thrust of Schumpeter's vision is that the form of capitalism that describes Western Europe and North America in the period since 1700 cannot be theorized about as a system in equilibrium. Rather, through entrepreneurial action and adaptation to those emergent novelties, it is system that is necessarily and continually transformed by a process that is internal to capitalism, and the manner of its transformation is evolutionary. One might, using the modern terminology, say more accurately that an innovation-dependent capitalism is always far from equilibrium, while accepting that it is always ordered according to specific economic and social norms and rules.[3] Thus there is a tension in Schumpeter's argument, a tension that we can resolve below by recognizing that an economic order can exhibit pattern and logic and not be in equilibrium in the strict sense of that term. Put crudely, systems in equilibrium experience no meaningful change, so they certainly do not evolve. Evolution is not change *simpliciter* but rather change that involves either or both of two separate causal logics, one based on the idea of an unfolding of interconnected possibilities, and the other based on a population-based dynamics of the differential growth of 'old' and 'new' activities. In Schumpeter's scheme the two forms interact, as they do in Marshall, to the effect that, over extended periods, the details of how economic activity is conducted and structured may come to have little in common. This is the high theme of development as creative destruction, a term that it is significant to note has deeper origins in German nineteenth-century economic thought (Renart and Renart, 2005; Santarelli and Pesciarelli, 1990; Streissler, 1994).

To summarize what is already well known, Schumpeter's primary source of variation is entrepreneurial activity defined as the introduction of novel ways of conducting a business, a process we might usefully equate with the formulation of business experiments. Innovations are the novelties, the impossibilities rendered actual, those experimental sources of economic variety that the prevailing order evaluates and adapts to according to the relative advantages that the new ways possess over the old. This is a theoretical scheme that makes a distinction between creative action or response and adaptive action or response contingent on whether or not innovation, 'the doing of new things or the doing of things that are already being done in a new way', is entailed (Schumpeter, 1947a, p. 151). Thus innovation is contrasted with those routine, habitual behaviours that give comfort to their followers but which also serve as a barrier to the acceptance of new activities, a barrier that is only overcome by the exceptional leadership that defines the exercise of the entrepreneurial function. It is no inconsistency when Schumpeter argues that it is the context of trying something new that forces on the entrepreneur the impossible attempt at rational calculation. Evolutionists would recognize this as a classic variation-cum-selection process in which the relative fitness values of different economic methods, old and new, are jointly determined and jointly adapted too, for the prevailing economic arrangements always provide the external environment in which the new can be tried and tested. Not all attempted innovations will succeed, but those that do have passed a test of profitability and, whether they are new forms of textile machinery or a new caviar product, the dynamic of adaptation is the same: it is a selection-driven, profit-induced process of transformation within a population of rival possibilities. In fact Schumpeter held the view that the majority of putative entrepreneurs never get their projects to fruition and, of those that do, 90 per cent fail to make a success of them (*BC*, p. 117). The differential profit advantages of those innovations that are viable in the prevailing order serve to stimulate investment in the form of imitative entry by less adventurous business minds, thus increasing the supply of the relevant class of commodity or service. In so doing, the system of output and input quantities and prices is transformed until the entrepreneurial profit is eliminated and this process, of necessity, changes the environment in which future entrepreneurial possibilities are conjectured and implemented. As he famously expressed the matter, entrepreneurial profit 'is at the same time the child and the victim of development' (*TED*, p. 154). The logic here is broader than often understood, in that an entrepreneur's profits are not only at risk from less adventurous imitators in the same field, but also from other entrepreneurs who have perceived yet another, different route to economic leadership. Thus entrepreneurial profit is not a form of income like wages or rents, it is the differential reward for advantageous innovation, it is transitory, it is a consequence of productive leadership and its amount is not to be determined on marginal productivity grounds, for these are the equilibrium notions that exclude its possibility (*TED*, p. 153). Entrepreneurial profit is a class of return that makes no sense in the circular flow; it is an expression of the value of novelty that cannot be known prior to the act of innovation. The interplay between order and innovation is the central feature of Schumpeter's vision: not only are innovations evaluated by the prevailing price structure to determine viability or failure; they lead to a development of the price and quantity structure, so adapting the innovation and the economy in mutual fashion. Thus entrepreneurial profit correlates with change or rather developmental change; it is an expression of the inadequacy of the current order now that more efficient ways of producing have emerged. Neither is it a reward for risk bearing; nor is it to be linked to the existence of differential rents accruing from long-standing differences in business ability and behaviour (*BC*, p. 153) and for which there is no tendency to equalization.

The transience of entrepreneurial profit carries clear implications for the innovating entrepreneurs, in particular, and for investors in innovative enterprises, in general, since few companies have a capacity for continued economic leadership. Schumpeter's firms, like Marshall's, do not maintain their entrepreneurial vigour indefinitely but slip into conservative routine, 'lingering in the fatally deepening dusk of respectable decay' (*BC*, p. 95). Death of firms is part and parcel of the adaptive process; it is the complement to innovative entry, and the repayment of capital is often concealed in dividends for the declining business. 'No industrial company of the type indicated gratifies its shareholders with a constant shower of gold; on the contrary it soon declines into a stage that has the most lamentable similarity with the drying up of a spring' (*TED*, p. 209). Hence the importance of 'new men' in the transformation process that is an important theme in Schumpeter's sociological evaluation of bourgeois capitalism; innovation-derived wealth brings high social position but, like the profits on which it is founded, those positions are transient and business dynasties are likely to be short lived, as they are in Marshall, with few exceptions to the rule of 'three generations from overalls to overalls' (ibid., p. 156). Flux in society parallels flux in business, with the rise and fall of firms in absolute and relative terms coexisting with innovation-based entry and innovation-induced exit.

It is here that Schumpeter alighted on a matter of the greatest importance: business experimentation is an investment process that requires resources to be committed in anticipation of results, and so depends on the terms and conditions under which credit is made available. Schumpeter's theory is a monetary theory, and the monetary system is not neutral in its real effects; credit creation to fund enterprise has a material determining effect on which innovations may be implemented, and thus on the evolution of the system. This is why Schumpeter is careful to distinguish between the investment theory of banking and finance, and the commercial theory of the funding of normal trade (*BC*, p. 115). The latter predominates numerically in banking activity, where it is a matter of administering the structures of the prevailing order, while it is the former that filters innovation and economic evolution. This is not the financing of routine working capital requirements in established channels, but rather the financing associated with the incalculable uncertainties carried by emergent novelty, and for which no offsetting assets can be offered directly by the entrepreneur to compensate for failure, for such assets are yet to be created. Schumpeter's identification of the role of capital and credit in funding and filtering emergent novelty is one of his major contributions to the understanding of innovation: no matter that he may have misunderstood the facts in relation to the finance of innovation in Austria, the innovation–finance connection is at the centre of the capitalist dynamic (Streissler, 1994). Hence the importance of competent bankers who can exercise independent judgement on the prospects for innovation-based enterprise. Consequently, a failure on the part of banks and the capital market to fund innovation will push enterprise into those established businesses able to deploy internal finance and offer collateral assets not immediately connected with the innovation in view, and, in so doing, bias the process against the 'new man'. The experimental nature of the system depends fundamentally in Schumpeter's scheme on the capacities of bankers and the workings of the money market: as he put it, the money market constitutes the 'headquarters of the capitalist system' (*TED*, p. 126).[4]

This naturally leads to a quite explicit perspective on competition not as perfect competition, a state of affairs, but entrepreneurial competition, a process that a company must engage in continually if it is to survive, not knowing from where or in what form rivals might emerge. For Schumpeter, competition is a process of transformation that can achieve and has achieved improvements in economic efficiency quite impossible to attain in conditions of perfect competition. The essential point is not to link competition with efficient resource allocation, but to identify it as an experimental discovery process that necessarily generates and requires above-normal profits as incentive and source of the funds to implement change. Consequently, to replace perfect competition by imperfect, monopolistic competition was no advance at all, for that still leaves competition as a state of affairs. It is not the number of competitors that counts, but their behavioural differences and their commitment to innovation-based variation 'so much more important that it becomes a matter of comparative indifference whether competition in the ordinary sense functions more or less promptly' (*CSD*, p. 85).

The perspective of competition as variation-cum-selection shades into the evolution as unfolding perspective. Innovations are rarely fully developed when they first appear, but rather offer up a space for exploration and further innovation to define a sequence or trajectory of related developments, a theme that is by now standard fare in the innovation literature (Dosi, 1982; Utterback, 1994). How this sequence is realized is not independent of the context in which the innovations are commercialized and spread, so the two perspectives of a development trajectory of related innovations and of a process of competitive selection of different innovations become intertwined. All of this fits together as a supply-side story. Indeed, one of the curiosities of Schumpeter's approach is that consumers, households that is, are treated as passive recipients of the innovations coming from new firms – no creative response for them. This is not only a gap in his reasoning; consumers, as matters of fact, do find new uses for products that are often unanticipated by their designers and innovators; it is also internally inconsistent to ignore the fact that firms are consumers too and that any innovation has consequences for the demand for inputs, including in these the products of other firms.

From another perspective, this is a model of knowledge-based economic transformation. Innovation as business experimentation is always a conjecture about a hypothetical, alternative economic structure. The carrying into effect of that conjecture depends on scarce leadership qualities, to give effect to novelty and overcome the manifold liabilities of newness (*TED*, pp. 86–7; *BC*, p. 100). In the process, new economic information and knowledge is generated, and it is the awareness of this new information that is generated within the system in response to the innovation that stimulates others to follow as imitators. So Schumpeter's capitalistic dynamic is a dynamic of knowledge and information, a point of considerable significance when we turn to Marshall. However, the new knowledge in question is not only, perhaps not even, a matter of high science and technology. Invention is not innovation, technology experiments are not business experiments, and, in a telling phrase, the innovation 'need not be of spectacular or of historic importance'; the humble innovation is quite essential to the business process (Schumpeter, 1947a, p. 151). Here one might find an interesting hint of Marshallian gradualism. With the passage of time, Schumpeter's sense of the agency that performs the entrepreneurial function extended from the creative individual to the corporate team, as trustified capitalism grew in relative importance and as salaried managers became the locus of the entrepreneurial function; yet in all cases it required the possibility of imagination to conceive of possible alternative economic worlds, as well as leadership and the sure evaluation of possibilities. Nor need the large firm completely dominate the innovation process. There is still room for the traditional entrepreneur, as the modern world of innovation in internet and bio-medicine so powerfully illustrates. No matter what the precise form of entrepreneurial agency, capitalism is not a system to preserve the *status quo*, but rather a self-transforming system in which transformation of knowing and transformation of acting run hand in hand.

One of the strengths of Schumpeter's approach is that his scheme of innovation is grounded in wider considerations. We have already noted one example of this kind: the idea that innovation may meet hostility from incumbents because the gains to novelty are necessarily losses to tradition, and so it is essential that the system is guided by institutions that are sufficiently open to accept the challenge from novelty. Capitalism cannot be conservative in its actions even though it must be conservative in its framing rules. The rules of the decentralized market process certainly facilitate openness and adaptation to innovation, but even they may need supplementing by regulatory action to prevent the suppression of enterprise. The social and instituted framing of capitalism matters in another dimension too, in relation to the cultural acceptance of the large rewards that can be associated with successful innovation. Inequality of outcomes is integral to the evolutionary process, success and failure are inevitably conjoined, and there is no requirement, *pace* the standards of Paretian welfare theory, for those who gain to compensate those who lose. Creative capitalism is uncomfortable capitalism, and unfettered competition 'red in tooth and claw' could rightly be dismissed by many as humanly unacceptable.[5] Exactly similar issues arise not in relation to profits and incomes more generally but in relation to the intrinsic instability of economic arrangements in innovation-driven systems: the source of much of the disruption that the system imposes on particular individuals in terms of loss of employment, obsolescence of skills, enforced change of locality or loss of capital value.

Here there is a paradox that Schumpeter forces us to confront: the stability of the price system, so important to the possibility of a coherent market order, must be set in the context of the instability posed by innovation.[6] Capitalism is a system in which all positions are potentially open to the challenge of creative destruction and will remain so under the present rules of the game. We are straying here into the ethical foundations of capitalism and of how a balance is to be struck between the beneficial effects of creation and the detrimental effects of destruction. It is not that Schumpeter offered solutions to such problems, but rather that he knew that an evolving cultural, social component would determine the continuing possibilities for innovation-led competition.[7] On average the system is progressive, but progress comes at a cost in terms of the unevenness of rewards generated by a restless capitalism.

Why is Schumpeter's capitalism restless? It is because it has metaphorically struck a Faustian bargain with knowledge. It is his identification of the connection between enterprise and new economic knowledge that is Schumpeter's enduring contribution to economics. Like Marshall, and indeed Hayek later, he was well ahead of his time, and economic theory has yet to fully absorb the implications of this conjunction of ideas. Indeed if progress, that is to say development and growth, involve 'putting productive resources to uses *hitherto untried in practice*, and withdrawing them from the uses they have served so far' (Schumpeter, 1928, p. 378, emphasis in original), this would present three major challenges to a theory of equilibrium economic states: the impossibility of predicting its evolution *ex ante* even when the general rules of its functioning are understood; the irreversible effects of the growth of knowledge and the impossibility of placing an economy in equilibrium if knowledge is not in equilibrium; and the inevitable link between individuality and personal knowledge such that socially situated individuals matter vitally to the evolution of the system. Economic agents are not homogeneous automata and, if they were, no progress would be possible and no history could await their discovery. It will not be lost on the reader that individual heterogeneity is a founding concept in evolutionary theory too. It is these three challenges that surprisingly connect Schumpeter with Marshall. As we shall claim in the conclusion, they also connect his thought with modern complexity thinking but that claim must be held in check for the moment.

ALFRED MARSHALL[8]

Although Marshall's first edition of his great work the *Principles of Economics* (1890) preceded Schumpeter's 1912 opus by fully two decades, it is quite remarkable how much they have in common in terms of a vision of a dynamics of capitalism based on evolutionary principles. Indeed, the common elements are in my view more important than the more obvious differences. The internally induced development of an economy is a central theme in Marshall's work, and, as in Schumpeter, the way in which it develops depends on the nature of its ordering processes. Evolution in Marshall depends on his evolutionary account of the market order but, unfortunately, Marshall's evolutionism was not taken seriously by his followers, who systematically replaced his dynamics of capitalism with a static jigsaw puzzle in which the economic problem is reduced to the explanation of the most appropriate place for each resource in the economic structure (Shove, 1930). With the benefit of a resurgent evolutionary economics post Nelson and Winter (1982), this dismissal of Marshall is no longer tenable. Marshall's evolutionary credentials should not be in doubt. As Schumpeter (1941 [1952]) suggests in his semi-centennial celebration of the *Principles*, Marshall is 'one of the first economists to realise that economics is an evolutionary science', his thought 'ran in terms of evolutionary change – in terms of an organic, irreversible process'. What is the evolutionary content of Marshall's thought?

In a remarkable way it runs parallel to Schumpeter's, although it is more formal in terms of its use of the demand-and-supply apparatus and marginal concepts. Innovation is a central part of the economic problem for Marshall just as much as for Schumpeter. For both, it equates to a capacity for business leadership that individuals are endowed with to different degrees and for both, business differentiation is a source of transient profit advantage. Marshall is just as capable as Schumpeter is of distinguishing invention from innovation, and in identifying great innovators, such as Henry Bessemer, as outstanding contributors to economic development. But, whereas Schumpeter draws attention to the activities of heroic leaders innovating to generate diversity, the role of enterprise in Marshall is *sotto voce*. For Marshall, innovation is a normal aspect of everyday business practice but its success depends on other creative dimensions of management, beyond the routine superintendence of labour that is downplayed by Schumpeter.[9] Marshall, however, is far less explicit than Schumpeter in conceiving of barriers to innovation and the resistance of established interests, perhaps a reflection of Schumpeter's wider sociological frame.

Like Schumpeter's, Marshall's theory presumes non-representative behaviour: in any trade there coexists a diversity of approaches to solving the problems of business. Just as Schumpeter used the stationary circular flow to describe what capitalism was not, so Marshall rejects the stationary state, including what we would now term proportional economic expansion, as a starting point for understanding capitalism. It is a chimera, and it is so because it abstracts from the particular processual nature of a knowledge-based economic system. At the heart of his rejection of stationary analysis lies Marshall's concern with knowledge and organization as the key concepts in his account of the growth and development of economies, and the explanation of growth and development is his primary objective. For an economy to be stationary, to follow the repetitive rhythm of the circular flow, knowledge would have to be stationary and neither Marshall nor Schumpeter could find any meaning in that stultifying notion. Thus we are told on the opening page of Book IV (*P*, IV, 1, p. 138) that knowledge and organization are the greater part of capital, that knowledge is the most powerful engine of production and that knowledge is aided by organization in its many different forms (Loasby, 2003). Organization and knowledge bring us not to Schumpeter's entrepreneur but to the manager of a business, although this in no way downplays the significance of enterprise, for knowledge and organization are the correlates of enterprise in Marshall. The reason for this is clear: the managerial function is a major route to explaining firm differentiation and firm dynamics, both of which are central to the long-run theory of value and to the role of differential profitability in economic change.[10]

In Book IV Marshall sets out the central evolutionary question thus: 'what are the causes which make different forms of management the fittest to profit from their environment, and the most likely to prevail over others . . .?' (*P*, IV, 9, p. 265). The answer is in two parts: first, in terms of the emergence of specialist managerial tasks and new divisions of managerial function, to reflect more complex organizational problems; and second, the specification of the principal tasks of management. These in turn fall within two broad categories of action: first, the ability to appoint and lead a team of subordinates and to make the most of their abilities while preserving order and unity in the plan of the business; and, second, to 'know the trade'. By this short phrase, Marshall means activities that are closely tied to enterprise and innovation, and included in this category are the ability to anticipate demand (expectations, as always, play an important role in Marshall's assessment of how people act, and different individuals hold substantively different expectations[11]), the facility to judge risks boldly but with care, and, finally, the capacity to innovate through the perception of opportunities to supply new commodities or improve methods of production. Indeed, managerial work can be very demanding in that it entails great mental strain 'in organising and devising new methods; or because it involves great anxiety and risk: and these two things frequently go together' (*P*, VI, 8, p. 612). It cannot be said that Marshall did not have innovation and enterprise, that is to say business leadership, very firmly in his grasp when he wrote about the distinctive contribution of management to economic organization. Two aspects of Marshall's argument are also relevant here. As with Schumpeter, capacities for leadership and innovation vary with age, the basis for the famous trees-in-the-forest metaphor of firm growth and decline, and, outside of the joint stock company, there may be serious problems of business succession. Equally significant from an evolutionary viewpoint are the differences in managerial ability that coexist in an economy. In broad terms, business leaders are divided into those who open up new and improved business methods and, as in Schumpeter, those who follow beaten tracks (*P*, VI, 7, p. 597).[12] Very few employers combine the multifarious managerial abilities to a high degree and scarcely any two owe their business success to the same combination of advantages. Consequently each business is an 'individual', differing in some degree from its rivals, for no two persons pursuing the same aims follow exactly the same route and, importantly, we are told, this tendency to variation is the chief source of progress (*P*, V, 4, p. 355). This telling phrase captures in a single step the deep evolutionary content of Marshall's thought.

What Marshall adds to our understanding is his famous periodization scheme, which is not to be read as descriptive of different kinds of equilibria but rather as a statement of different contemporaneous forces acting with different velocities. More radical forms of innovation in Marshall are the province of the secular period, but the predominant focus of the *Principles* is the long period, when time allows the forces of investment and of innovation in established channels, drawing on established principles, to work their effects. It is in terms of the long-period method that Marshall makes a connection between profitability and structural development that parallels Schumpeter's account of adaptation to an innovation. However, for Marshall, innovation is not the cataclysmic event it is for Schumpeter, but, rather a reflection of his gradualist approach in which new ways are continually being introduced throughout the many different sectors of the economy. Innovation is endemic in the system, and the process by which firms expand and contract their capacity to supply particular goods and services is at the core of Marshall's principle of substitution in which more profitable firms prosper at the expense of their weaker brethren. Outcomes are tested in the market so that 'society substitutes one undertaker for another who is less efficient in proportion to his charges' (1920, V, 3, p. 341). Indeed, in introducing a discussion of profit in relation to business ability, Marshall is quite explicit that this principle of substitution is a 'special and limited application of the law of 'the survival of the fittest' (1920, VI, 7, p. 597). We are surely justified in claiming that Marshall's principle of substitution is the logical equivalent of Schumpeter's sequences of creative destruction through innovation and imitation.

The whole apparatus depends, as it does in Schumpeter, on recognizing the differentiation of firms within a trade, but Marshall has more to say on the many possible sources of business variation. The immediate consequences of real differences in the ability of business leaders are differences in the profitability of their business organizations and their prospects for survival, such that average ability brings forth quite low returns but exceptional ability allows fortunes to be amassed. Differential ability translates

into differential profitability, and, by making good profits, a firm blessed
with exceptional managerial ability and energy (*P*, VI, 8, p. 614) not only
adds to own capital but increases the willingness of others to lend to it on
more advantageous terms. The converse happens for weaker businessmen
so that selection, via the product market directly and the capital market
by remove, we are told, results in an unexpected correlation between size
and business ability (*P*, IV, 12, p. 312). In a further passage that could well
have come from the *Theory of Economic Development*,[13] we find Marshall
arguing that 'A manufacturer of exceptional ability and energy will apply
better methods and perhaps better machinery than his rivals: he will
organise better the manufacturing and the marketing sides of his business',
and as a consequence, 'he will obtain increasing return and also increasing
profit: for if he is only one among many producers, his increased output
will not materially lower the price of his goods, and nearly all the benefit
of his economies will accrue to himself.' (*P*, VI, 8, pp. 614–15). It is no
accident that this passage comes not from the discussion of management
and organization in Book IV, but rather from the chapters in Book VI
dealing with profitability and its decomposition into interest and the
gross and net earnings of management. The relation between prospective
business profitability and sources of capital is as important to Marshall's
long-period analysis as it is to Schumpeter's discussion of innovation and
credit. The further aspect of this is that the process of market evolution
depends on the operation of the capital market in its general support of the
investment process, not simply in relation to the financing of innovations
and new men, although we may note in passing that the term 'new men'
is frequently resorted to by Marshall. In Marshall too, differences in the
ability to conceive of and conduct a business are of the first importance to
the dynamics of the system's evolution.

As soon as we emphasize the distribution of business ability we are led
automatically to the problem of how economic change is to be connected
to diversity and its source in innovation. It is here that Marshall made a
major theoretical innovation, namely the representative firm, which serves
as the fulcrum around which non-representative firms are rising and
falling relatively and absolutely, and in relation to which the prospects of
entry are judged.[14] The representative firm is Marshall's way of managing
the flux that is characteristic of any industry and it is of course a statistical notion not to be confused with the idea of the uniform representative
agent of modern theory. Marshall's depiction of market order thus distinguishes the marginal firm from the representative firm; the former is the
measure of the market-clearing price in any long-period market order; the
latter is the measure of the average profitability of the industry and thus
the long-period rate of transformation of that order. Marshall realized

that evolution is not random change but rather a process that presupposes an economic structure, a regular order that can evolve. This is why the demand-and-supply economics of static, partial equilibrium play such a central role in his analysis: they describe the order and form the substrate on which evolutionary forces can operate. The fact that different forces work with different velocities is not the basis for a description of different kinds of equilibria, but rather a device to account for the connection between structural change and historical time. This is one of Marshall's great contributions to economics, for when different components of the system change at different velocities, this necessarily revises, restructures the prevailing order, and the prevailing order is all we ever have.

Schumpeter and Marshall also hold in common a processual vision of the central place of competition in the self-transformation of capitalism within an instituted frame that keeps the process open.[15] In Marshall, it is not perfect competition at all but a matter of rivalry (racing is his alternative description), a contest between competitors of different and changing abilities, grounded in the fundamental characteristics of modern industrial life – self-reliance, deliberation and an awareness of the possible future consequences of actions. Competition is not a dull, equilibrium state, but rather a creative force promoting spontaneity of action; it is a matter, as he put it, of 'Economic Freedom' (1920, I, 1, p. 10), that is to say, the freedom to use knowledge and capability for economic advantage.[16] Furthermore, innovation is inseparable from the competitive process, for the advantages of economic freedom 'are never more strikingly manifest than when a business man endowed with genius is trying experiments, at his own risk, to see whether some new method or combination of old methods, will be more efficient than the old' (1920, V, 8, p. 406). The relation runs two ways and mutually reinforces the links between free competition and business experimentation. Nor is the idea of competition to be confused with the perfection of the market, which is greatly influenced by the prevailing transport and communications technologies, improvements that have sharpened the forces that establish common prices for common goods and services.

This is Marshall's theory of the competitive process in which differentiated business traits, including those in relation to innovation, are connected to differential profitability and thus access to resources from the capital market. Yet Marshall's Darwinian credentials are sophisticated: there is no necessary implication that the most profitable activity in terms of time and place is necessarily the best activity when considered from a wider perspective. This is the dynamic significance of external effects: selection is via the price mechanism and the price mechanism does not extend to everything that is of value, especially innovations as yet unborn.

The final strand of Marshall's thought that needs our attention lies in the role of the wider instituted frame in shaping the evolution of the system. The education system is of vital importance in this regard, but it is Marshall's exposition of an innovation systems perspective, grounded in a quite remarkably evolutionary take on the growth of knowledge, that marks him out as an economist who understood the interplay between the evolution of knowledge and the evolution of economic activity. Education serves an important social purpose: to enhance vertical mobility and prevent that 'wasteful negligence which allows genius that happens to be born of lowly parentage to expend itself in lowly work' (1920, IV, 6, p. 212). It also serves to supply the new skills needed for an industrial society in which machinery displaces low-skilled activities. While a liberal education adapts the mind to use its best faculties in business, a technical education develops the skills to master the details of particular trades, and important national differences are evident to Marshall. The German system, for example, is better fitted for developing middle ranks of industry and for imparting scientific training. But, in a passage that is manifestly Schumpeterian in spirit, he claims that the English system is better for developing daring energy and restless enterprise (1920, IV, 6, p. 209). That the supply of enterprise may rest in education is Marshall's point, and the economic value of one genius, a Bessemer, Pasteur, Jenner or Darwin, Shakespeare or Beethoven, can repay the cost of their education many times over.

In relation to innovation and the growth of knowledge, Marshall offers an analysis that is thoroughly modern in outlook. As with the treatment of management, the organic perception of the division of labour holds sway but now in relation to the generation of new knowledge, and with regard to the internal and external organization of the firm. Given this frame, it is not surprising to find Marshall claiming in *Industry and Trade* that the advances in the chemical, electrical and biological sciences will open up the prospect of increasing returns to effort for many generations to come. Knowledge for Marshall develops cumulatively in paradigm fashion in chains of related sequences of discoveries, 'each new knowledge being the offspring of others that went before, and the parent of many that follow' (*IT*, II, 2, p. 206). Moreover, knowledge production has to be organized in such a way that '*imagination* creates movement; *caution* checks reason by working out parallel but independent chains of thought, and each general rule is *confirmed or discredited* by experiments or observations of specific facts' (ibid., p. 203, my emphasis). This is not too far removed in broad outline from a variation–selection view of the growth of knowledge that a modern evolutionary epistemologist might hold.[17]

Marshall's crucial insight in his account of innovation is that it is no longer sufficient to focus on the firm in isolation; its external organization in relation to the growth of knowledge matters. So it is not an overstatement to see Marshall as propounding an innovation systems perspective that, of course, is simply another angle on the division of labour and its coordination. But in order to benefit from external economies, the firm needs an external organization; external economies do not come for free and access to them has to be organized and coordinated. Innovation is not confined to the new firm: Marshall's established firms are innovators and such a firm's internal knowledge-generating processes are embedded in Marshall's thought in a broader matrix of national and sectoral arrangements of two broad kinds, the industrial district and the national system of research. The first is well known: the co-location of firms facilitates the communication of information; hence it correlates knowledge so that 'the mysteries of the trade become no mysteries' and ideas are readily interchanged and, crucially, become 'the source of further new ideas', a perfect Marshallian combination of restless knowledge and restless activity (1920, V, 10, p. 271). The second knowledge-generating structure is not so well known perhaps because it is only found in *Industry and Trade* (1919). It is articulated in terms of a tripartite ecology of research laboratories: those of the first order, charged with extending knowledge in the large and normally the province of publicly funded universities, the primary originators of scientific advances that revolutionize the methods of industry; those of the second order, charged with generating knowledge directed at the requirements of a particular branch of industry and either organized by single giant businesses or in collaborative association between businesses;[18] and those of the third order, quality control laboratories for particular establishments that check that their output meets the standards required. As with any division of labour, its functioning depends on how it is interconnected, not in this case by markets but by personal scientific contact and reference to the published literature. The technical research laboratory of an industry benefits from keeping in touch with the chief scientific laboratories, and 'the latter may gain much and lose nothing' by keeping in touch with the industries whose methods may be improved by the fruits of fundamental research.

Before leaving Marshall, we may note that it is somewhat of a surprise to find that even the mature Schumpeter never fully accepted the Marshallian vision, or rather, as he put it the Smith–Mill–Marshall theory of economic growth (1947b, p. 7), a conclusion that he had reached much earlier. The famous 1928 article gives a perfectly fair account of Marshall's theory: the interdependence there is contained between investment in capacity and the development of new wants; an endogenous expansion of the system in which the interplay between saving and investment is shaped by the distribution of increasing returns and coordination of activities. Schumpeter's objection to this is clear: expansion cannot explain expansion, a self-exciting system needs a stimulus and that stimulus comes from the new combinations. This is surely correct, but it is not accurate as a criticism of Marshall; innovation and invention are part of his scheme too.

In drawing this discussion of Marshall to a close, I do not want to hide the more obvious differences between the two great scholars: on the existence of a rate of interest, on the mechanics of money and credit, and on the business cycle they cannot be conjoined. But these differences should not hide what they shared: a vision of an innovation-led, evolving capitalism within a specific set of instituted rules that sustain a market order. This said, it is appropriate to turn to some wider consequences of this view and to connect it to more modern themes.

THE WIDER CONSEQUENCES

The most important line of approach that Schumpeter and Marshall share is their reliance on an evolutionary understanding of the development of capitalism. For both scholars the bedrock of their approaches is a variation-cum-selection model of order and transformation. Variation is generated via enterprise, and the vehicles of emergent novelty are the innovations, or more precisely the business experiments, that flow from business leadership. The new is to be compared with the old, and it is the market process that carries out this valuation and applies the test of economic viability to the business experiment. Valuation is one thing; adaptation is quite another and depends, as both recognized, on the responses of consumers, on the investment strategies of the innovating and imitating firms, and on the responses of the suppliers of productive services. In short, the market is a process of stimulating and adapting to change, not an instituted means to quieten the world. How quickly these adjustments to new opportunities can take place is not entirely covered by the theories of market order that they separately developed, but the general processes at work are clear and depend primarily on the profitability and the utility of the innovation in question. Thus Schumpeter and Marshall are at their most cogent when analysing the process of adaptation consequent upon economic variation, but they necessarily have less to say when it comes to explaining the number and kinds of innovations. I say necessarily because the act of innovation falls within the realm of creative action, and while we can understand how a particular order signals the scope for innovation, we cannot hope to treat innovation as if it were containable within a closed system of explanation. Rather we are dealing with an open system that renders impossible any concept of predictable, endogenous innovation. The 'within' must live with the 'without', as Schumpeter well understood.[19]

One of the fundamental issues here is the question of equilibrium. Neither Marshall nor Schumpeter saw capitalism as a system in equilibrium, but for both of them it was a system structured by powerful ordering processes, in particular the market process and the price mechanism. Market order is a product of relatively durable instituted frames for economic action, but those orders are necessarily transient and possess no durable, unique attractors. To say that an economic system has a durable attractor of any kind or number is equivalent to stating that the state and distribution of human knowledge has durable attractors too, but this is not what history tells us. The economy is an open system because knowledge is also an open system, and it could not be otherwise within the instituted frame of capitalism. Is this, as Popper suggests, the price we pay for being curious humans? Pre-capitalism lacked this restless dynamic because the constituent orders on which evolution might work was too fragmentary and so a series of unconnected, virtually, stationary states was a logical and practical possibility. As soon as trade and its instituted frame emerged, this possibility disappeared; for trade, more than anything else, developed new knowledge and began the restless movement that would fitfully but gradually accelerate and, post renaissance and reformation, there could be no turning back. Isaiah Berlin captures the essential point: when writing of Vico and his understanding of history, he tells us: 'man is a self transforming creature, the satisfaction of each set of needs alters his character and breeds new needs and forms of life'; he cannot therefore live his life 'according to unvarying, timeless principles, for then there would be no growth, no historical change, only eternal repetition as in the lives of animals' (Berlin, 2000, p. 65). This is precisely the impossibility that Schumpeter and Marshall point us away from; it is the core of the link between the development of knowledge and the development of an economy, the link that ties together self-transformation with self-organization, evolution with order.

The reasoning that flows from a conjoined Marshall–Schumpeter vision is that information and new knowledge are inevitable joint products of the operation of the market process and are created internally. Individuals engaged in the market process are continually revising their knowledge as a consequence of their engagement with that market process, and the more entrepreneurially minded among them are foreseeing ways in which the prevailing order can be transformed. Thus the peculiar property of a stationary state or circular flow is not simply its repetitive nature, but the fact that it is a state without learning or conjecture on anyone's part: it is a world of automata who agree on everything. Only by assuming that the beliefs and knowledge of all individuals are frozen and held in common can we make sense of the idea, and, while this may be a useful abstract exercise, it is not what Schumpeter and Marshall have in mind, for it is the very antithesis of life in capitalism. Knowledge is the most powerful engine of production, *once its application is organized*, and capitalism provided a remarkably fruitful system for generating the required organization through firm and market. This positive feedback process leads us to complexity and results in the co-evolution of knowledge and economic action. As Marshall (1879), and Popper much more recently (1995), recognized, economic activity changes human beliefs and knowledge directly and indirectly, and every change in knowledge opens up the conditions for changes in activity and thus further changes in knowledge *ad infinitum*, that is, without knowable limit. Like any autocatalytic process, the output of knowledge becomes the input into new knowledge, and one idea results in another although the connection may only become transparent after the event. In the modern economy, of course, this is reinforced by the practice of allocating a non-trivial portion of the economy's resources to the acquisition of knowledge, off line, and the dissemination of information, together with its embodiment in the population via processes of education and training. These are key institutional developments that enable society to allocate its resources to the purposeful exploration of the unknown, with a profound effect on the conduct of economic life, for it builds into the system a further powerful, quasi-independent source of novelties. Consequently, with the passage of time, an increasingly refined division of labour has emerged in the production, dissemination and application of laboratory-based knowledge. As we have seen, Marshall recognized that new fields of knowledge have emerged together with a complex skein of systemic interrelation between laboratories in firms, their customers and suppliers, universities and other public and private research organizations. While Schumpeter realized that these independent sources of knowledge make more vital the distinction between invention and innovation to the degree that the supply of possible sources of invention was effectively unlimited, only the forces stimulating and limiting innovation became the rate-determining aspects of development.

Here we must face a paradox that the institutions of capitalism generate and resolve. Economic order depends on a very high degree of commonality of understanding at different levels of economic action, yet progress and the transformation of order depend on the breakdown of that commonality of understanding. If beliefs are too fluid, order will descend into chaos; if beliefs are too rigid, then order descends into lifeless equilibrium. Once again Isaiah Berlin captures the point with perfect clarity when he writes that, like all Utopias, equilibrium is a fiction, at best a satire, a state of perfection within which 'all is still and immutable and eternal' (Berlin, 1991, p. 22). Marshall and Schumpeter faced this paradox and understood that capitalism evolves too and develops institutional structures that establish sufficient order for the individuals to imagine how the present constellation of activities can evolve into a new constellation without the system breaking down into chaos. These innovations emerge on a small scale in local contexts but at least some have the capacity to stimulate widespread adoption and large-scale transformation. Thus Marshall and Schumpeter understood well that 'history versus equilibrium' is a false dichotomy; the changing economic order writes history and leads to history dependence without any resort to equilibrium.

The corollary of their vision is that economic development is always shrouded in uncertainty as to how it will develop. The system gives confidence for the immediate future but no confidence at all as the horizon extends into longer time spans, and so we have no secure expectation about the future order other than it will be different from our present and past experience. The point is familiar and need not be elaborated further, but it does bear on the idea that the Schumpeter and Marshall visions are thoroughly modern in purpose; to express it rather grandly, they have an air of complexity about them. I take the essence of complexity to be the idea that relatively simple sets of rules generate unpredictable behaviour, unpredictability that is reflected in the emergent novelties that we call innovations. Complexity, though, is an emergent system property that depends on the connections between components. The components are knowledgeable and socially situated individuals, and it is the distributed nature of knowledge and personal differences in knowing and conjecturing, the most important aspects of individuality, that make innovation possible. For individuation to generate complexity the individuals need to be connected in a system, and that system must be open to the possibility of and adaptive to innovation. The process is evolutionary in the sense described above, with micro events generating the novelties and meso and macro processes constraining the adaptive response in a synthesis of bottom-up and top-down processes.[20] The institutions of the market economy have precisely the required characteristics, with a distributed system of innovation and a systemic market response by consumers and producers to the challenges and opportunities represented by innovation. The unpredictability and genuine uncertainty as to the future order follow from these properties. Concepts of calculable risk do not work here because the state space of the future cannot be prespecified: to put it differently, a characteristic of complexity, as of economic life, is the non-computability of possible futures.[21]

CONCLUDING REMARKS

Although all economies are necessarily knowledge based, not all instituted arrangements are compatible with endogenous development. It is here that the characteristics of post-seventeenth-century capitalism seem to be of paramount importance in that they not only generate ordered patterns of economic activity; they also create incentives to innovate and adapt to the consequences of emergent novel behaviours. It is the peculiar property of the instituted rules of capitalism, and the political systems and ethical structures in which they are embedded, that, in generating economic order, they also create the incentives and means to transform those orders. This is the great insight that shapes the thought of Schumpeter and Marshall: capitalism is an ordered system but it is an open system; that is, it is first and foremost a system for the generation and application of new knowledge.

NOTES

1. In referring to the respective writings of Marshall and Schumpeter, I have used the following abbreviations. For Marshall: *P – The Principles of Economics* (8th edn, 1920); and *IT – Industry and Trade* (1919). For Schumpeter: *TED – The Theory of Economic Development* (1912; English translation 1934); *BC – Business Cycles* (1939); and *CSD – Capitalism, Socialism and Democracy* (1942).
2. See Jolink (1996) for an interesting account of evolutionary ideas in Walras, ideas essentially focused on the concept of evolution as a cumulative unfolding of phenomena.
3. Prof. Shionoya draws attention to the fact that in the second German edition of the work, subsequently translated into English as *TED*, Schumpeter claims that equilibrium and development are incompatible concepts; equilibrium arises only in a static economy. The reference is to p. 541 of *Theorie der Wirtschaftlichen Entwicklung* (1912) as quoted in Shionoya (1997), p. 39. This is not the place to enter into the debate about the difference between a static and a stationary economy, although we return to the issue in the final section.
4. The recently instituted innovations associated with the growth of venture capital and corporate venturing in the USA, in particular, can be interpreted as an instituted Schumpeterian innovation in the banking system, a response to the highly uncertain nature of business experimentation in the context of radically new technologies and markets (Freeman, 2005). At the time of writing, an international financial crisis associated with the development of securitized lending instruments reflects a far less successful innovation in finance.
5. From a modern viewpoint two instituted responses have been invoked to meliorate the effects of competition. One is the resort to high rates of progressive taxation to equalize more fully *ex post* outcomes, but this threatens the very link between enterprise and profitability. The alternative is a welfare state safety net that buffers the vicissitudes of innovation-driven competition on individuals and localities without undermining the *primum mobile* of the system. This tension between progress and the distribution of its effects is, of course, a central theme in Hayek (1944).
6. It is no accident that the famous paper (Schumpeter, 1928) that must have brought his ideas to the attention of most English-speaking audiences is called 'The instability of

capitalism', and that it plays on the distinction between institutional durability in the round and the transience of particular arrangements in the small.

7. Schumpeter (1943) is the place where his fears that the internal questioning of the system might destroy it from within are expressed.
8. The following account has been shaped greatly by the work of Raffaelli (2003) and of the encyclopaedic volume edited by Rafaelli et al. (2006), to whom all Marshall scholars must be indebted.
9. See *TED*, pp. 20–21.
10. I have explored these themes more fully in Metcalfe (2007a and 2007b), to which I refer the reader.
11. See Loasby (1990) for further elaboration. We note in passing that a business does not expect to make profits, or losses for that matter, by having the same expectations as rivals. At a minimum, rational expectations in relation to business prospects must mean variform expectations.
12. Not that leadership in innovation necessarily brings a full reward to the innovator: those that pioneer new paths may confer on society benefits that are disproportionate to their personal gains even if they 'have died millionaires' (*P*, VI, 7, p. 598).
13. See *TED*, pp. 129–33.
14. I have explored the theory of the representative firm more fully in Metcalfe (2007a, b), to which the interested reader is referred.
15. Here Marshall is demonstrating that his roots lie in Adam Smith. See Richardson (1975) for a compelling account of Smith's dynamic theory of competition.
16. For further discussion the reader is referred to Groenewegen (2003).
17. Vincenti (1990), for example.
18. Marshall, who was generally enthusiastic about cooperative arrangements, notes that it may be advisable for such a cooperative research venture to be partly funded by the public in order to exercise a degree of control and prevent the emergence of cartels (*IT*, I, 5, p. 101).
19. On this see Shionoya (1997, p. 186) for Schumpeter's defence against Kuznets's review of *Business Cycles* in which he criticized Schumpeter's failure to close the system by providing a theory of innovation.
20. See Dopfer and Potts (2007) for further development of this theme.
21. See the interesting paper on this theme by Boschetti and Gray (2007) and Metcalfe and Ramlogan (2005) for further elaboration.

REFERENCES

Berlin, I. (1991), *The Crooked Timber of Humanity: Chapters in the History of Ideas* (edited by Henry Hardy), London: Fontana Press.

Berlin, I. (2000), *The Power of Ideas* (edited by Henry Hardy), Princeton, NJ: Princeton University Press.

Boschetti, F. and R. Gray (2007), 'Emergence and computability', *Emergence, Complexity and Organisation* (*E:CO*), vol. 9, pp. 120–30.

Dopfer, K. and J. Potts (2007), *Micro–Meso–Macro: Foundations for Evolutionary Economics*, London: Routledge.

Dosi, G. (1982), 'Technological paradigms and technological trajectories', *Research Policy*, **11**, 147–62.

Freeman, J. (2005), 'Venture capital and modern capitalism', in V. Nee and R. Swedberg (eds), *The Economic Sociology of Capitalism*, Princeton, NJ: Princeton University Press, pp. 144–67.

Groenewegen, P. (2003), 'Competition and evolution: the Marshallian conciliation enterprise', in R. Arena and M. Quere (eds), *The Economics of Alfred Marshall*, Basingstoke: Palgrave, pp. 113–35.

Hayek, F.A. (1944), *The Road to Serfdom*, Chicago, IL: Chicago University Press.

Jolink, A. (1996), *The Evolutionist Economics of Leon Walras*, London: Routledge.

Loasby, B.J. (1990), 'Firms, markets and the principle of continuity', in J. Whitaker (ed.), *Centenary Essays on Alfred Marshall*, Cambridge: Cambridge University Press, pp. 108–26.

Loasby, B.J. (2003), 'Efficiency and time', in R. Arena and M. Quere (eds), *The Economics of Alfred Marshall*, Basingstoke: Palgrave, pp. 202–20.

Marshall, A. (1879 [1930]), *The Pure Theory of Foreign Trade. The Pure Theory of Domestic Values*, reprints of Scarce Tracts in Economic and Political Science, London: London School of Economics.

Marshall, A. (1919), *Industry and Trade*, London: Macmillan.

Marshall, A. (1920), *Principles of Economics*, 8th edn, London: Macmillan.

Metcalfe, J.S. (2007a), 'Alfred Marshall and the general theory of evolutionary economics', *History of Economic Ideas*, **15** (1), 81–110.

Metcalfe, J.S. (2007b), 'Alfred Marshall's Mecca: reconciling the theories of value and development', *Economic Record*, **83**, Supplement 1, September, S1–22.

Metcalfe, J.S. and R. Ramlogan (2005), 'Limits to the economy of knowledge and knowledge of the economy', *Futures*, **37**, 655–74.

Nelson R.R. and S. Winter (1982), *An Evolutionary Theory of Economic Change*, Cambridge, MA: Belknap Press of Harvard University Press.

Popper, K. (1995), *A World of Propensities*, Bristol: Thoemmes.

Raffaelli, T. (2003), *Marshall's Evolutionary Economics*, London: Routledge.

Raffaelli, T., G. Becattini and M. Dardi (eds) (2006), *The Elgar Companion to Alfred Marshall*, Cheltenham, UK and Northampton, MA, USA: Edward Elgar.

Renart, H. and E.S. Renart (2005), 'Creative destruction in economics: Nietzsche, Sombart, Schumpeter', mimeo, Cambridge University.

Richardson, G.G. (1975), 'Adam Smith on competition and increasing returns', in A.S. Skinner and T. Wilson (eds), *Essays on Adam Smith*, Oxford: Oxford University Press, pp. 350–60.

Santarelli, E. and E. Pesciarelli (1990), 'The emergence of a vision: the development of Schumpeter's theory of entrepreneurship', *History of Political Economy*, **22** (4), 667–96.

Schumpeter, J.A. (1912 [1934]), *The Theory of Economic Development*, Oxford: Galaxy Books.

Schumpeter, J.A. (1928), 'The instability of capitalism', *Economic Journal*, **38**, 361–86.

Schumpeter, J.A. (1939), Business Cycles, Volumes I & II, New York: McGraw-Hill.

Schumpeter, J.A. (1941 [1952]), 'Alfred Marshall (1842–1924)', in J.A. Schumpeter (ed.), *Ten Great Economists*, London: George Allen & Unwin, pp. 91–109.

Schumpeter, J.A. (1943), *Capitalism, Socialism and Democracy*, London: George Allen & Unwin.

Schumpeter, J.A. (1947a), 'The creative response in economic history', *Journal of Economic History*, **7** (2), 149–59.

Schumpeter, J.A. (1947b), 'Theoretical problems of economic growth', *Journal of Economic History*, **7**, 1–9.

Shionoya, Y. (1997), *Schumpeter and the Idea of Social Science*, Cambridge: Cambridge University Press.

Shove, G.F. (1930), 'The representative firm and increasing returns', in 'Increasing returns and the representative firm: a symposium', *Economic Journal*, **40**, 94–116.

Streissler, E.W. (1994), 'The influence of German and Austrian economists on Joseph A. Schumpeter', in Y. Shionoya and M. Perlman (eds), *Schumpeter in the History of Ideas*, Ann Arbor, MI: University of Michigan Press, pp. 13–38.

Utterback, J.M. (1994), *Mastering the Dynamics of Innovation: How Companies Can Seize Opportunities in the Face of Technological Change*, Boston, MA: Harvard University Press.

Vincenti, W. (1990), *What Engineers Know and How They Know It*, Baltimore, MD: Johns Hopkins University Press.

PART II

Finance in Modern Economics

4.   The co-evolution of technologies and financial institutions

Pier Paolo Saviotti and Andreas Pyka

1.   INTRODUCTION

The mutual dependencies of the industrial and financial realms of economies are at the heart of comprehensive neo-Schumpeterian economics (CNSE) (Hanusch and Pyka, 2007a). The relationships between these two pillars are characterized by subtle conditions, in particular stemming from the financial markets, which allow for only a narrow corridor of mutual support with respect to prolific economic development (Hanusch and Pyka, 2007b).

In a series of papers (Saviotti and Pyka, 2004a, 2004b, 2004c), we have developed a model of economic development by the creation of new sectors, which allows us to study the mutual impact of industry development and financial availability on macroeconomic growth performance. In this chapter, we focus on the dynamics of the co-evolution of technologies and of financial institutions (Nelson, 1994). We examine the possibility that co-evolutionary forces can give rise to irregular and chaotic behaviour. In the framework of CNSE, this is more than a methodological exercise. In fact, the existence of deterministic chaos can be expected to affect patterns of economic development.

The idea that biological evolution could occur at the edge of chaos has been formulated during the early years of the Santa Fe Institute by Langton (1990) and Kauffman (1993), among others (Mitchell Waldrop, 1992). The logic behind this idea was that, in the vicinity of chaos, evolution has a better chance to succeed in creating the complex and adaptable structures that characterize biological life than either in a very ordered state (e.g. a crystal) or in a completely chaotic one. The possibility that such an idea might be applied to the evolution of economic systems had been mentioned at that time but was never explored explicitly. Here, by using our model of economic development, we explore whether the co-evolution of technologies and of financial institutions can lead to chaotic behaviour, whether the onset of chaos has an impact on economic development, and whether economic evolution can occur better at the edge of chaos than in chaotic or pre-chaotic regions.

2.   A MODEL OF ECONOMIC DEVELOPMENT BY THE CREATION OF NEW SECTORS

The model of development that we describe in this section has been developed over the past seven years and has already undergone a number of modifications (see Saviotti and Pyka, 2004a, 2004b, 2004c, 2005). We will give first a brief verbal description of the model and then introduce the equations most central for this study. For a detailed description of the formal structure, we refer to the respective references.

In the model, each sector is generated by an important innovation. Such an innovation creates a potential market and gives rise to what we call an adjustment gap. The term adjustment gap is due to the fact that, as soon as a potential market is created, it is in fact empty: neither the productive capacity nor the demand for the innovation is present. They are gradually constructed during the life cycle of the new sector. As the new sector matures, the adjustment gap is continuously closed: a productive capacity, which in the end matches demand, is created. When this happens, the sector enters its saturation phase. The productive capacity is generated by Schumpeterian entrepreneurs establishing new firms initially induced by the expectation of a temporary monopoly and related extraordinary profits. The success of the innovation gives rise to a bandwagon of imitators. The number of firms in the new sector gradually rises, but this also raises the intensity of competition in the sector, thus gradually reducing the inducement to further entry. After the intensity of competition in the new sector reaches levels comparable to those of established sectors, the new sector is no longer innovating but becomes part of the circular flow. When a sector achieves maturity in the way described above, an inducement exists for Schumpeterian entrepreneurs to set up a new niche, which can eventually give rise to the emergence of a new industry. In other words, the declining economic potential of maturing sectors induces the creation of newer and more promising ones. Competition plays a very important role in this process of creation of new industries. Entrepreneurs are induced to establish new firms by the expectation of a temporary monopoly, that is, by the absence of competition. However, the new sector could not achieve its economic potential unless imitative entry took place. As a result, the intensity of competition rises, thus reducing the inducement to further entry. An additional contribution is made to the dynamics of our artificial economic system by inter-sector competition. Inter-sector competition

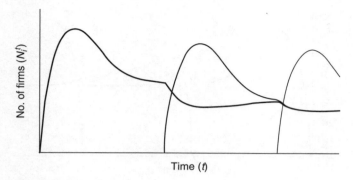

Figure 4.1a   Number of firms

arises when two sectors produce comparable services. Inter-sector competition is an important component of contestable markets (Baumol et al., 1982) and can keep the overall intensity of competition of the economic system high, even when each sector achieves very high levels of industrial concentration.

In our model, the variety of the economic system plays an essential role. Economic variety is approximated by the number of different sectors. By raising variety, the creation of new sectors provides the mechanism whereby economic development can continue in the long run. In this way, the economic system can escape the trap generated by the imbalance between rising productivity and saturating demand (Pasinetti, 1981, 1993; Saviotti, 1996), which would occur in a system at constant composition. This also affects the macroeconomic employment situation: in particular, this artificial economic system can keep generating employment, even when employment creation is falling within each sector (Saviotti and Pyka, 2004b).

In order to illustrate qualitatively the developments generated by our model, Figure 4.1a shows the development of the number of firms in a certain industry. Within a wide range of conditions, the number of firms in each sector grows initially, reaches a maximum and then falls to a fairly low value. Within these conditions, each sector seems to follow a life cycle, similar to the ones detected by Klepper (1996), Jovanovic and MacDonald (1994), Utterback and Suarez (1993). However, in our model, this industry life cycle is created by variables very different from those used by the previous authors in their models, which include increasing returns to R&D, radical innovations and the emergence of dominant designs. In our case, the cyclical behaviour is caused only by the combined dynamics of competition and of market saturation. We do not wish to say that cyclical

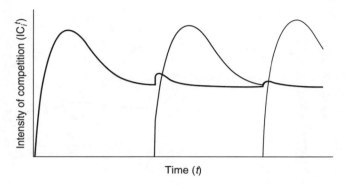

Figure 4.1b   Intensity of competition

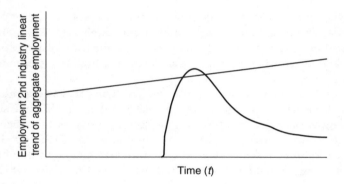

Figure 4.1c   Employment in a single industry

behaviour cannot arise under the conditions identified by the previous authors. We simply say that it can also arise from the interplay of competition and of market saturation. Figure 4.1b displays the development of the intensity of competition, and one clearly sees the impact of intra-industry dynamics as well as the additional effect of inter-sector competition after the emergence of the new sector. Figure 4.1c then shows the course of development of employment in a single industry – which first strongly increases, but in the shake-out period also is reduced considerably – and the trend of the aggregate employment on the macroeconomic level, which can be positive despite the decrease of sectoral employment.

In the following paragraphs, we describe briefly the main formal aspects of our model. A complete description can be found in Saviotti and Pyka (2004a, 2004b). The main equation governing the dynamics of each sector in the model is:

$$dN_i^t = k_1 \cdot FA_i^t \cdot AG_i^t - IC_i^t - MA_i^t \qquad (4.1)$$

where N_i^t is the number of firms in sector i at time t, AG_i^t is the adjustment gap at time t, IC_i^t is the intensity of competition at time t, and MA_i^t is the number of mergers and acquisitions at time t. Equation (4.1) represents the rates of entry ($FA_i^t \cdot AG_i^t$) and exit (IC_i^t, MA_i^t) into and out of sector i. Thus ΔN_i^t is the net entry of firms in sector i at time t. In this equation, co-evolution is represented by the term $FA_i^t \cdot AG_i^t$.

The exit term IC_i^t includes inter- and intra-industry competition. (For a detailed description, see Saviotti and Pyka, 2008.) The second exit term MA_i^t includes, besides exits via mergers and acquisitions, failure and bankruptcy (see Saviotti et al., 2007).

$$AG_i^t = Dmax_i^t - D_i^t \qquad (4.2)$$

The adjustment gap AG_i^t (exemplarily displayed in Figure 4.2c) is very large right after the creation of the sector, and later it decreases gradually, although not continuously. It is in fact possible for the adjustment gap to grow during certain periods if innovations, following the one creating the sector, improve either the performance of the product or the efficiency with which it is produced, or both. In our model, search activities affect both the maximum possible demand ($D^t_{max,i}$) and the instant demand (D^t_i) in a sector i. If we consider that, analytically, the adjustment gap (equation 4.2) is defined as the difference between these two types of demand, we can understand that the time path of the adjustment gap depends on those of $D^t_{max,i}$ (Figure 4.2b) and of D^t_i (Figure 4.2a). During particular periods, it is possible for $D^t_{max,i}$ to grow more rapidly than D^t_i, thus enlarging the adjustment gap, or delaying the saturation of the market. In the long run,

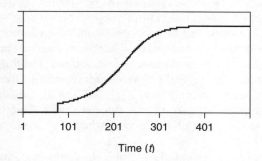

Time (t)

Figure 4.2a   Demand of sector i

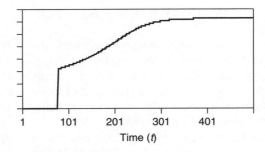

Figure 4.2b   Maximum demand of sector i

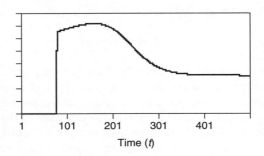

Figure 4.2c   Adjustment gap of sector i

we expect the adjustment gap to be reduced to zero or to a constant value, or the market to become saturated.

FA_i^t represents financial availability, the amount of money present in the economic system that financial institutions are prepared to allocate to sector i at time t. Thus FA_i^t depends on money as well as on the presence of financial institutions capable of judging the prospects of growth and development of sector i at time t. It is in principle possible for an economic system to have enough money but to lack the financial institutions capable of assessing the potential of a new sector. The role of financial institutions has been crucial in the process of economic development, and financial innovations have been required several times to adapt these institutions to changes in the economic environment (Perez, 2002, 2007). AG_i^t, the adjustment gap, is the size of the potential market of sector i at time t. Co-evolution of the technology of sector i and of FA_i^t occurs when FA_i^t grows with AG_i^t and AG_i^t grows with FA_i^t.

An example of how this could happen is the following. Financial operators monitor the performance of the economic system and at a given time they notice that sector i is growing much faster than the average. As a consequence, they decide to allocate resources to sector i based on its differential rate of growth with respect to the average of the economy. If then AG_i^t were to grow at a rate proportional to the amount of financial resources allocated to it, each of these two variables would increase with any rise in the other. What could seem a permanent virtuous circle would have been created. However, such a virtuous circle could not be indefinitely stable. If it were to continue, in time all resources of the economic system would be allocated to sector i, which sounds unrealistic. Furthermore, the allocation of resources to sector i by financial institutions depends on a judgement that is subject to uncertainty. This uncertainty is particularly high in the early phases of the life of a new sector. It is thus possible for financial institutions to either underestimate or overestimate the potential of a new sector. Stunted development would occur in the former case and financial bubbles in the latter. The economy would drop out of the Schumpeterian corridor.

Summarizing, we can expect financial availability to constrain the development of technologies and markets by allowing these technologies and markets to reach their full economic weight when resources are invested wisely, but to overshoot and lead to bubbles when uncertainty mutates into bullish optimism (Perez, 2002, 2007).

In previous versions of this model, we did not exploit the co-evolution of technologies and financial institutions. There we simply assumed FA_i^t to be a constant. Here we introduce a new expression for it, according to which FA_i^t-depends on the difference between the differential rate of growth of the number of firms in sector i and in the whole economy (equation 4.3).

$$FA_i^t = k_3 \cdot \left[1 + k_x \cdot \left(dN_i^t - \frac{1}{n-1} \cdot \sum_{\substack{j=1 \\ j \neq i}}^{n} dN_i^t \right) \right] \qquad (4.3)$$

where dN_i^t is the differential of the number of firms in sector i at time t. The term in brackets represents the difference between the instantaneous rate of growth of the number of firms in sector i and in the average sector in the economy. Equation (4.3) can be considered a form of replicator dynamics (see Metcalfe, 2007). Equation (4.3) tells us that the amount of financial resources allocated to sector i, FA_i^t, will depend on the differential rate of growth of the number of firms in sector i and in the average sector in the economy. We can observe in equation (4.3) that FA_i^t depends also on the two constants k_3 and k_x. For a given value of the difference $dN_i^t - 1/n - 1 \cdot \sum_{j=1 \, j \neq i}^{n} dN_j^t$ higher values of k_3 and k_x can be expected to lead to higher values of FA_i^t. However, while this can be expected on the basis of equation (4.2), the behaviour of our artificial economic system will turn out to be very different.

In section 3, we show the results of experiments carried out by varying the values of constants k_x and k_3. These two constants jointly determine the 'sensitivity' of operators to the performance of sector i. Very low values of k_3 and k_x correspond to the inability of financial institutions to assess the potential of sector i and lead to insufficient development. Very high values of k_3 and k_x correspond to excessive expectations by institutions and are likely to lead to a bubble. In particular, k_3 represents the resources available to financial institutions in the economy, a fraction of which can be allocated to sector i. The constant k_x gives the sensitivity of financial institutions to the performance of sector i, i.e. the resources financial institutions are prepared to allocate to sector i for a given improvement in its performance. The best development performance is likely to be included between these two extremes when the system develops within the neo-Schumpeterian corridor (Hanusch and Pyka, 2007a). In our experiments, we use employment creation as an indicator of the performance of the economic system.

The dynamics of employment enter our model by means of the expected relationship between firm size and employment per unit of output. This relationship has been observed empirically in a very large number of cases and it is compatible with at least some of the models of industry life cycle, such as those of Abernathy and Utterback (1975). We assume employment per unit of output to fall as total output increases within each sector:

$$l_i^t = \frac{k_i}{Q_{ia}^t} = \frac{k_i}{\dfrac{Q_i^t}{N_i^t}} = (k_i \cdot N_i^t)/Q_i^t \qquad (4.4)$$

where l_i is average employment per unit of output in sector i, k_i is a constant proportional to the capacity of sector i to create employment at any given level of output, and Q_{ia} is the average output of firms in sector i at time t, Q_i is the total output of sector i at time t, L_i is total employment in sector i and:

$$l_i^t = \frac{L_i^t}{Q_i^t} \qquad (4.5)$$

The constant k_i measures the intrinsic capability of sector i to create employment at equivalent output. Thus we can expect it to be related to the capital intensity of the sector.

As a consequence of the previous assumption, we can expect employment creation within each sector to be higher in the early stages of the life cycle. Average output per firm can be expected to increase during the life cycle, at least after the maximum number of firms has been reached. These intuitions were confirmed in previous experiments, in which we obtained the interesting result that employment can keep growing in the economic system even when it falls within each of the sectors. This proves that variety growth, as measured by the growth in the number of sectors, can lead to a positive macroeconomic employment growth profile. Of course, variety growth is only a necessary and not a sufficient condition for self-sustaining economic development. In order for that to happen, an adequate inter-sector coordination must occur. In other words, the emergence and growth of new sectors needs to occur when old, maturing sectors start declining.

3. EXPERIMENTS ON THE CO-EVOLUTION OF TECHNOLOGIES AND FINANCIAL INSTITUTIONS

In the experiments described here, we assess the impact of changes in the values of the constants k_x and k_3 on the creation of firms in each sector and on the rate of creation of employment. Figures 4.3, 4.4 and 4.5 show the effect of varying k_x from 0.1 to 0.3 for $k_3 = 1$. It can be clearly seen that, for values of k_x above 0.1, the economic system's ability to create new firms collapses. Given that economic development cannot be expected to proceed without the creation of firms, the previous result leads us to expect that the overall process of economic development will stop for k_x above a given threshold value.

However, the threshold value of k_x rises with growing values of k_3. In Figures 4.6, 4.7 and 4.8, we show the results of similar experiments for higher values of k_3 ($k_3 = 2$), which means a higher availability of financial resources for all sectors. Now the strange fluctuations emerge for k_x-values around 0.5. Higher general financial availability (k_3) accordingly allows for faster economic development, as single sectors can obtain larger portions (k_x) of the available financial resources without detrimental effects to other industries.

The emergence of strange behaviour is also confirmed for employment creation. In this case as well, and for the same values of k_x and k_3, the behaviour of the system becomes strange as we raise k_x (Figures 4.9, 4.10 and 4.11). These results show that the behaviour of the system changes markedly and becomes strange for values of k_x above a threshold value. This led us to suspect that the strange behaviour could in fact be chaotic. We decided to carry out tests for the presence of chaotic behaviour. It

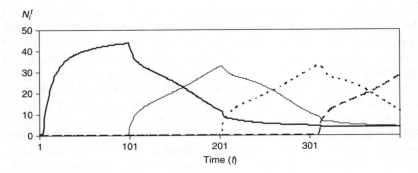

Figure 4.3   Number of firms ($k_3 = 1$; $k_x = 0.1$*)*

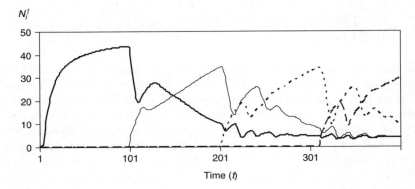

Figure 4.4   Number of firms ($k_3 = 1$; $k_x = 0.2$*)*

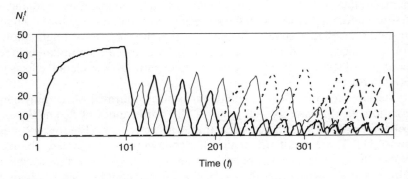

Figure 4.5   Number of firms ($k_3 = 1$; $k_x = 0.3$*)*

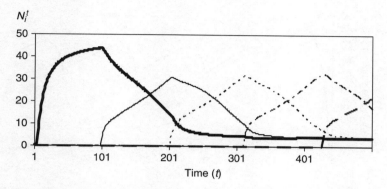

Figure 4.6   *Number of firms for* $k_x = 0.2$ *and* $k_3 = 2$

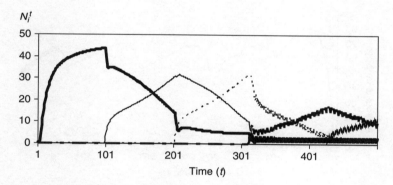

Figure 4.7   *Number of firms for* $k_x = 0.5$ *and* $k_3 = 2$

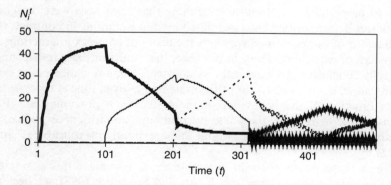

Figure 4.8   *Number of firms for* $k_x = 0.5$, $k_3 = 3$

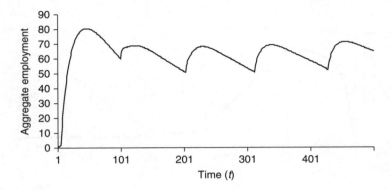

Figure 4.9   Employment creation for $k_x = 0.1$ *and* $k_3 = 1$

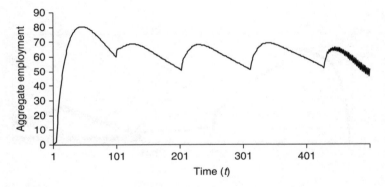

Figure 4.10   Employment creation for $k_x = 0.15$ *and* $k_3 = 1$

has to be pointed out from the beginning that these tests were designed to detect deterministic chaos generated by one equation. In contrast, the behaviour of our economic system is the result of complex interactions in a system of equations. Thus, in our case, the results of these tests cannot be fully conclusive. To start with, we construct some so-called phase portraits, in which the behaviour of the system at a given time is represented as a function of the behaviour of the system at a previous time. For non-chaotic behaviour, the phase portraits are smooth curves, while, in chaotic regions, they become strange and apparently inexplicable (Figure 4.12).

Since these phase portraits resemble those of time series characterized by deterministic chaos (e.g. Kantz and Schreiber 1997), we decided to perform some econometric tests estimating the Lyapunov-exponents which describe the sensitive dependence on initial conditions. Lyapunov-

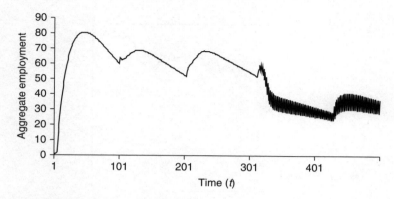

Figure 4.11   Employment creation for $k_x = 0.35$ *and* $k_3 = 1$

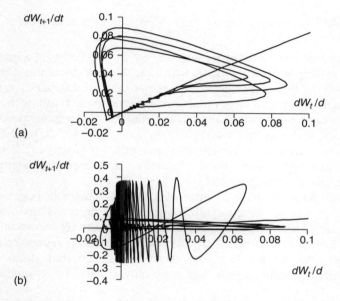

Figure 4.12   Phase portrait for employment creation: (a) $k_x = 0.1$ *and (b)*
  $k_x = 0.2$

exponents below zero characterize systems with stable fixed points, whereas exponents larger than zero indicate chaos, in the sense of the unpredictability of the future despite a deterministic development (see Kantz and Schreiber, 1997, ch. 5).

The econometric tests are performed with the chaos package in *R*. For this purpose, we first have to simulate long time series (1500

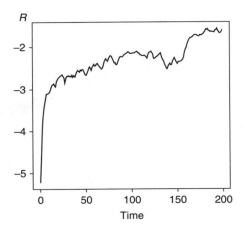

*Figure 4.13   Lyapunov-exponents (*s = 200*) for* $k_3 = 1$, $k_x = 0.1$

periods). For our standard scenario, $k_3 = 1$, $k_x = 0.1$, we get a maximum Lyapunov-exponent $R = -1.558$, which excludes the possibility of chaotic behaviour in this case. Figure 4.13 shows that the Lyapunov-exponent remains negative for a large number of iterations, which follow the neighbours of each point under consideration, i.e. the system remains within its trajectory. When we increase slightly, k_x ($k_3 = 1$, $k_x = 0.2$), the estimated maximum Lyapunov-exponent becomes positive ($R = 2.62$), indicating that our system now shows a behaviour that resembles deterministic chaotic behaviour (Figure 4.14).

At this point, to have a better idea of the changes in behaviour we could expect as we varied k_x and k_3, we explore more systematically the parameter space of these two constants. The results are shown in Figure 4.15. There it can be seen that, for low values of k_3 system behaviour becomes 'chaotic' for very low values of k_x, and that values of the Lyapunov-exponents higher than 1 are only attained for k_3 smaller than 2.5.

Figure 4.16 displays Lyapunov-exponents from experiments varying k_x for different values of k_3. The general result of these experiments confirms our expectations from observing the development of sector evolution as well as employment evolution, and shows that the region where the behaviour of our economic system is pre-chaotic when we vary k_x becomes wider for higher values of k_3, although the effect of k_3 is not linear.

So far we have proved that the behaviour of our economic system can become 'chaotic' as a result of the co-evolution of technologies and of financial institutions. An increasing intensity of feedback between

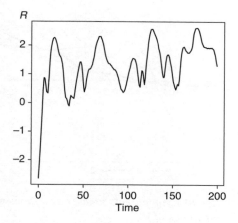

Figure 4.14 Lyapunov-exponents (s = 200) for $k_3 = 1$, $k_x = 2$

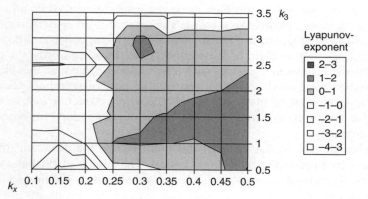

Note: White regions correspond to normal behaviour, while grey regions of increasing darkness correspond to 'chaotic' behaviour.

Figure 4.15 Emergence of 'chaotic' behaviour as a result of the joint variation of k_x and of k_3

technologies and financial institutions can accelerate the process of economic development, but beyond a given intensity, the system moves to a 'chaotic' regime and loses its ability to develop further. A higher intensity of feedback occurs when, for a given differential rate of growth of the number of firms in sector i with respect to the average sector in the economy, financial institutions allocate a greater amount of resources to sector i. When such an amount of resources, which is subject to a high

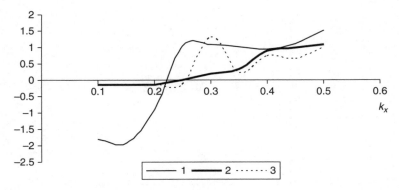

Figure 4.16   Variation of Lyapunov-exponents as a function of k_x *for different values of* k_3

uncertainty, is too low, the system will not achieve its full potential. If the amount of feedback is too high, financial institutions allocate an excessive amount of resources to sector i. The amount is excessive if it cannot achieve an adequate rate of return, thus leading to the collapse of financial institutions and, in turn, of the whole system. In other words, the onset of chaotic behaviour coincides with a bubble-like behaviour in which an overestimate of the development potential of particular technologies and markets by financial institutions leads the whole economic system to an at least temporary collapse. 'Chaotic' behaviour is not good for economic development.

What we still do not know at this point is how the behaviour of our system changes in the pre-chaotic region. The results of further experiments carried out to explore this point are shown in Figures 4.17 and 4.18.

In Figure 4.17, we can see that the range of values of k_x for which non-chaotic behaviour occurs becomes wider when k_3 rises from 1 to 2 and to 3. We can also see that, in the pre-chaotic range, employment growth reaches its maximum value just before the onset of the chaotic regime and the consequent collapse of economic development. In other words, these results seem to indicate that the best conditions for economic evolution occur at the edge of chaos.

Figure 4.18 finally shows that, in the space defined by the two parameters k_x and k_3, there is a non-chaotic corridor (white or light grey) where economic development is possible, surrounded by a chaotic region (dark grey) where economic development would collapse. By attaching to this diagram a third dimension, we can imagine that the two white regions are sinks that would absorb and prevent any development, while the light grey

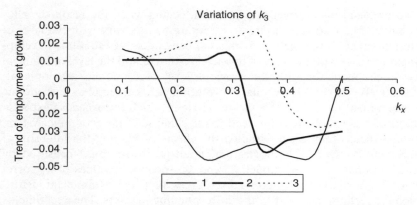

Figure 4.17   Trend of employment growth as a function of k_x *for different values of* k_3

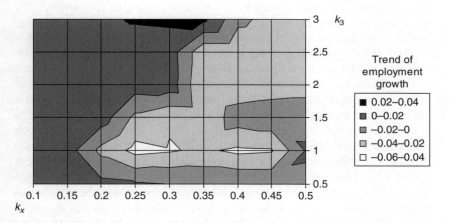

Figure 4.18   Employment growth trend as a function of k_x *and* k_3

region is the only one where development can proceed surrounded by high and impervious chaotic mountains.

4.   SUMMARY AND CONCLUSIONS

In this chapter, we studied the possibility that chaotic behaviour could arise in our artificial economic system from the co-evolution of technologies and financial institutions. Co-evolution occurs when the resources allocated by financial institutions to emerging sectors vary with the level of development of the sectors. If this happens, rates of economic development increase with the level of financial resources and the level of financial resources increases with the previous level of economic development. Intuitively, we can expect this co-evolution either to accelerate economic development or to lead to a vicious circle in which the excessive expectations of financial institutions lead to the collapse of the economic system. Given these premises, we studied the effects of varying the intensity of feedback between technologies and financial institutions, measured by two parameters of our model, k_x and k_3. Increasing values of k_x correspond to a rise in the amount of resources allocated by financial institutions to technologies and to the corresponding markets. The experiments we carried out for this chapter show that, when we raise the value of k_x, our artificial economic system starts behaving in a strange way and rapidly loses its capacity to create new firms and employment. There is a threshold value of k_x below which system behaviour is normal and above which the behaviour becomes strange and the economic system stops developing. The threshold value of k_x turns out to increase with growing values of k_3.

After these preliminary results, we tested more systematically for the presence of chaotic behaviour by generating time series of employment creation and by calculating the corresponding Lyapunov coefficients. With the proviso that the tests we used are designed for deterministic chaos created by single equations and that our artificial economic system is defined by a system of equations, the results of these tests confirm our intuitions. What we called strange behaviour is in fact chaotic. As the chaos threshold is attained, the economic system loses its capacity to create new firms and employment, or to develop. We find that in the parameter space defined by k_x and k_3 there is a non-chaotic corridor, where the system can develop, surrounded by a chaotic region, where development becomes impossible. Furthermore, we find that the capacity of the system to create employment increases in the pre-chaotic region as we approach the chaos threshold and collapses after we enter the chaotic region. The development potential of our economic system improves as we move towards chaos and reaches its best conditions just before we enter the chaotic region. In other words, evolution occurs at the edge of chaos.

REFERENCES

Abernathy, W.J. and J.M. Utterback (1975), 'A dynamic model of process and product innovation', *Omega*, **3**, 639–56.

Baumol, W.J., J.C. Panzar and R.D. Willig (1982), *Contestable Markets and the Theory of Industry Structure*, San Diego, CA: Harcourt, Brace Jovanovich.

Hanusch, H. and A. Pyka (2007a), 'The principles of neo-Schumpeterian economics', *Cambridge Journal of Economics*, **31** (2), 275–89.

Hanusch, H. and A. Pyka (2007b), 'Manifesto for comprehensive neo-Schumpeterian economics', *History of Economic Ideas*, **15**, 11–29.

Jovanovic B. and G.M. MacDonald (1994), 'The life cycle of a competitive industry', *Journal of Political Economy*, **102**, 322–47.

Kantz, H. and T. Schreiber (1997), *Nonlinear Time Series Analysis*, Cambridge: Cambridge University Press.

Kauffman, S.A. (1993), *The Origins of Order*, New York: Oxford University Press.

Klepper S. (1996), 'Entry, exit growth and innovation over the product life cycle', *American Economic Review*, **86**, 562–83.

Langton, C.G. (1990), 'Computation to the edge of chaos: phase transitions and emergent computation', *Physica,* **42D**: 12.

Metcalfe, J.S. (2007), 'Replicator dynamics', in H. Hanusch and A. Pyka (eds), *The Elgar Companion to Neo-Schumpeterian Economics*, Cheltenham, UK and Northampton, MA, USA: Edward Elgar, pp. 440–52.

Mitchell Waldrop, M. (1992), *Complexity: The Emerging Science at the Edge of Order and Chaos*, New York: Viking.

Nelson, R.R. (1994), 'Economic growth via the co-evolution of technologies and institutions', in L. Leydesdorff and P. Von Besselaar (eds), *Evolutionary Economics and Chaos Theory: New Directions in Technology Studies*, London: Pinter, pp. 21–32.

Pasinetti, L.L. (1981), *Structural Change and Economic Growth*, Cambridge: Cambridge University Press.

Pasinetti, L.L. (1993), *Structural Economic Dynamics*, Cambridge: Cambridge University Press.

Perez, C. (2002), *Technological Revolutions and Financial Capital*, Cheltenham, UK and Northampton, MA, USA: Edward Elgar.

Perez, C. (2007), 'Finance and technical change: a long-term view, in: H. Hanusch and A. Pyka (eds), *The Elgar Companion to Neo-Schumpeterian Economics*, Cheltenham, UK and Northampton, MA, USA: Edward Elgar, pp. 775–9.

Saviotti, P.P. (1996), *Technological Evolution, Variety and the Economy*, Cheltenham, UK and Brookfield, USA: Edward Elgar.

Saviotti, P.P. and A. Pyka (2004a), 'Economic development by the creation of new sectors', *Journal of Evolutionary Economics*, **14**, 1–35.

Saviotti, P.P. and A. Pyka (2004b), 'Economic development, variety and employment', *Revue Economique*, **55** (6), Special Issue on Structural Change and Growth (eds J.L. Gaffard and P.P. Saviotti).

Saviotti, P.P. and A. Pyka (2004c), 'Economic development, qualitative change and employment creation', *Structural Change and Economic Dynamics*, 15, 265–87.

Saviotti, P.P. and A. Pyka (2005), 'Micro and macro dynamics in economic development: the influence of industry life cycles and of inter-sector coordination', paper presented at the workshop Innovation, Structural Change and Economic Development, LES TREILLES, 16–21 June.

Saviotti, P.P. and A. Pyka (2008), 'Product variety, competition and economic growth', *Journal of Evolutionary Economics*, **18** (3–4), 323–47.

Saviotti, P.P., A. Pyka and J. Krafft (2007), 'On the determinants and dynamics of industry life cycles', paper presented at the EAEPE conference in Porto.
Utterback, J.M. and F.F. Suarez (1993), 'Innovation, competition and industry structure', *Research Policy*, **22**, 1–21.

5. The role of information and risk sharing for R&D investment, technological change and economic welfare

Burkhard Drees and Bernhard Eckwert*

1. INTRODUCTION

The founding of the Schumpeter Society in 1986 and the annual scientific conferences that the society has organized have had a considerable impact on how economists think about technological change and the evolution of economies. Horst Hanusch, one of the founding members of the Schumpeter Society, has witnessed and, to a considerable extent, shaped the change of paradigms in evolutionary economics over the past two decades (see Hanusch, 1993). His work and his scientific activities within the Schumpeter Society have stimulated research interest in the economics of innovation and technological development. While most of Hanusch's contributions are firmly rooted in a Schumpeterian theoretical framework (Hanusch, 1994; Cantner and Hanusch, 1997; Greiner and Hanusch, 1998; Balzat and Hanusch, 2004; Hanusch and Pyka, 2007), he has also influenced strands of the literature in other areas. Examples include the growing literature on European integration, financial market development, and international trade (Hanusch and Cantner, 1993; Hanusch, 1998, 2001; Balzat and Hanusch, 2004; Hanusch and Sommer, 2007).

This chapter examines a specific aspect of the evolution of economies. We analyse technological development and economic welfare when, in the process of economic integration, the dissemination of information throughout the economy becomes more effective and more reliable. It turns out that the implications of more reliable information are not always straightforward or benign. Instead, these implications are determined by complex market interactions, and they depend critically on the financial structure of the economy. An early partial equilibrium study of informational aspects with special emphasis on the the supply of local services can be found in Hanusch (1985). Since then, the literature on the role of public information in economic models has grown rapidly and has highlighted the importance of information systems for decision making and market coordination.

Our chapter pays special attention to the role of the financial sector and the risk sharing it provides in shaping technological development. The literature that has investigated this link with the help of standard models of stochastic economic growth includes the work by Becker and Zilcha (1997), who study a stationary setting, and the more recent study by Böhm and Chiarella (2005), which examines a non-stationary setting. The nexus between technological development and financial structure has also been examined in the literature of endogenous growth (Greenwood and Jovanovic, 1990; Romer, 1990; Greenwood and Smith, 1996). These studies identified and clarified various transmission channels, but they also produced a number of inconclusive results. In particular, the causality of the interaction between technological development and the financial sector is still in dispute. Is the financial structure the driving force that affects technological development? Or does the financial structure endogenously adjust to technological changes? The answer to these questions may depend on how efficiently information is being transmitted in the economy and how precise the available information is. Some theoretical evidence in support of the importance of informational effects can be found in the papers by Greenwood and Jovanovic (1990), De la Fuente and Marin (1996), and Blackburn and Hung (1998).

Any meaningful analysis of the interactions between information structures, technological development and the financial system requires a general equilibrium framework. This insight implies a shift of paradigm, because traditionally evolutionary Schumpeterian economics has predominantly been cast in terms of partial equilibrium. In the early 1990s, Hanusch (1994, 1995) suggested that the Schumpeterian approach to technological change and innovation could be combined with general equilibrium modelling techniques. Our chapter acts on this suggestion.

We build a simple general equilibrium overlapping generations model with technological uncertainty to identify the channels through which the precision of information about production technologies affects the evolution of the economy. Our dynamic model has four key components: (i) individual agents with production projects whose qualities differ randomly; (ii) an information system that conveys signals about the quality of the production projects; (iii) intertemporal technological externalities; and (iv) a financial system that, to a certain degree, provides opportunities to share production risks.

In the early stage of an agent's two-period life, when the quality of his production project is still unknown, he decides on his investment in R&D. In the second period of life, R&D investment and the project's quality jointly determine the output of the project. The R&D decision is made after the agent has received a noisy signal about the quality of his project. Investment in R&D will therefore be conditional on the screening information (signal). In this model, the aggregate output of all projects that have been carried out in a given period serves as a proxy for the level of technological development in the next period. This proxy variable captures the technological externality between generations: higher aggregate output today will reduce the cost of R&D investment in the next period and will thereby affect output in all subsequent periods.

An information system is a correlation structure between the signal and the project quality, which is not observable at the time of the R&D decision. The strength of the correlation measures the informativeness of the system. Yet the investment decisions depend not only on the information signals, but are also affected by the financial structure of the economy, because the agents' decisions depend on the degree of existing risk-sharing opportunities.

We analyse the interaction between the precision of the information about project qualities and technological development under two different financial structures (i.e. risk-sharing scenarios). The first structure precludes any risk sharing among agents, while the second leads to efficient risk sharing conditional on the revealed information.

We find that, in the absence of risk sharing, better information raises the level of technological development and increases welfare if the economy is moderately risk-averse. In highly risk-averse economies, by contrast, the level of technological development declines and welfare may decline as well. With conditionally efficient risk-sharing arrangements, better information always raises the level of technological development but may, at the same time, reduce economic welfare through adverse risk effects: with more precise information, agents have to bear more of the production risk themselves.

2. THE MODEL

We consider an overlapping-generations economy with a single commodity and a continuum of two-period-lived agents in each generation. The generation that consists of all individuals born at time $t - 1$ is denoted by G_t, $t = 0, 1, \ldots$. All generations have the same size, which is normalized to one.

Each agent is a consumer–producer pair. Within a given generation, individuals differ by the production projects that nature has randomly assigned to them. In his first period of life, each agent invests research and development (R&D) effort, x, into his project. In the next period, the project delivers a return $q(x, \tilde{A}) = x + \tilde{A}$, which depends on the R&D investment, x, and on the random quality of the project, $\tilde{A}$. The random variable $\tilde{A}$ can assume a high value A_H and a low value A_L, $A_H > A_L > 0$, each with probability $\frac{1}{2}$. If the realization of $\tilde{A}$ is A_H, the project has high quality; and if the realization is A_L, the project quality is low. The output belongs to the owner of the project, who can consume it.

When an agent makes his R&D investment decision in the first period of life, he perceives the quality of his project as uncertain. This individual quality risk is identical across the projects of all agents and, by a version of the law of large numbers, there is no aggregate uncertainty, i.e. *ex post* the fractions of high-quality projects and of low-quality projects are both equal to $\frac{1}{2}$.[1]

Before an agent chooses R&D investment, his project undergoes a costless quality test. The test produces a publicly observable signal $\tilde{y}$ that contains noisy information about the project's quality. The signal $\tilde{y}$ is a random variable with realizations y_H and y_L, which are correlated with the project's quality $\tilde{A}$. The signals assigned to projects with quality A_H and A_L are distributed according to the probabilities $[f(y_H|A_H), f(y_L|A_H)]$ and $[f(y_H|A_L), f(y_L|A_L)]$, respectively. Clearly, by construction, the distributions of signals and the distributions of qualities are correlated. Therefore the signal assigned to a project reveals some, albeit noisy, information about the project's unknown quality. The agent uses the screening information to update his expectations about the project quality in a Bayesian way. The individual R&D investment thus takes into account the conditional distribution of the project quality given the observed signal.

An information system specifies for each quality level a conditional probability distribution over the signals. Thus, in our framework an information system can be described by a column-stochastic matrix

$$\begin{pmatrix} f(y_H|A_H) & f(y_H|A_L) \\ f(y_L|A_H) & f(y_L|A_L) \end{pmatrix} \tag{5.1}$$

of conditional signal probabilities. For convenience, we restrict our analysis to the class of symmetric information systems, i.e. we only consider information systems that satisfy the restriction $f(y_H|A_H) = f(y_L|A_L) = p \geq \frac{1}{2}$,

$$\begin{pmatrix} f(y_H|A_H) & f(y_H|A_L) \\ f(y_L|A_H) & f(y_L|A_L) \end{pmatrix} = \begin{pmatrix} p & 1-p \\ 1-p & p \end{pmatrix}. \tag{5.2}$$

The restriction $p \geq \frac{1}{2}$ implies that the information system possesses the monotone likelihood ratio property (MLRP) in the sense of Milgrom

(1981), which means the higher signal y_H induces a better (in the sense of first-order stochastic dominance) posterior distribution over the project's quality levels than the lower signal y_L. By construction, p is the probability that the project has high quality if it tested favourably, as well as the probability that the project has low quality if it tested unfavourably. Thus p measures the reliability of the test and can therefore be interpreted as the informativeness of the information system. With $p = \frac{1}{2}$, the signals are uniformly distributed, regardless of the project quality. In this case, the signal and the project's quality are uncorrelated, and thus the information system is completely uninformative. With $p = 1$, by contrast, a high (low) signal is a perfectly reliable predictor of high (low) project quality. More generally, within our class of information systems, p measures informativeness in the sense of Blackwell's (1953) sufficiency criterion.

When R&D investment decisions are made, agents do not know the qualities of their projects, but they do know the value of p and correctly understand that the signals and project qualities are correlated according to (5.2). Therefore the evaluation of a project will be based on the project's signal (y_H or y_L), which will be used to update the prior quality distribution ($\frac{1}{2}, \frac{1}{2}$) according to

$$v(A|y) = \frac{f(y|A)}{f(y|A_H) + f(y|A_L)} = f(y|A), \, A = A_H, A_L; y = y_H, y_L \quad (5.3)$$

Combining (5.2) and (5.3), the updated posterior distributions of project qualities are

$$\begin{pmatrix} v(A_H|y_H) & v(A_H|y_L) \\ v(A_L|y_H) & v(A_L|y_L) \end{pmatrix} = \begin{pmatrix} p & 1-p \\ 1-p & p \end{pmatrix} \quad (5.4)$$

The unconditional probabilities of signals that agents of generation G_t receive are

$$\mu(y_L) = \mu(y_H) = \frac{1}{2}[p + (1 - p)] = \frac{1}{2} \quad (5.5)$$

The average quality of projects with good signals is

$$\overline{A}(y_H) = A_L + p(A_H - A_L) \quad (5.6)$$

and the average quality of projects with bad signals is

$$\overline{A}(y_L) = A_H - p(A_H - A_L) \quad (5.7)$$

From $p \geq \frac{1}{2}$ we conclude that $\bar{A}(y_H) \geq \bar{A}(y_L)$, i.e. the average quality of projects with favourable test results (good signals) is higher than the average quality of projects with unfavourable test results (bad signals).

All agents of generation G_t have identical preferences that are described by the von Neumann–Morgenstern lifetime utility function

$$U(c,x;Q_{t-1}) = -e^{-ac} - \frac{x^{2-\beta}}{Q_{t-1}} \tag{5.8}$$

where $\beta \in (0, 1)$, $x \in [\underline{x}, \bar{x}] \subset \mathbb{R}_{++}$. The term $(-e^{-ac})$ measures the utility derived from consumption, c, in the second period of life. The parameter $a > 0$ is the coefficient of absolute risk aversion. The term $-(x^{2-\beta})/(Q_{t-1})$ represents the utility cost imposed on the agent in his first period of life by R&D investment effort, x. The aggregate output in the previous period $t - 1$, Q_{t-1}, will be used as a proxy for the level of technological development at time t. Higher technological development reduces the utility cost associated with R&D investment through a positive technological externality.

2.1   The Information Economy without Risk Sharing

As mentioned above, the agents make their investment decisions in their first periods of life when the qualities of their projects are still unknown. At this time, the agents in generation G_t differ only by the signals they have received about their projects. If an agent in G_t has received the signal y, his investment and consumption decisions are determined by

$$\max_{x, \tilde{c}} E\left[-\frac{x^{2-\beta}}{Q_{t-1}} - e^{-a\tilde{c}} \,\middle|\, y \right], \; y = y_H, y_L$$

$$\text{subject to } \tilde{c} = x + \tilde{A} \tag{5.9}$$

Note that, in the absence of risk-sharing arrangements, each agent consumes the entire output of his project, i.e. $\tilde{c} = q(x, \tilde{A}) = x + \tilde{A}$. Denote by x_H and x_L the optimal R&D investment levels when the good signal was received ($y = y_H$) and when the bad signal was received ($y = y_L$). The first-order conditions for the agent's decision problem are

$$x_H^{1-\beta} e^{ax_H} = \frac{aQ_{t-1}}{2 - \beta}\left[pe^{-aA_H} + (1 - p)e^{-aA_L} \right] =: \frac{aQ_{t-1}}{2 - \beta} \vartheta_L(p) \tag{5.10}$$

$$x_L^{1-\beta} e^{ax_L} = \frac{aQ_{t-1}}{2 - \beta}\left[(1 - p)e^{-aA_H} + pe^{-aA_L} \right] =: \frac{aQ_{t-1}}{2 - \beta} \vartheta_H(p) \tag{5.11}$$

From $p > \frac{1}{2}$, we conclude that $\vartheta_H(p) > \vartheta_L(p)$ and, hence, $x_L > x_H$.

In addition, $\vartheta'_H(p) > 0$ and $\vartheta'_L(p) < 0$ hold, which implies that x_L is strictly monotone increasing in the signal's informativeness, p, and that x_H is strictly monotone decreasing in p.

From (5.10) and (5.11), we can also derive upper and lower bounds for R&D effort. Let $\overline{x}$ and $\underline{x}$ be defined by

$$\overline{x}^{1-\beta}e^{a\overline{x}} = \frac{aQ_{t-1}}{2-\beta}e^{-aA_L}; \quad \underline{x}^{1-\beta}e^{a\underline{x}} = \frac{aQ_{t-1}}{2-\beta}e^{-aA_H} \tag{5.12}$$

Note that the bounds $\overline{x}$ and $\underline{x}$ are independent of the information system and that $\{x_H, x_L\} \subset [\underline{x}, \overline{x}] \subset \mathbb{R}_{++}$.

Let $\overline{q}_t(y_H)$ and $\overline{q}_t(y_L)$ denote the average output of all projects with signals y_H and y_L, respectively, in period t:

$$\overline{q}_t(y_H) := x_H + \overline{A}(y_H) \tag{5.13}$$

$$\overline{q}_t(y_L) := x_L + \overline{A}(y_L) \tag{5.14}$$

Aggregate production at date t can then be written as

$$Q_t := \overline{q}_t(y_H)\mu(y_H) + \overline{q}_t(y_L)\mu(y_L) = \frac{1}{2}(A_H + A_L + x_H + x_L) \tag{5.15}$$

Note that a higher level of technological development in $t - 1$ raises the level of technological development in t. This follows from (5.15) and the fact that x_H and x_L are both increasing in Q_{t-1}.

We use a standard equilibrium concept for the dynamic economy that requires that all agents behave optimally and that the process of technological development satisfies the accumulation equation (5.15).

Definition 5.1 *(equilibrium): Given the initial level of aggregate production, Q_0, an equilibrium consists of a sequence of R&D investment and consumption $\{(x_H^i, x_L^i, \widetilde{c}^i)_{i \in G_t}\}_{t=1}^{\infty}$ such that:*

(i) *At each date t, given Q_{t-1}, the optimum for each agent $i \in G_t$ in problem (5.9) is given by $(x_H^i, x_L^i, \widetilde{c}^i)$.*
(ii) *The levels of technological development Q_t, t=1,2,..., satisfy (5.15).*

Next we shall analyse the welfare implications of more reliable information systems. In our economy, all agents of generation G_t are identical *ex ante*, i.e. they do not differ before they have received their signals. We may, therefore, define the welfare of generation G_t as the level of *ex ante* expected utility (before the signals are observed), which is the same for all members of that generation. An information system, $\bar{f}$, will be ranked higher than an information system $\hat{f}$, if all generations attain higher welfare under $\bar{f}$ than under $\hat{f}$.

Let $V_t(y_H, Q_{t-1})$ and $V_t(y_L, Q_{t-1})$ be the value functions of an agent in generation G_t with a project that has received the signal y_H and y_L, respectively:

$$V_t(y_H, Q_{t-1}) := -\frac{x_H^{2-\beta}}{Q_{t-1}} - pe^{-a(x_H + A_H)} - (1-p)e^{-a(x_H + A_L)} \tag{5.16}$$

$$V_t(y_L, Q_{t-1}) := -\frac{x_L^{2-\beta}}{Q_{t-1}} - (1-p)e^{-a(x_L + A_H)} - pe^{-a(x_H + A_L)} \tag{5.17}$$

For example, $V_t(y_H, Q_{t-1})$ represents the conditional expected utility of a member of generation G_t who carries out a project with signal y_H. Using the value functions in (5.16) and (5.17), we define the welfare of generation G_t by

$$W_t(p, Q_{t-1}) := E[V_t(\tilde{y}, Q_{t-1})] = \frac{1}{2}[V_t(y_H, Q_{t-1}) + V_t(y_L, Q_{t-1})] \tag{5.18}$$

$W_t(p, Q_{t-1})$ represents the level of *ex ante* expected utility of agents in generation G_t before they observe the signals, if the economy operates under the information system parameterized by p.

Obviously, individual investment decisions as well as technological development and welfare depend on the economy's information system. What are the effects of a more reliable information system on welfare and on technological development? In our model, welfare and technological development are not independent of one another because the level of technological development exerts an externality on future generations. For this reason, our model highlights two channels through which an information system may affect economic welfare. The first channel, which we shall call the uncertainty channel, is based on the link between information and the implied reduction of uncertainty under which agents make their choices: with better information, agents can be expected to make better decisions. The second channel works through the technological externality, and we therefore call it the externality channel: the reliability of the information system affects the path of technological development and – through this externality – the welfare of future generations. We shall study these two channels separately and investigate under which conditions they both work in the same direction.

Proposition 5.1. *For a given level of technological development Q_{t-1}, $W_t(p, Q_{t-1})$ is increasing in p, i.e. more reliable information leads to higher economic welfare for generation G_t.*

Proof. Differentiating (5.16) and (5.17) with respect to p and using the envelope theorem yields

$$\frac{\partial}{\partial p}[V_t(y_H, Q_{t-1})] = e^{-ax_H}[e^{-aA_L} - e^{-aA_H}] \tag{5.19}$$

$$\frac{\partial}{\partial p}[V_t(y_L, Q_{t-1})] = e^{-ax_L}[e^{-aA_L} - e^{-aA_H}] \tag{5.20}$$

Combining (5.19) and (5.20) with (5.18), we arrive at

$$\frac{\partial W_t(p, Q_{t-1})}{\partial p} = \frac{1}{2}[e^{-aA_L} - e^{-aA_H}][e^{-ax_H} - e^{-ax_L}] > 0$$

where the inequality follows from $x_L > x_H$ and $A_H > A_L$.

The result in Proposition 5.1 is quite intuitive. Welfare increases under a better information system because more reliable information allows agents to improve their R&D investment decisions. Since individuals face less uncertainty when they receive more reliable information, we call this effect 'uncertainty-related'. Thus the uncertainty-related welfare effect of better information is unambiguously positive.

The above proposition does not imply, however, that in equilibrium all generations benefit from a better information system. After all, there is a second channel through which information affects welfare because the externality, Q_{t-1}, is not constant but depends on the information system.

Both effects are positive and thus overall welfare increases only if the better information system leads to a higher level of technological development.[2]

The following technical lemma will be useful for a characterization of the 'externality-related' welfare effect.

Lemma 5.1. *The function $\varphi: [\underline{x}, \overline{x}] \to \mathbb{R}_{++}$,*

$$\varphi(z) = e^{az}[(1 - \beta)z^{-\beta} + az^{1-\beta}]$$

is
(i) strictly increasing, if $a \geq 1/4\underline{x}$; and
(ii) strictly decreasing, if $a \leq \beta(1 - \beta)/2\overline{x}$.

Proof. Differentiating $\varphi(\cdot)$ and rearranging terms yields

$$\varphi'(z) = e^{az}z^{-(1+\beta)}[2a(1-\beta)z + a^2z^2 - \beta(1-\beta)] \qquad (5.21)$$

It is straightforward to verify that the term in brackets has a negative sign if $a \leq \frac{(1-\beta)\beta}{2\bar{x}}$. This proves part (ii). In order to prove part (i), we rewrite (5.21) as

$$\varphi'(z) = e^{az}z^{1-\beta}\left[\left(a + \frac{1-\beta}{z}\right)^2 - \frac{1-\beta}{z^2}\right] \qquad (5.22)$$

The term in brackets in (5.22) is non-negative for all z, whenever $a \geq \frac{1}{\underline{x}}[\sqrt{1-\beta} - (1-\beta)]$ is satisfied. The term $[\sqrt{1-\beta} - (1-\beta)]$ is bounded above by $\frac{1}{4}$ (attained at $\beta = \frac{3}{4}$). Therefore $\varphi'(z)$ is non-negative for all z, if $a \geq \frac{1}{4\underline{x}}$.

The next proposition characterizes the externality-related welfare effect and indicates circumstances in which this effect has the same sign as the uncertainty-related welfare effect.

Proposition 5.2. *More reliable information*
(i) *raises the level of technological development, Q_t, for all $t \geq 1$ if $a \leq \beta$* $(1-\beta)/2\bar{x}$;
(ii) *lowers the level of technological development, Q_t, for all $t \geq 1$ if* $a \geq 1/4\underline{x}$.

Proof. To prove the proposition, we need to show that $Q_t := \frac{1}{2}[A_H + A_L + x_H + x_L]$ is strictly increasing in p under the restriction in (i), and strictly decreasing in p under the restriction in (ii). By the first-order conditions (5.10) and (5.11), the investment decisions x_H and x_L satisfy

$$x_H^{1-\beta}e^{ax_H} + x_L^{1-\beta}e^{ax_L} = \frac{aQ_{t-1}}{2-\beta}(e^{-aA_L} + e^{-aA_H}) = C_1 \qquad (5.23)$$

where C_1 is a positive constant. If we use the notation $x := x_L + x_H$, (5.23) may be rewritten as

$$(x - x_L)^{1-\beta}e^{a(x-x_L)} + x_L^{1-\beta}e^{ax_L} = C \qquad (5.24)$$

Both x and x_L depend on p, and as we concluded earlier from equation (5.11), x_L is strictly increasing in p. Therefore x is strictly increasing (decreasing) in p, if the left-hand side in (5.24) is strictly decreasing (increasing) in x_L. Differentiating the left-hand side (LHS) in (5.24) with respect to x_L yields

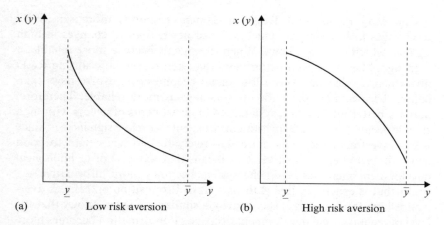

Figure 5.1 Investment function if risk aversion is (a) low; (b) high

$$\frac{\partial \, \text{LHS}(5.24)}{\partial x_L} = \varphi(x_L) - \varphi(x_H) \tag{5.25}$$

where the function φ has been defined in Lemma 5.1.

If the restriction in part (i) of the proposition is satisfied, then, by Lemma 5.1, $\varphi(\cdot)$ is strictly decreasing. Therefore, since $x_L > x_H$ holds, the derivative in (5.25) is negative and hence x is strictly increasing in p. Similarly, if the restriction in part (ii) of the proposition holds, then, again by Lemma 5.1, $\varphi(\cdot)$ is strictly increasing, which implies that the derivative in (5.25) is positive. x is therefore strictly decreasing in p. Since Q_t and $x = x_L + x_H$ differ only by an additive constant, the proof is complete.

According to Proposition 5.2, better information raises the level of technological development, if the consumers' absolute risk aversion is sufficiently small; and better information lowers the level of technological development, if absolute risk aversion is high. These effects can be understood intuitively by examining the curvature of the investment function x. We illustrate the argument for the general situation where the signals are drawn from a continuous set $Y = [\underline{y}, \overline{y}]$. The two-signal specification in this chapter constitutes a special case of this more general formulation.

It can easily be verified that the investment function, $x(y)$, is convex in the signal if risk aversion is small (see Figure 5.1a), and the function is concave if risk aversion is high (see Figure 5.1b). For the purpose of illustration, let us consider the case of low risk aversion, i.e. a convex curvature of $x(\cdot)$.

Convexity means that R&D investment responds more sensitively to changes in low signals, which are bad news, than to changes in high signals, which are good news. When the signals become more reliable, a high signal becomes even better news than before, thereby causing R&D investment to decline. And a low signal becomes even worse news than before, because now the unfavourable news is more reliable. Therefore, under a better information system, R&D investments of agents with high signals decline, and R&D investments of agents with low signals rise. Since R&D investment responds more sensitively to bad news than to good news, the net effect is positive. This means that the level of technological development increases when the system becomes more informative – a result that is exactly in line with part (i) of Proposition 5.2. If risk aversion is high (and thus $x(y)$ is concave), a similar argument shows that the level of technological development decreases if information becomes more reliable.

Propositions 5.1 and 5.2 imply that the second channel (the externality-related effect) through which information affects economic welfare reinforces the first channel (the uncertainty-related effect), if the economy is moderately risk-averse. We may, therefore, conclude, as a corollary, that the welfare of all generations increases under a more reliable information system if the economy is moderately risk-averse.

Corollary 5.1. *If the economy is moderately risk-averse, that is, if $a \leq \beta(1 - \beta)/2\bar{x}$, then better information raises the welfare of all generations.*

2.2 The Information Economy with Risk Sharing

In the absence of risk sharing, we have seen that the degree of risk aversion plays a critical role in the interaction between information, technological development and welfare. If risk-sharing arrangements exist that allow agents to hedge their project risk, we might expect that risk aversion matters much less.[3]

To address this conjecture, we introduce a specific risk-sharing mechanism into the economy: a financial intermediary offers insurance contracts that are fairly priced, conditional on the projects' signals. More precisely, if the signal $y = y_H, y_L$ has been assigned to an agent's project, the agent can sell forward the project's future random output, or part of it, at a price reflecting its current fair value conditional on the signal.

In other words, each agent can buy insurance contracts from the intermediary on the following terms. Each contract involves the obligation for the agent to pay A_H or A_L units of the consumption good to the intermediary next period, depending on the realized project quality. In return, depending on the realized signal today, the agent receives a predetermined payment $\overline{A}(y_H)$ or $\overline{A}(y_L)$ (defined in equations (5.6) and (5.7)) from the intermediary next period. Note that, at the time the insurance contract is concluded, the signal has already been observed, while the project's quality is still unknown. Nonetheless, the intermediary always breaks even because the law of large numbers holds and the contracts are fairly priced.

An agent of generation G_t who has received the signal y solves the problem.

$$\max_{x,\tilde{c},h} E\left[-\frac{x^{2-\beta}}{Q_{t-1}} - e^{-a\tilde{c}}\bigg|y\right], y = y_H, y_L$$

subject to $\tilde{c} = x + \overline{A} + h[\overline{A}(y) - \tilde{A}]$ \hfill (5.26)

where h denotes the number of insurance contracts the agent buys.

The first-order conditions for this problem are

$$x^{1-\beta}e^{ax} = \frac{aQ_{t-1}}{2-\beta}e^{-a\tilde{A}(y)}; \; y = y_H, y_L$$

$$h = 1 \hfill (5.27)$$

Let $\hat{x}_H$ and $\hat{x}_L$ be the optimal investment levels for $y = y_H$ and $y = y_L$. Since $\overline{A}(y_H) > \overline{A}(y_L)$ (see (5.6) and (5.7)), equation (5.27) implies that $\hat{x}_L > \hat{x}_H$. Furthermore, $\hat{x}_L$ is strictly increasing and $\hat{x}_H$ is strictly decreasing in p because $\overline{A}(y_L)$ is strictly decreasing and $\overline{A}(y_H)$ is strictly increasing in p.

Given these risk-sharing opportunities, how does the level of technological development respond to changes in the informativeness of the system?

Proposition 5.3. *Better information raises the level of technological development, Q_t, for all $t \geq 1$.*

Proof. In view of (5.15), we need to show that $\hat{x} := \hat{x}_L + \hat{x}_H$ is strictly increasing in p. By (5.7), $\overline{A}(y_L)$ is strictly decreasing in p. Equation (5.27), then, implies that $\hat{x}_L$ is strictly increasing in p. Now, combining the two equations in (5.27), we obtain

$$[(\hat{x} - \hat{x}_L)\hat{x}_L]^{1-\beta}e^{a\hat{x}} = \left(\frac{aQ_{t-1}}{2-\beta}\right)^2 e^{-a(A_L+A_H)} = C_2 \hfill (5.28)$$

where C_2 is a positive constant. Therefore, since $\hat{x}_L$ is strictly increasing in p, $\hat{x}$ must be strictly increasing in p if we can show that the left-hand side in (5.28) is strictly decreasing in $\hat{x}_L$. This however, is readily verified by differentiating the left-hand side of (5.28) with respect to $\hat{x}_L$ and noting that $\hat{x} - 2\hat{x}_L = \hat{x}_H - \hat{x}_L < 0$.

Since Proposition 5.2 stated that better information slows technological progress in the absence of risk sharing unless absolute risk aversion in the economy is sufficiently low, the more sweeping claim in Proposition 5.3 is quite surprising: the risk-sharing arrangement eliminates the ambiguity in the interaction between technological development and the precision of information. Better information always stimulates technological development regardless of individual attitudes towards risk and, hence, the externality-related welfare effect is always positive.

The situation is, however, quite different with regard to the uncertainty-related welfare effect. Under risk sharing, the value functions of an agent in generation G_t take the form

$$\hat{V}_t(\overline{A}(y_H), Q_{t-1}) := -\frac{\hat{x}_H^{2-\beta}}{Q_{t-1}} - e^{-a[\hat{x}_H + \overline{A}(y_H)]} \tag{5.29}$$

$$\hat{V}_t(\overline{A}(y_L), Q_{t-1}) := -\frac{\hat{x}_L^{2-\beta}}{Q_{t-1}} - e^{-a[\hat{x}_L + \overline{A}(y_L)]} \tag{5.30}$$

and the *ex ante* welfare attained by generation G_t is

$$\hat{W}_t(P,Q_{t-1}) := E[\hat{V}_t(\overline{A}(\tilde{y}),Q_{t-1})] = \frac{1}{2}[\hat{V}_t(\overline{A}(y_H),Q_{t-1})$$
$$+ \hat{V}_t(\overline{A}(y_L),Q_{t-1})] \tag{5.31}$$

The impact of p on $\hat{W}_t(\cdot)$ captures the uncertainty-related welfare effect of better information, which is characterized in the next proposition.

Proposition 5.4. *For a given level of technological development, Q_{t-1}, ex ante welfare $\hat{W}_t(P,Q_{t-1})$ is decreasing in p, i.e. more reliable information leads to lower economic welfare for generation G_t.*

Proof. Differentiating (5.29) and (5.30) with respect to p and using the envelope theorem, we get

$$\frac{\partial}{\partial p}\left[\hat{V}_t(\overline{A}(y_H),Q_{t-1})\right] = (A_H - A_L)\frac{2-\beta}{Q_{t-1}}\hat{x}_H^{1-\beta} \tag{5.32}$$

$$\frac{\partial}{\partial p}\left[\hat{V}_t(\overline{A}(y_L),Q_{t-1})\right] = (A_L - A_H)\frac{2-\beta}{Q_{t-1}}\hat{x}_L^{1-\beta} \tag{5.33}$$

Differentiation of (5.31) in combination with (5.32) and (5.33) yields

$$\frac{\partial \hat{W}_t(p, Q_{t-1})}{\partial p} = \frac{2 - \beta}{2Q_{t-1}} (A_H - A_L)(\hat{x}_H^{1-\beta} - \hat{x}_L^{1-\beta}) < 0, \qquad (5.34)$$

where the inequality follows from $\hat{x}_L > \hat{x}_H$.

According to Proposition 5.4, risk-sharing arrangements reverse the direction in which information affects welfare through the uncertainty channel. The uncertainty-related welfare effect is now negative, while it was positive in the absence of risk sharing. This result is based on a fairly simple mechanism: more reliable signals mean that the agents are exposed to less uncertainty at the time they choose their hedging positions. As a consequence, fewer risks can be hedged, which imposes welfare costs on risk-averse agents. The overall risk allocation, therefore, becomes less efficient from an *ex ante* point of view, which explains the result in Proposition 5.4. Of course, this mechanism operates only when risk sharing takes place conditional on the observed information signals.

Propositions 5.3 and 5.4 together imply that, under conditional risk sharing, the overall welfare effects of better information about project qualities are ambiguous. The welfare effects through the uncertainty channel and through the externality channel have unambiguous signs, but they work in different directions. The first generation, i.e. generation G_0, loses welfare under a better information system, because this generation is only affected through the uncertainty channel. For all other generations, the overall outcome depends on the relative strength of the effects resulting from the positive externality and from the deterioration of the equilibrium risk allocation in an *ex ante* perspective.

3. CONCLUSION

The Walrasian model of perfect competition does not capture the essential features of entrepreneurial decision making in an uncertain and evolving economic environment where agents compete dynamically for market shares and technological margins. The Schumpeterian approach to economic dynamics and evolution offers a new perspective for a deeper understanding of the mechanisms shaping the growth paths of modern economies. Evolutionary models in the Schumpeterian tradition, however, as Hanusch (1994) pointed out, tend to use partial equilibrium analysis and they largely ignore the role information for investment decisions and economic development.

This chapter is an attempt to overcome these shortcomings. We incorporate information about technological uncertainties into a dynamic general equilibrium model with an intertemporal production externality between generations. We find that the implications of a better information system depend critically on the risk-sharing capacity of the economy's financial systems. More precise information affects economic welfare through an uncertainty channel and through an externality channel. The latter channel captures the interaction between technological development and the welfare of future generations. In the absence of risk sharing, both transmission channels work in the same direction and improve welfare if the agents in the economy are moderately risk-averse. By contrast, under conditionally efficient risk sharing through financial intermediaries, the two channels always counteract each other. In this case, a more reliable information system can raise or reduce overall welfare depending on the strength of the technological externality and on the agents' degree of risk aversion.

Our analysis has shown that the role of information for technological development and economic welfare depends sensitively on the financial structure of the economy, which determines the degree of risk-sharing opportunities that are offered to the agents. In this study, we have examined only the extreme cases where the financial system either allows fully efficient conditional risk sharing or no risk sharing at all. A study of intermediate cases where the financial system allows some but less than complete sharing of technological risks is left for future research. This extension would accommodate a richer structure of financial instruments and risk-sharing arrangements.

NOTES

* The views expressed are those of the authors and should not be attributed to the International Monetary Fund, its Executive Board, or its management.
1. See Feldman and Gilles (1985) for details.
2. Note that the value function $V_t(\cdot)$ is increasing in Q_{t-1}.
3. In fact, it is well known that better information can be welfare reducing if risk sharing takes place (Hirshleifer, 1971, 1975; Schlee, 2001; Eckwert and Zilcha, 2001, 2003, 2004; Drees and Eckwert, 2003).

REFERENCES

Balzat, M. and H. Hanusch (2004), 'Recent trends in the research on national innovation systems', *Journal of Evolutionary Economics*, **14**, 197–210.

Becker, R. and I. Zilcha (1997), 'Stationary Ramsey equilibrium under uncertainty', *Journal of Economic Theory*, **75**, 122–40.
Blackburn, K. and V.T.Y. Hung (1998), 'A theory of growth, financial development, and trade', *Economica*, **65**, 107–24.
Blackwell, D. (1953), 'Equivalent comparison of experiments', *Annals of Mathematical Statistics*, **24**, 265–72.
Böhm, V. and C. Chiarella (2005), 'Mean variance preferences, expectations formation, and the dynamics of random asset prices', *Mathematical Finance*, **15**, 61–97.
Canter, U. and H. Hanusch (1997), 'Evolutorische Ökonomik-Konzeption and Analytik', *wisu*, **8–9**, 776–85.
De la Fuente, A. and J.M. Marin (1996), 'Innovation, bank monitoring, and endogenous financial development', *Journal of Monetary Economics*, **38**, 269–301.
Drees, B. and B. Eckwert (2003), 'Welfare effects of transparency in foreign exchange markets: the role of hedging opportunities', *Review of International Economics*, **11** (3), 453–63.
Eckwert, B. and I. Zilcha (2001), 'The value of information in production economies', *Journal of Economic Theory*, **100**, 172–86.
Eckwert, B. and I. Zilcha (2003), 'Incomplete risk sharing arrangements and the value of information', *Economic Theory*, **21**, 43–58.
Eckwert, B. and I. Zilcha (2004), 'Economic implications of better information in a dynamic framework', *Economic Theory*, **24**, 561–81.
Feldman, M. and C. Gilles (1985), 'An expository note on individual risk without aggregate uncertainty', *Journal of Economic Theory*, **35**, 26–32.
Greenwood, J. and B. Jovanovic (1990), 'Financial development, growth, and the distribution of income', *Journal of Political Economy*, **98**, 1076–107.
Greenwood, J. and B. Smith (1996), 'Financial markets in development, and the development of financial markets', *Journal of Economic Dynamics and Control*, **21**, 145–81.
Greiner, A. and H. Hanusch (1998), 'Growth and welfare effects of fiscal policy in an endogenous growth model with public investment', *International Tax and Public Finance*, **5**, 249–61.
Hanusch, H. (1985), 'Information problems and the efficient management of the supply of local services', *Dokumentatieblad*, **4**, Ministerie van Financien, Belgie.
Hanusch, H. (1993), 'Zurück zur Wirklichkeit, Ökonomische Theorie: Wissenschaft vor dem Paradigmenwechsel – Bilanz einer ZEIT-Serie', in *Die ZEIT*, No. 47, 19 November. See also *ZEIT-Punkte Zeit der Ökonomen. Eine kritische Bilanz volkswirtschaftlichen Denkens*, Vol. **3**, pp. 112–14.
Hanusch, H. (1994), 'Technologie und Wachstum', *Der Rotarier*, **44** (521), 17–32.
Hanusch, H. (1995), 'Die neue Qualität des wirtschaftlichen Wachstums', in H. Hanusch and W. Gick (eds), *Ansätze für ein neues Denken in der Wirtschaftspolitik* Berichte & Studien. Band 70 Reihe Wirtschaftspolitik, Akademie für Politik und Zeitgeschehen, Hanns-Seidel-Stiftung e.V., pp. 13–26.
Hanusch, H. (1998), 'Die Europäische Währungsunion – Politische Vision und wirtschaftliche Realität', in *Koncepcje Wspólczesnych Reform Podatkowych. Europa na Drodze Do Wspólnej Waluty* (Ksiazka wydana z okazji 40-leica pracy naukowej Prof. Dr. Hab. Andrzeja Komara) (Festschrift für Prof. A. Komar), Poznan: Wydawnictwo Wyzszej Szkoly Bankowej, 1998, pp. 167–81.
Hanusch, H. (2001), 'The dynamics of European integration: some Schumpeterian

perspectives', in J.E. Bigio (ed.), *Europe's New Destiny*, Lisbon: Universidade Autónoma de Lisboa, pp. 61–75.

Hanusch, H. and U. Cantner (1993), 'Process and product innovations in an international trade context', *Economics of Innovation and New Technology*, **2**, 217–36.

Hanusch, H. and A. Pyka (2007), 'Principles of neo-Schumpeterian economics', *Cambridge Journal of Economics*, **31** (2), 275–89.

Hanusch, H. and J. Sommer (2007), 'Kapitalmarktmodelle', in C. Herrmann-Pillath and M. Lehmann-Waffenschmidt (eds), *Handbuch zur evolutorischen Ökonomik*, Berlin: Springer Verlag, pp. 181–98.

Hirshleifer, J. (1971), 'The private and social value of information and the reward to incentive activity', *American Economic Review*, **61**, 561–74.

Hirshleifer, J. (1975), 'Speculation and equilibrium: information, risk and markets', *Quarterly Journal of Economics*, **89**, 519–42.

Milgrom, P.R. (1981), 'Good news and bad news: representation theorems and applications', *Bell Journal of Economics*, **12**, 380–91.

Romer, P.M. (1990), 'Endogenous technological change', *Journal of Political Economy*, **98**, 71–102.

Schlee, E. (2001), 'The value of information in efficient risk sharing arrangements', *American Economic Review*, **91** (3), 509–24.

6. Bubbles, crashes and the psycho-economic forces behind them

Friedrich Kugler

When 'normal' sentiment gives way to collective 'group think', we have to look at nonlinear forces to understand market fluctuations' (Vaga, 1990, p. 36)

1. INTRODUCTION

Bubbles and crashes in speculative markets are considered as economic facts whose existence is accepted by empirical as well as by theoretical studies. Well-known historical examples are the Dutch Tulipmania, England's South Sea bubble and the US Stock Market crash of 1929. Recently, the crashes of 1987 and 1989 and the real-estate bubble in Japan towards the end of the 1980s have turned out to be more prominent. The end of the vision of a 'New Economy' is often quoted as an additional contemporary example. The Nasdaq Index which, until mid-March 2000, had climbed to unprecedented heights in less than two years, lost 35 per cent of its value in one month. This so-called dot-com crash had effects on every stock exchange in the world. The bursting of speculative bubbles had consequences not only for the financial markets, but also for the real economy. Binswanger (1999) even goes so far as to regard bubbles as an integral part of modern economic development, and Eichengreen (2002, p. 4) states that such economic crises must be viewed as ´an unavoidable concomitant of the operation of financial markets'.

Literature presents complex explanations for market inefficiencies, market anomalies and financial instabilities. Based on the efficient market theory, which assumes solely rational market participants, these are attributed to the non-unique solution of the system of equations behind it, in case bubbles exist at all. For the bursting of these seemingly rational bubbles, external forces are used, such as the acceptance of exogenous crash probabilities (Blanchard and Watson, 1982; Binswanger, 1999). The assumption of solely rationally acting individuals is certainly most controversial. Approaches developed which suggested easing the restrictions of the homogeneous behaviour of the market participants. In the noisy trader models, different groups of investors are observed, whereby only one group, if any at all, shows rational behaviour (for an overview see Unser, 1999). Consequently, speculative bubbles arise through the interaction of heterogeneous traders (Fernandez-Rodriguez et al., 2002). Due to these types of models, there is widespread agreement among economists that rational as well as irrational market participants determine the dynamics, especially in speculative markets (Brunnermeier and Nagel, 2004).

This recent perspective is accompanied by studies that focus on the expectation formation process and the resulting behaviour of participants. Following Shiller's (2000) arguments, price deviations from the fundamentals are driven by an irrational euphoria among the investors, supported by corresponding reports in the media.

Explanations emerged, ascribing bubbles to speculative markets due to the presence of social pressure or crowd behaviour. Accompanied by excessive media reports, a sentiment arises, making people jump onto the bandwagon for fear of missing a chance. At the same time, controversial points of view have more or less disappeared or have been intentionally neglected (Bowden and McDonald, 2005). Characteristic of this are keywords such as collective expectations, social learning, mimetic contagion and herd behaviour (cf. Banerjee, 1992; Lux, 1995; Flieth and Foster, 2002).

Such phenomena are often accompanied by non-linear forces (Shiller, 1991; Vaga, 1990; Fernandez-Rodriguez et al., 2002; Peters, 1996, 2003; Sornette, 2003). As a result, a dynamic develops at the macro level which, depending on certain influential factors, provides for a complex range of market results (Boldrin, 1988; Abhyankar et al., 1995). Johansen et al. (2000) presented a link between crashes and the critical behaviour of complex systems even in rational markets. Kugler and Hanusch (1993) developed a psycho-economic model of a stock market which, at certain parameter constellations, endogenously generates the formation and collapse of speculative bubbles.

Besides this non-linear dynamic at the macro level (be it stochastic or deterministic), the decision behaviour at the micro level also plays an essential role. According to the notions of the efficient market theory, the stock market should be the ideal 'playground' for *homo oeconomicus*. Here, free from any individual psychological behaviour restrictions, he can act as a rational individual, driven only by self-interest and the ambition to maximize his profit. Consequently, the results have to be efficient and are darkened only by randomness.

Theoretical, empirical and experimental studies show that this is not the case. Bubbles and crashes are viewed as psychological overactions of individuals, groups and crowds in the marketplace. In consequence, people turn away from normal investment behaviour. Therefore speculative markets should be an excellent laboratory for social scientists to study such deviations from behavioural norms. However, particularly in financial modelling, these behavioural aspects are considered rather inadequately. Research works in behavioural finance mainly point out that decision making is influenced more by heuristic methods (Peters, 2003). Also, evolutionary economics models are marked by a renunciation of the strict rationality postulate (for an example see Grebel et al., 2004). All of these perspectives are more or less contradictory to the neoclassical view, which models the decision-making process of a rational individual strictly with the expected utility theory.

Economists are interested in market behaviour and/or results, as well as in the psychology of the individual decision making and the interactions in progress. For this purpose, I suggest in this chapter a microfoundation of a stock market model. However, instead of the usual approach, in which modelling is carried out from the micro to the macro level, the opposite approach is pursued. Starting with the existence of bubbles and crashes at the macro level and the assumption that these phenomena are controlled by a non-linear dynamic, I shall explain the forces behind them. This may provide some insight behind the scenes of market results and the underlying interaction of the psycho-economic factors at the micro–macro level.

The chapter is structured as follows: in section 2, I describe the stock market macro model that illustrates the link between economical and psychological variables. In section 3, I offer a decision model and demonstrate the combination of neoclassical and behavioural elements. Having shed light on the decision process, I connect the micro and the macro levels in section 4. In section 5, I present simulation results. Section 6 concludes and points to possible extensions.

2.   THE MACRO-SPHERE: A PSYCHO-ECONOMIC APPROACH

It is not quite usual in this kind of research to start with the macro level. In many publications on financial markets, the stock market in particular is described as a market with complicated dynamics and is characterized as a result of the interaction by feedback processes (Shiller, 1991).

Kugler and Hanusch (1993) developed such a model of a stock market and described it with the following non-linear system of differential equations:

$$\dot{y} = -v_1 (4y^3 + 2ky + l), \tag{6.1a}$$

$$\dot{k} = v_2 (\varphi(y) + l), \tag{6.1b}$$

$$\dot{l} = v_3 (\Lambda - k - \mu l + \phi(l)). \tag{6.1c}$$

The model contains economic as well as psychological variables. As such, y describes the deviation of the market index from its fundamental value (see also Vaga, 1990), k the scepticism about market development, and l the market sentiment, which can be optimistic ($l < 0$) as well as pessimistic ($l > 0$). The exogenously given adjustment rates are denoted by v_1, v_2 and v_3. Each equation is explained briefly below (for a detailed description see Kugler and Hanusch, 1993).

Social Imitation

Equation (6.1a) demonstrates the adaptation of the individual market participant to the majority. In the behavioural science context, the social pressure of the mass on the individual is portrayed. In recent behavioural finance literature on herd behaviour and social network approaches, such behaviour is considered to be unquestioned, empirically as well as theoretically.

Modelling this behaviour, a distribution function is assumed for y, the density of which over time undergoes several phase transitions. As such, Vaga (1990) points out in his coherent market hypothesis linked to studies in natural sciences (the Ising model of ferromagnetism) that single market states, in line with the theory of social imitation, can be described with the help of a dynamically changing probability distribution. A function showing these characteristics is the general Q-distribution, the density of which in qualitative simplification is given by:[1]

$$f_t^Q(y|k, l) = \exp[-(y^4 + k_t y^2 + l_t y)] \tag{6.2}$$

Depending on the values of the parameters k and l, this density can change its form as shown in Figure 6.1. In a mix of empirical observations and theoretical consequences Vaga describes the market states thus generated as follows:

Case 1: True random walk (efficient market state, $k > 0$, $l = 0$)
In this stadium, the market is not conducive to social pressure. There is no scepticism and the sentiment is neutral, and therefore this market state is regarded as being relatively stable and efficient, as can also be found in the random walk theory.

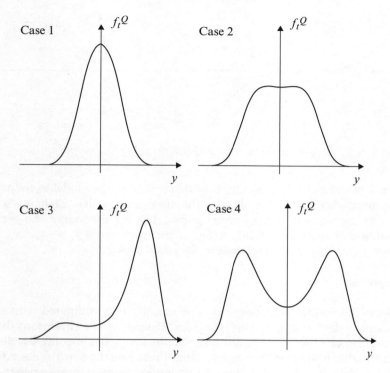

Figure 6.1   Four states of the market

Case 2: Unstable transition (inefficient market state, $k = 0, l = 0$)
This is described as the critical transition threshold from the efficient to the inefficient market. Due to increasing scepticism, the variance becomes very large, and market development is characterized as having no sense of direction.

Case 3: Coherent market ($k < 0, l < 0$)
Here the risk to underperform the market average increases, so the market becomes conducive to social pressure. Combining scepticism with an optimistic sentiment, the density function has a bimodal shape with a strong bullish influence.

Case 4: Chaotic market (quasi-efficient market state, $k < 0, l = 0$)
This market state is referred to as 'dangerous'. Due to the crowd behaviour, with equally strong bullish and bearish influences, the sentiment here can change abruptly. This particular constellation can lead to crashes.

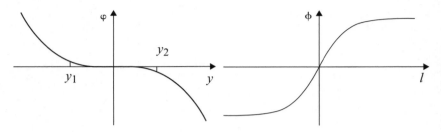

Figure 6.2   Indirect influences on scepticism and optimism/pessimism

The adjustment to the majority now takes place in the model as follows: The maximization of the density function ensures that each investor follows the opinion of the general public. The corresponding first-order condition is shown in (6.1a). A fast adjustment speed $v_1 \gg 1 > v_2, v_3$ ensures an immediate adaptation to the social pressure.

Scepticism

This psychological component is economically best compared with the 'chance of the lost opportunity' (Day and Huang, 1990). This means that, in the market, there are certain reservations about the ongoing development that can dissipate or increase over time. Equation (6.1b) describes this development. It can be seen that the optimism/pessimism parameter l has a direct influence, i.e. the higher the degree of optimism in the market ($l < 0$), the more the scepticism will grow ($k < 0$) as to whether the optimistic expectations will be fulfilled in the future.

In contrast, the influence of the economic component y is not so clear, although it effects the scepticism indirectly via the function φ, which is shown in the left part of Figure 6.2.

A positive (negative) deviation from the market index acts as scepticism-encouraging (reducing). However, the influence of the function is relatively weak within the interval $[y_1, y_2]$. As such, for example, a slight overvaluation $0 < y \le y_2$ leaves little room for a sceptical attitude regarding ongoing positive development.

Market Sentiment

The development of the second psychological component l describes equation (6.1c). Analogous to studies of behavioural finance, sentiments in the market are granted a high significance.

The parameter $\Lambda \ne 0$, which can be positive as well as negative, reflects a certain basic sentiment on the stock market. Furthermore, similar to equation (6.1b), (6.1c) is determined by direct and indirect influences, namely $\mu\,l$, $\mu > 0$, and $\phi\,(l)$. The right side of Figure 6.2 illustrates function ϕ.

Due to the specific shape of ϕ, increasing optimism ($l < 0$) lets optimism continue to increase. In contrast, decreasing optimism ($l > 0$) leads to an increase in pessimism. This development is, however, reversed by $\mu\,l$. The parameter μ acts somewhat as a stabilizing element on the respective development. In the model, it is interpreted as a type of cautionary parameter. Since the first systematic analysis of Kaldor (1939), there has been disagreement as to whether speculative behaviour has a stabilizing or destabilizing effect. The efficient market theory argues for a more stabilizing tendency. Accordingly, rational investors attack speculative bubbles by acting against them. Theoretically, and also empirically, this behaviour is ambiguous. For some time it can be optimal for rational investors to ride a bubble (Abreu and Brunnermeier, 2003; Brunnermeier and Nagel, 2004). In the following investigation, I shall show that, with the appropriate selection of the parameter μ, the model can handle both views.

Kugler and Hanusch (1993) analysed the dynamic behaviour of the non-linear model generally and specifically for certain model constellations. In particular, they showed that price or index deviations can result endogenously, depending on certain parameter values. This can even lead to the formation of a price bubble, which bursts at a certain point in time due to endogenous development. But first I shall reflect on the micro-structure of the market in the next section and especially on the function $\phi\,(l)$.

3. THE MICRO-SPHERE: COMBINING NEOCLASSICAL AND BEHAVIOURAL ELEMENTS

There is a large number of descriptions of the stock market microstructure (for an overview see O'Hara, 1995; Madhavan, 2000). Most of them deal with expectation formation or the related provision, processing and diffusion of information. For many, to a certain extent *ad hoc* behaviour is implied for the decision process. In this section, another approach is pursued. I derive the microstructure of the market from a neoclassical decision model based on expected utility theory. Admittedly, this is not undisputable and thus there are numerous papers from the fields of psychology as well as economics that show controversial views on the closeness of this theory to reality. As such, predominantly psychologists hold the view that deviations from rational behaviour do not always occur randomly, as is claimed in the theory of the efficient markets, but arise mainly systematically (Barber and Odean, 1999).

There are, however, also integrating approaches, and, accordingly, Camerer (1999) pointed out correlations between expected utility theory and prospect theory employed in behavioural economics. The main difference here is in the interpretation of probabilities. Whereas in expected utility theory, the probabilities are given objectively, they are formed subjectively in prospect theory, based on experience, learning effects, etc. This aspect will be taken up later.

Otherwise, the microeconomic model is based on the state-preference model of Arrow (1964) and was adopted in Kugler et al. (1996) originally for a simulation study. I shall reflect its main features below and integrate the fundamental elements and propositions in the non-linear model discussed above.

In an economy, there are $i \in I = \{1, N\}$ investors with initial wealth $\overline{w}_i$. Each investor has to make a decision in period 0 about his portfolio of security holdings in the following period. There are only two securities available: the risk-free security O and the risky asset M. The latter can be a share or an index fund. Furthermore, it is assumed that the consumption decision is independent of the investment decision and has already been made. The prices of both securities in period 0 are known and scaled to 1. The budget restriction of investor i is thus

$$m_i + o_i = \overline{w}_i \qquad (6.3)$$

While the individuals know the price of the risk-free security in the following period, they have to form expectations regarding the price of the risky investment. For each market participant, only two states for M are of interest: state 1 reflects an expected gain situation, and state 2 an expected loss situation. The following expectation matrix E_p summarizes the agent's price expectations or expected returns:

$$E_p = \begin{bmatrix} e_{11} & e_{12} \\ \vdots & \vdots \\ e_{N1} & e_{N2} \end{bmatrix} \qquad (6.4)$$

In this $N \times 2$ matrix, e_{is}, $s \in \{1, 2\}$ denotes the price expectations of investor i if he presumes that state s will arise. Depending on the state of nature, the investor's expected wealth for the following period is given by

$$w_{is} = m_i e_{is} + o_i p_O \qquad (6.5)$$

where m_i (o_i) denotes the demand of security M (O) and p_O the price of O in the next period. In order to be able to describe the expected profit or loss situation analytically, $0 \leq e_{i2} < 1 < e_{i1} < \infty$ must hold. Furthermore, it is assumed that the price of the risk-free investment does not change over time.

The investor now makes an investment decision in the present period with regard to his expectations for the following period. The individual's preferences are represented in the following risk utility function:[2]

$$V_i(w_{is}) = \sum_s \pi_{is} U_i(w_{is}) \tag{6.6}$$

Furthermore, the subjective assessment or estimation of the occurrence of the two possible states is denoted by π_{is}, $\sum_s \pi_{is} = 1$.

Due to the formal similarity, this variable is not to be confused with the probability in the original model in which all possible states are known *a priori*. As market participants act according to their expectations and the prevailing sentiment in the market, they themselves generate the state that will arise in the next period. However, this may not necessarily be consistent with the expected states. While in the state-preference model, the state arising represents, in a way, an 'either–or' restriction which is determined exogenously, here the realization is dependent on the expectations and sentiments in the market. This subjective estimation thus presents a behaviour component characterized to a high degree by interactivity. In a sense, the uncertainty concept as per Knight (1921) and the view of behavioural economics (Camerer, 1999) are adopted due to this distinction.[3]

Regarding the individual utility functions, the formal characteristics of the linear risk tolerance are assumed. As a result, I fall back on the following relatively risk-averse utility function for the exact modelling of the microstructure:[4]

$$U_i(w_{is}) = \frac{n_i}{1 - n_i} \beta_i w_{is}^{1-n_i} \quad \text{with} \quad n_i := \frac{1}{\beta_i}, \beta_i > 1 \tag{6.7}$$

Here, n_i gives a measure for the investor's relative risk tolerance. In the further course, it is evident that the use of this class of utility functions allows a larger modelling generality with respect to individual risk behaviour.

The decision problem of an investor can now be formulated as follows:

$$\max_{(w_{i1},w_{i2})} V_i(w_{i1},w_{i2}) = \max_{(w_{i1},w_{i2})} \sum_s \pi_{is} U_i(w_{is}) = \max_{(m_i,o_i)} \sum_s \pi_{is} U_i(m_i e_{is} + o_i p_o)$$

subject to $m_i + o_i = \overline{w}_i$. $\tag{6.8}$

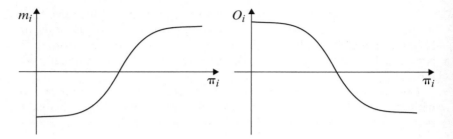

Figure 6.3   The demand functions for the risky and risk-force securities

The solution of (6.8) leads to the optimal condition:[5]

$$-\frac{\pi_i U_i'(w_{i1})}{(1-\pi_i)\,U_i'(w_{i2})} = T_i, \quad T_i := \frac{e_{i2}-1}{e_{i1}-1} \qquad (6.9)$$

Consequently, three components are important for the optimal decision of an individual: the individual assessment π_i, his price expectations e_{i1} or e_{i2}, and his initial wealth $\overline{w}_i$. The realized price and the achieved wealth are also added to a dynamic variant of the model (see Sommer and Kugler, 1997). For reasons of clarity it is, however, disregarded.

The two demand functions for investors i can now be calculated as follows:

$$m_i = \left(\frac{1}{e_{i1}-1}\right)\left(\frac{\overline{w}_i\,(1-\tau_i^{\beta_i})}{\tau_i^{\beta_i}-T_i}\right) \quad \text{and} \quad o_i = \overline{w}_i - \left(\frac{1}{e_{i1}-1}\right)\left(\frac{\overline{w}_i\,(1-\tau_i^{\beta_i})}{\tau_i^{\beta_i}-T_i}\right),$$
$$(6.10)$$

where $\tau_i := -\dfrac{1-\pi_i}{\pi_i}\,T_i,\ \beta_i > 0$

Figure 6.3 illustrates these two curves dependent on the individual assessment π_i.

Changes in wealth, risk attitude and return expectations are relevant for further analysis. Especially due to the latter two aspects, a separation of risk attitude, i.e. the propensity to take risks, and risk perception, i.e. how the gain or loss risk is assessed individually, is possible. Research on risk behaviour confirms a correlation between risk perception and return expectations (for an overview see Byrne, 2005). In the initial expected utility theory, a blending of the two risk aspects takes place (Unser, 1999). In order to elucidate the consequences of the mentioned changes, the demand curve of the risky asset m_i is examined. The results hold analogously for o_i.

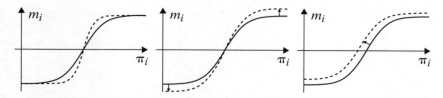

Figure 6.4   Changes in the demand function due to parameter variations

Proposition 6.1   If an investor's risk attitude changes *ceteris paribus*, then the slope of the security demand function changes to such an extent that it increases (decreases) with decreasing (increasing) relative risk aversion.

Proposition 6.2   If an investor's wealth increases (decreases), then the individual security demand curve expands (contracts). Analogously to equation (6.3) in the dynamic version, the change in wealth corresponds to the change in the realized asset price via

$$w_{i,t} = m_{i,t-1}p_{t-1} + o_{i,t-1}. \tag{6.11}$$

Proposition 6.3   An increase in an investor's return expectations (due either to an increase in e_{i1}, e_{i2} or both) causes a shift of the security demand curve to the left via the parameter T_i.

Figure 6.4 illustrates these propositions.[6]

In the left part, it is clear that the riskier the investor is (decrease in the relative risk aversion), the steeper is his demand curve. The middle part shows that the more wealth the investor possesses, the more wide-ranging is his security demand. Finally, the right part demonstrates the effects of changed risk perceptions. An increase in the agent's expected returns *ceteris paribus* causes a shift of the security demand curve m_i to the left.

In the following, I shall apply these statements to the non-linear macro model (6.1a–6.1c) from the previous section. First, I will observe the complementary function that is the demand function of the risk-free asset o_i. Subject to the best assessment, namely $(1 - \pi_i)$, the curve shape follows as in Figure 6.5. Likewise, Propositions 6.1 to 6.3 hold analogously. It has already been mentioned that the subjective estimation, π_i, presents a behaviour component that, to a high degree, is characterized by inter-activity. Naturally, this individual assessment correlates with the general market sentiment. The more optimistic is the sentiment on the market, the

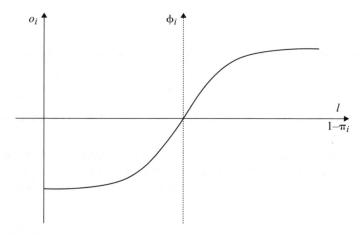

Figure 6.5   Transformation from o_i $(1 - \pi_i)$ to $\phi_i(l)$

more advantageously are future states assessed. As a result, a qualitative analogy arises from $(1 - \pi_i)$ to l, the optimism/pessimism parameter of the dynamic model. This is shown via the transformation of coordinates in Figure 6.5.

If the investor assesses the future situation optimistically, $(l < 0)$, he will shift his portfolio in favour of stocks or index funds. An investment in risk-free assets is the case for a pessimistic assessment $(l > 0)$.

As a one-to-one integration of this demand function into the dynamic model of the stock market is not easy to do for technical reasons, the qualitative aspects at the micro level are to be applied with the aid of topological equivalence.[7] The following function $\hat{\phi}$ shows a topological equivalence to the demand function in Figure 6.5:

$$\hat{\phi}_i\,(l|\hat{w}_i,\,\hat{\beta}_i,\hat{T}_i) \;=\; \frac{\hat{w}_i}{1 + \exp\,(-\,\hat{\beta}_i l + \hat{T}_i)} \;-\; \frac{\hat{w}_i}{2} + \hat{T}_i,\, \hat{\beta} > 0 \quad (6.12)$$

Here it involves a slightly expanded version of the sigmoid function, which also finds application in artificial neural nets (Zimmermann, 1994). Furthermore, the increase in $\hat{w}_i$ expands the function, analogous to the wealth in $o_i(1 - \pi_i)$. An increase in $\hat{\beta}_i$ changes the slope analogously to the previous decrease in the relative risk aversion. Finally, an increase in the expected return (expressed by an decrease in $\hat{T}_i$) shifts the curve to the top left. Figure 6.6 shows the qualitative analogy.

Therefore, in the basic model of the stock market (6.1a–6.1c), besides scepticism and optimism/pessimism, a further economic variable can be

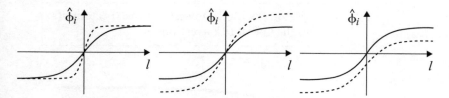

Figure 6.6   The analogy of ϕ_i and $\hat{\phi}_i$

integrated with investor's wealth, a psycho-economic one with the individual risk perception and an additional psychological one with individual risk propensity.

4   THE MICRO–MACRO CONNECTION

An investor's decision about the holdings of risky assets takes place at the individual state space. Under the assumption that all market participants act according to the basics of the state preference model, the aggregated state space, i.e. the macrostructure of the stock market, can be described fully (cf. in this respect Kugler et al., 1996). Figure 6.7 reflects the aggregated state space in which market activities take place. If wealth is distributed equally, it is limited in the optimistic range ($l < 0$) by the demand function(s) for a risk-free security of the investor(s) with the lowest; in the pessimistic range ($l > 0$) by the function(s) of the investor(s) with the highest return expectation(s). As can be seen, the borders are also determined by the respective risk attitudes.

The aggregation results via the function:

$$\hat{\phi}\,(l\,|\hat{w},\hat{\beta},\hat{T})\ =\ \sum_i \hat{\phi}_i(l\,|\hat{w}_i,\hat{\beta}_i,\hat{T}_i) \qquad (6.13)$$

In order to elucidate the effects of the micro-structure at the aggregate level, I shall observe the following three cases:

Case 1: *All investors have identical return expectations, risk attitudes and capital*   This case is consistent with the representative agent in neoclassical theory. The above aggregate function becomes

$$\hat{\phi}\,(l\,|\hat{w},\hat{\beta},\hat{T})\ =\ N\hat{\phi}_i(l\,|\hat{w}_i,\hat{\beta}_i,\hat{T}_i) \qquad (6.14)$$

From the left part of Figure 6.8 it is clear that this case is identical with the increase in wealth.

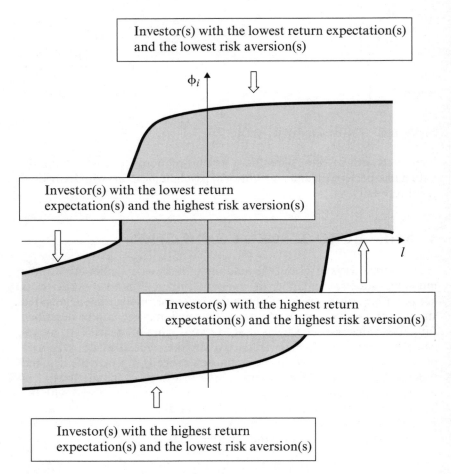

Figure 6.7   The macrostructure of the stock market

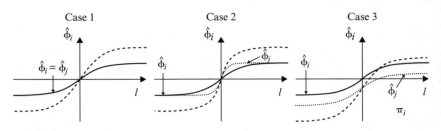

Figure 6.8   The three aggregation cases

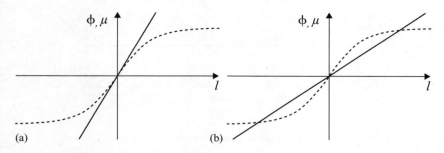

Figure 6.9   Stabilizing and destabilizing effects

Case 2: *All investors have identical expected returns and wealth*   They differ in their risk propensities. The effects are shown in the middle part of Figure 6.8. Without loss of generality, it is assumed that the risk attitude of investor *i* is as in case 1 and investor *j* is relatively more risk-tolerant. Besides the effect of the increase in wealth, it can be seen that the slope of the aggregated function $\hat{\phi}$ is steeper than in case 1.

Case 3: *All investors have identical risk attitudes and wealth*   They differ in their risk perceptions. The right part of Figure 6.8 illustrates the changes as opposed to case 1. Here investor *i* has the return expectations of case 1. For investor *j*, $e_{j1} > e_{i1}$ and $e_{j2} > e_{i2}$ are assumed. Besides the effect of the increase in wealth, the aggregated function $\hat{\phi}$ shifts to the bottom right.

To sum up, it remains to note that the macro-structure of the market can be portrayed qualitatively by the same function as in (6.12).

5. RESULTS

The main influence on the dynamic behaviour of the original macro model (6.1a–6.1c) acts on the coaction of μl and $\phi(l)$. In case a) of Figure 6.9 there is always an adaptation to the equilibrium. As $\phi'(l) \leq \mu$, $\forall l$ holds, the stabilizing effect outweighs. This corresponds to the efficient market theory.[8]

Continuous fluctuations (over- and undervaluation) as well as price bubbles with discontinuous correction are possible in case (b). The latter always occurs when there is crowd behaviour with equally strong bullish and bearish influences, i.e. the opinion of the majority is ambiguous. In this case, the density function is bimodal with equal extreme values due to the development of *k* and *l* (see Figure 6.1: case 4). The corresponding index movements are shown in Figure 6.10.

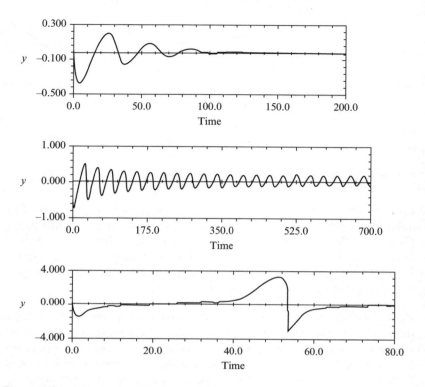

Figure 6.10   Three possible dynamical patterns

However, a further dynamic behaviour investigation is not the object of this chapter (for further details see Kugler and Hanusch, 1993).

In the following, I shall analyse the case of the speculative bubble and the corresponding microeconomic influences with simulation runs, using in (6.15) a numerical specification of the system (6.1a–6.1c) combined with (6.12):

$$\dot{y} = -v_1 (4y^3 + 2ky + l),$$

$$\dot{k} = v_2(-0.016y^3 + l), \qquad (6.15)$$

$$\dot{l} = v_3\left\{ \Lambda - k - \mu l + \left(\frac{\hat{w}}{1 + \exp(-\hat{\beta} l + \hat{T})} - \frac{\hat{w}}{2} + \hat{T} \right) \right\}$$

See Table 6.1 for the parameter values.

Whereas in the original model dynamic behaviour was generated solely by variation of the caution parameter μ, this is now held constant. For

Table 6.1   Parameter values

v_1	v_2	v_3	Λ	μ
5.0	0.2	0.2	2.0	0.7

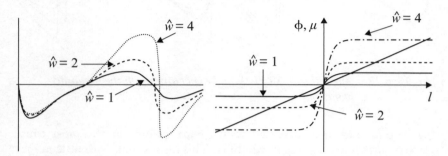

Figure 6.11   The influence of wealth on the dynamic behaviour

the initial situation, I assume the original equilibrium condition, i.e. $\phi'(l) \leq \mu, \forall l$.

The wealth in the market is regarded as the major influence factor arising from the microeconomic level. That is, the more speculative money there is in the market, the more the danger of a speculative bubble increases. As shown in the previous section, the aggregation is always connected with a wealth increase in the market. If the market, due to its development, now experiences a colossal popularity at the micro level, the behaviour shown in the left part of Figure 6.11 arises at the macro level. In addition, there is more wealth in the market when share prices increase rapidly, as can be seen in equation (6.11). In the simulation behind it, the original wealth was doubled and quadrupled. The right part of Figure 6.11 shows the corresponding coaction between μl and $\phi(l)$.

What influence do the other microeconomic parameters now have? In the right part of Figure 6.12, I assume a crash situation with quadruple wealth. A step-by-step increase in the relative risk aversions, by reducing $\hat{\beta}$ from 8 to 1, curbs the bubble. It disappears completely for $\hat{\beta} = 0.5$. A similar behaviour can be observed for changes in return expectations. Increased return expectations thus cause the bubble to expand, whereas low return expectations have the observed curbing effect. Figure 6.12 demonstrates both effects.

Examined individually, changes in the risk attitudes as well as in the return expectations have little effect at the macro level. A relatively risky

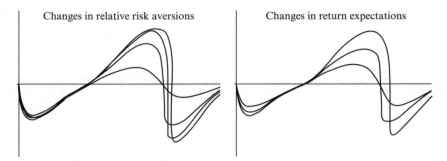

Figure 6.12   The influences of risk and expectations on the dynamic behaviour

behaviour, and also increased return expectations, at the most cause *ceteris paribus* an increase in volatility. This means that, with little money in the market ($\hat{w} = 1$), increased risk propensity and/or higher return expectations can only trigger increased volatility.

To sum up, it can be noted that of all microeconomic parameters, wealth in the market has the greatest effect at the macro level. On the other hand, a dangerous constellation can arise and, in the case of a small relative risk aversion together with increasing expected returns, less money would be sufficient to induce a bubble. With regard to such a price bubble, stabilizing as well as destabilizing effects can be assumed by both, as shown in Figure 6.12.

However, the isolated specified influences cannot be separated in reality, as they are highly interdependent. If the interdependence is taken into account at the macro level, the complex structure of the whole system becomes clear. In the following, I shall describe a conceivable scenario:

Step 1: The return expectations in the market increase   The volatility of the market index increases.

Step 2: Optimism increases   The attitude towards risk decreases. New investors and new firms appear on the market. Speculative money increases, and thus the probability of a bubble.

Step 3: Optimism continues to increase, but also scepticism   The expected returns continue to increase, and the stream of new investors persists. Speculative money increases due to reinvested profits. A bubble arises, whose lifetime and extent are increased by lower risk aversions, higher return expectations and, if rational investors ride the bubble, a decrease in the stabilizing caution parameter μ.

Step 4: An increase in scepticism leads to a sentiment that can change abruptly   Profits are capitalized, sentiment changes, the bubble bursts.

6.   SUMMARY AND OUTLOOK

Speculative markets are subjects for extensive research in human psychology, as it is alleged that all market actions are controlled by human sentiments. The intention of this chapter is therefore to establish microeconomically a dynamic macro model of a stock market that contains such sentiments. Moreover, it can generate bubbles and crashes endogenously by linking the complex dynamics of the market and the individual decision behaviour. In order to model the latter, I include basic elements of the state-preference approach. I show that, besides the parameters for optimism/pessimism and scepticism at the macro level, the aggregation of the individual wealth in the market, risk attitude and investors' return expectations are significant, especially in the case of a speculative bubble. Whereas the latter only have strengthening or curbing effects, from a microeconomic view it is especially the highly increased speculative money in the market that is responsible for the development of these market anomalies or financial instabilities. For example, particularly before the dot-com crash in the year 2000, it could be observed that employees had multimillion-dollar stock option portfolios. It is obvious that this type of instant wealth is illusory, and this is one of the prime characteristics of an impending stock market crash.

There are many possibilities to extend this model. Besides a stochastic expansion, in particular the meso level could be examined in more detail with the help of the noisy trader approach which divides the market into two groups – the 'smart money' or rational investors and the 'dumb money' or irrational investors. The first group is usually said to have a stabilizing role. In order to model this, the caution parameter should be founded microeconomically as well. As during the course of a bubble the border between the two groups floats (see Brunnermeier and Nagel, 2004), accordingly this can be endogenized dynamically. Furthermore, the individual decision behaviour could be expanded by a larger integration of behavioural finance aspects combined with recent results of neuro-economic studies. Suitable for this would be the separation of risk propensity and risk perception. The latter could be expanded, especially by overconfidence phenomena. In spite of all these expansions, the main questions still remain as to whether or not the duration, the extent or the critical point of bubbles can be predicted.

NOTES

1. In order to keep the model as simple as possible, it is sufficient to observe only the exponential term, as it is responsible for the shape of the underlying density function.
2. The usual neoclassical assumptions about monotony and concavity hold (see Kugler et al., 1996).
3. Cf. also the distinction between objective uncertainty and true uncertainty in Peters (2003).
4. Subject to β_i, the whole class of the linear risk-tolerant utility functions can be described qualitatively (Sommer and Kugler, 1997). For a detailed discussion of the linear risk-tolerant utility functions, see Ohlson (1987).
5. For the uniqueness and existence of the optimum, see Kugler et al. (1996). Furthermore, border solutions are disregarded as economically not relevant.
6. For the proofs of these propositions, see Kugler et al. (1996).
7. The topological equivalence describes the qualitative similarity of functions.
8. To be consistent with the original model, the function $\hat{\phi}$ is shown in this section without a 'hat'.

REFERENCES

Abhyankar, A., L.S. Copeland and W. Wong (1995), 'Nonlinear dynamics in real-time equity market indices: evidence from the United Kingdom', *The Economic Journal*, **105** (July), 864–80.
Abreu, D. and M.K. Brunnermeier (2003), 'Bubbles and crashes', *Econometrica*, **71** (1), 173–204.
Arrow, K. (1964), 'The role of securities in the optimal allocation of risk bearing', *Review of Economic Studies*, **31**, 91–6.
Banerjee, A.V. (1992), 'A simple model of herd behaviour', *The Quarterly Journal of Economics*, **107** (3), 797–817.
Barber, B.M. and T. Odean (1999), 'The courage of misguided convictions', *Financial Analysts Journal*, November–December, 41–55.
Binswanger, M. (1999), *Stock Markets, Speculative Bubbles and Economic Growth*, Cheltenham, UK and Northampton, MA, USA: Edward Elgar.
Blanchard, O.J. and M.W. Watson (1982), 'Bubbles, rational expectations and financial markets', in P. Wachtel (ed.), *Crisis in the Economic and Financial Structure*. Lexington, MA: Lexington Books, pp. 295–316.
Boldrin, M. (1988), 'Persistent oscillations and chaos in economic models: notes for a survey', in P.W. Anderson, K.J. Arrow and D. Pines (eds), *The Economy as an Evolving Complex System*, Redwood City, CA: Addison-Wesley, pp. 49–76.
Bowden, M. and S. McDonald (2005), 'The effect of social interaction and herd behaviour on the formation of agent expectations', mimeo, School of Economics, University of Queensland.
Brunnermeier, M.K. and S. Nagel (2004), 'Hedge funds and the technology bubble', *The Journal of Finance*, **59** (5), 2013–40.

Byrne, K. (2005), 'How do consumers evaluate risk in financial products?', *Journal of Financial Services Marketing*, **16** (1), 21–36.
Camerer, C. (1999), 'Behavioral economics: reunifying psychology and economics', *Proceedings of the National Academy of Sciences of the USA*, Vol. 96, pp. 10575–77.
Day, R.H. and W.J. Huang (1990), 'Bulls, bears and market sheep', *Journal of Economic Behaviour and Organization*, **14**, S.299–329.
Eichengreen, B. (2002), *Financial Crises (and what to do about them)*, Oxford: Oxford University Press.
Fernandez-Rodriguez, F., M.D. Garcia-Artiles and J.M. Martin-Gonzalez (2002), 'A model of speculative behaviour with a strange attractor', *Applied Mathematical Finance*, **9**, 143–61.
Flieth, B. and J. Foster (2002), 'Interactive expectations', *Journal of Evolutionary Economics*, **12** (4), 375–95.
Grebel, T., H. Hanusch and E. Merey (2004), 'Schumpeterian dynamics and financial market anomalies', Working Paper No. 264, University of Augsburg.
Johansen, A., O. Ledoit and D. Sornette (2000), 'Crashes at critical points', *International Journal of Theoretical and Applied Finance*, **3** (2), 219–55.
Kaldor, N. (1939), 'Speculation and economic stability', *Review of Economic Studies*, **7**, 1–27.
Knight, F. (1921), '*Risk, Uncertainty and Profit*', reprinted in 1971, Chicago, IL: University of Chicago Press.
Kugler, F. and H. Hanusch (1993), 'Stock market dynamics: a psycho-economic approach to speculative bubbles', Working Paper No. 92, University of Augsburg.
Kugler, F., J. Sommer and H. Hanusch (1996), 'Capital markets from an evolutionary perspective: the state preference model reconsidered', Working Paper No. 155, University of Augsburg.
Lux, T. (1995), 'Herd behaviour, bubbles and crashes', *The Economic Journal*, **105**, 881–96.
Madhavan, A. (2000), 'Market microstructure: a survey', *Journal of Financial Markets*, **3**, 205–58.
O'Hara, M. (1995), *Market Microstructure Theory*, Cambridge, MA: Blackwell.
Ohlson, J.A. (1987), *The Theory of Financial Markets and Information*, New York: North-Holland.
Peters, E.E. (1996), *Chaos and Order in the Capital Markets: A New View of Cycles, Prices, and Market Volatility*, 2nd edn, New York: John Wiley & Sons.
Peters, E.E. (2003), 'Simple and complex market inefficiences: integrating efficient markets, behavioral finance, and complexity', *Journal of Behavioral Finance*, **4** (4), 225–33.
Shiller, R.J. (1991), *Market Volatility*, Cambridge, MA: The MIT Press.
Shiller, R.J. (2000), *Irrational Exuberance*, Princeton, NJ: Princeton University Press.
Sommer, J. and F. Kugler (1997), 'Endogenous expectations and market sentiments on the basis of the state preference model', Working Paper No. 160, University of Augsburg.
Sornette, D. (2003), *Why Stock Markets Crash: Critical Events in Complex Financial Systems*, Princeton, NJ: Princeton University Press.
Unser, M. (1999), *Behavioral Finance am Aktienmarkt: empirische Analysen zum Risikoverhalten individueller Anleger*, Bad Soden: Uhlenbruch Verlag.

Vaga, T. (1990), 'The coherent market hypothesis', *Financial Analysts Journal*, November–December, 36–49.
Zimmermann, H.G. (1994), 'Neuronale Netze als Entscheidungskalkül – Grundlagen und ihre ökonometrische Realisierung', in H. Rehkugler and H.G. Zimmermann (eds), *Neuronale Netze in der Ökonomie*, München: Verlag F. Vahlen, pp. 1–87.

7.   Corporate currency hedging and currency crises*

**Andreas Röthig, Willi Semmler and
Peter Flaschel**

1.   INTRODUCTION

One of the key ingredients in financial crises according to Krugman
(2000) is foreign-currency-denominated debt. Given such sort of debt, a
sudden currency depreciation – a rising price of foreign exchange – could
have serious consequences for the balance sheets of firms. Those negative
balance-sheet effects may cancel out positive effects arising from the trade
balance, as described by the Marshall-Lerner condition.

Krugman (2000) sketches two possible solutions for avoiding financial
crises. The first is based on a growing integration of markets for goods
and services. This would weaken the contractionary balance-sheet effect
of a currency depreciation and strengthen the positive effects on exports.
The second solution concerns encouraging foreign direct investment.
Multinational firms, which have subsidiaries in different countries and
deal with a portfolio of different currencies, are more likely to resist pressures arising from a specific currency. Promoting foreign direct investment
serves to reduce negative effects of adverse trends in foreign exchange
markets. Hence both solutions focus on strengthening the independence of
a firm's balance sheet in respect of adverse exchange rate movements.

This chapter pursues a new approach for reaching this objective. The
main idea is that some independence of a firm's balance sheet from adverse
exchange rate movements can be achieved by corporate risk management.
In contrast to our firm-based approach, other authors, such as Burnside
et al. (2001), focus on the role of banks in currency crises. These authors
investigate the conflict between government guarantees and banks' hedging
activities and conclude that the presence of guarantees eliminates banks'
incentives to hedge. As the government guarantee serves as a kind of protection, additional risk management is dispensable.[1]

Usually there are no government guarantees to firms. Therefore firms
depend on financial markets to hedge their currency exposure. We

examine the impact of risk management activities of non-financial firms on economic stability by introducing corporate hedging in a Mundell–Fleming–Tobin type model. More specifically, we here extend the Flaschel and Semmler (2006) model to include hedging. Firms' hedging activity is modelled depending on firm size as well as hedging costs. Referring to the channels mentioned by Krugman (2000), the primary advantage of corporate risk management is the fact that, in general, it is not necessary officially to encourage risk management because it is a natural constituent of business. Furthermore, nowadays, financial derivatives are available in great variety, providing almost perfect hedging possibilities. Hedging currency risk with financial derivatives gives companies a powerful protection tool, and might be a key instrument for avoiding 'private sector crises' (Goodhart, 2000, p. 108).

The chapter is organized as follows. Section 2 implements corporate risk management into a Flaschel and Semmler (2006) type Mundell–Fleming–Tobin model.[2] The decision whether to hedge or not is given exogenously by assuming that only large firms can hedge their currency exposure, while small companies depend completely on foreign exchange markets. In section 3, all firms can hedge, and the hedging decision depends on hedging costs and expected losses due to currency depreciations. Section 4 contains concluding remarks. In the appendix, we discuss hedging strategies using currency forwards and futures as well as some empirical facts concerning currency derivatives' market size and the availability of financial derivatives in emerging markets.

2.   FIRM SIZE APPROACH

In this section, corporate hedging activity depends solely on firm size. The only hedging instruments available are linear over-the-counter (OTC) currency forward contracts. OTC products are 'custom-made' (Neftci, 2000, p. 6) and allow, therefore, for perfect currency hedging. However, the main disadvantage of OTC products is the fact that they are not traded on organized exchanges. The products are not standardized and therefore generally not available to a large number of customers. Furthermore, OTC derivatives, in general, deliver large amounts of the underlying asset. Smaller amounts of foreign exchange compatible with specific capital flows of smaller non-financial firms cannot be hedged perfectly with these products. Hence, in addition to restricted access to OTC derivatives, the contract size of OTC products poses a barrier to small firms' hedging activity. In our model, we assume that only large firms have access to OTC derivatives and use these products to hedge their currency exposure perfectly. Small firms do not hedge at all. Empirical evidence supports this approach (see Fender, 2000b). Mian (1996, p. 437) investigates corporate hedging policy and concludes:

> I find robust evidence that larger firms are more likely to hedge. This evidence supports the hypothesis that there are economies of scale in hedging and that information and transaction considerations have more influence on hedging activities than the cost of raising capital.[3]

Our model is based on the following assumptions:

1. There are two types of firms: large ones and small ones.
2. Only large firms can hedge their currency exposure, and they hedge it perfectly. Small firms cannot hedge at all. Large firms are completely independent of exchange rate movements, while small firms are subject to adverse developments in foreign exchange markets.
3. There are no hedging costs.
4. Small and large firms are equal, except regarding their ability to hedge.
5. Banks and trading partners recognize hedged and unhedged firms by their size.

2.1 The Investment Function

In our model, hedging activity affects the investment function. The investment function of firm i is given by $I_i(\theta, e)$, where the hedging coefficient θ and the exchange rate e enter in a multiplicative form ($\theta * e$). The term $\theta * e$ represents the sensitivity of investment to changes in the exchange rate, with hedging coefficient θ:

$$\theta = \begin{cases} 0 & \text{if firm } i \text{ is perfectly hedged (large firm)} \\ 1 & \text{if firm } i \text{ is not hedged (small firm)} \end{cases} \tag{7.1}$$

A perfectly hedged firm's investment function is, therefore, insensitive to exchange rate movements, while unhedged firms are exposed to developments in the foreign exchange markets.

$$I_i = \begin{cases} \bar{I} & \text{if firm } i \text{ is perfectly hedged (large firm)} \\ I(e) & \text{if firm } i \text{ is not hedged (small firm)} \end{cases} \tag{7.2}$$

Figure 7.1 shows a firm's payoff (a) and the investment function in the case without corporate hedging (b). This investment function is on a par with Krugman's (2000) type investment function, in which investment negatively depends on the nominal exchange rate e. The underlying idea is that

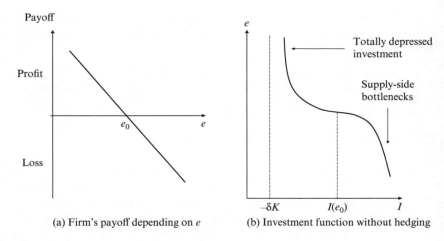

(a) Firm's payoff depending on e (b) Investment function without hedging

Figure 7.1 Economy consisting of small firms

firms in many developing countries have large amounts of debt denominated in foreign currency. A currency depreciation will worsen these firms' balance sheets, which will reduce their net wealth, leading to an investment contraction. The result of such a development might be a balance-sheet-driven crisis in which sufficiently strong negative balance-sheet effects outweigh positive competitiveness effects, leading to a backward-bending goods-market curve (see Krugman, 2000, pp. 82–4).

The payoff function in Figure 7.1(a) represents any cash flow connected to the liabilities held in foreign currency. In the case of a depreciation of the domestic currency, the value of the liabilities increases, resulting in a loss, while an appreciation of the domestic currency reduces the value of the liabilities, which can be taken as profit. The payoff function in Figure 7.1 is linear for simplicity, in order to introduce simple linear hedging techniques to potentiate perfect hedging possibilities.[4] However, the investment function is not linear due to the balance-sheet effect connected to the financial accelerator mechanism, as discussed in Bernanke et al. (1996), see also Proaño et al. (2005).

Figure 7.2 corresponds to the first line of equation (7.2), where $I_i = \bar{I}$. The payoff function shows a simple, linear currency forward hedging strategy. Here, the central idea is that the forward position generates profits if the spot position generates losses. Profits and losses sum to zero. If the spot position generates profits as the result of an appreciation, the forward position generates losses, again summing to zero.[5]

Since foreign liabilities are perfectly hedged against adverse currency movements, the investment function shown in Figure 7.2 is independent

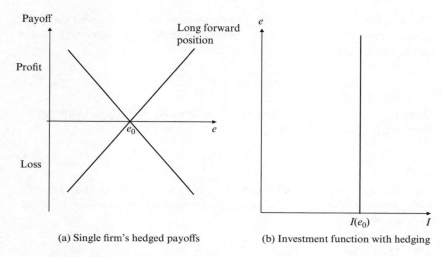

(a) Single firm's hedged payoffs   (b) Investment function with hedging

Figure 7.2   Economy consisting of large firms

of the exchange rate. Large firms that have access to financial derivatives will hedge their currency exposure and, hence, surrender potential gains by an appreciation. Fender (2000a, p. 10) describes the reasoning as follows: 'It is a fundamental insight, that under uncertainty, risk-averse decision-makers will prefer stable income and consumption streams to highly variable ones.' Furthermore, trading partners as well as banks recognize a hedged firm just by the fact that this specific firm is large. By knowing this, negative balance-sheet effects can be avoided, even if the hedge position is off balance sheet. Assuming that there are n firms in the economy, the investment function depends on the average hedging coefficient of the economy:

$$\phi = \frac{1}{n}\sum_{i=1}^{n}\theta_i, 0 \leq \phi \leq 1 \qquad (7.3)$$

In a perfectly hedged economy, where all n firms hedge their currency exposure perfectly, the investment function is constant: $I(\phi, e) = \overline{I}$. In the case that no firm hedges, the investment function is $I(\phi, e) = I(e)$.

2.2   The Goods Market

We get the following representation of goods-market equilibrium:

$$Y = C(Y - \delta\overline{K} - \overline{T}) + I(\phi, e) + \overline{G} + NX(Y, \overline{Y}^*, e) \qquad (7.4)$$

The shape of the IS curve with the dependent variable Y, and the independent variable e, is given by the implicit function theorem (see Flaschel and Semmler, 2006):

$$Y'(e) = -\frac{I_e + NX_e}{C_Y + NX_Y - 1} \qquad (7.5)$$

Since $C_Y + NX_Y < 1$ by assumption, the term $C_Y + NX_Y - 1$ is negative. Hence $Y'(e)$ is upward sloping if

$$NX_e > I_e \qquad (7.6)$$

Equation (7.6) always holds true if $\phi = 0$, which means that all firms hedge their currency exposure perfectly. In this case, there is no backward-bending IS curve.

2.3   The Financial Markets

The financial markets are fully described by the following equations (see Flaschel and Semmler, 2006; Proaño et al., 2005):

Private wealth: $W_p = M_0 + B_0 + eF_{p0}$ (AA1)

LM curve: $M = m(Y, r)$, $m_Y > 0, m_r < 0$ (AA2)

Demand for foreign bonds: $eF_p = f(\xi, W_p)$, $f_\xi < 0, f_{W_p} \in (0, 1)$
                                                                 (AA3)

Demand for domestic bonds: $B = W_p - m(Y, r) - f(\xi, W_p)$ (AA4)

Expected depreciation: $\varepsilon = \beta_\varepsilon(\frac{e_0}{e} - 1)$, $\varepsilon_e \le 0$ (AA5)

Risk premium: $\xi = r - \bar{r}^* - \varepsilon$ (AA6)

Foreign exchange market: $\bar{F}^* = F_p + F_c$ (AA7)

with the domestic interest rate r, the foreign interest rate $\bar{r}^*$, private foreign bond holdings eF_p, and the central bank's foreign bond holdings F_c. Equation (AA5) presents a typical formulation of regressive expectations, as discussed in Rødseth (2000, p. 21), with $\varepsilon_e \le 0$ and $\varepsilon(e_0) = 0$ for the steady-state exchange rate level e_0. Economic agents have perfect knowledge of the future equilibrium exchange rate and, therefore, expect the actual exchange rate to adjust to the steady-state value after the occurrence of a shock. Flaschel and Semmler (2006) call these expectations allowing agents to behave in a forward-looking way 'asymptotically rational'.

Solving equation (AA2) for r, inserting the result in equation (AA6), and inserting further equation (AA6) as well as equation (AA1) in equation (AA3), gives the financial markets equilibrium curve (AA curve):

$$eF_p = f\left(r(Y,M_0) - \bar{r}^* - \beta_\varepsilon\left(\frac{e_0}{e} - 1\right), M_0 + B_0 + eF_{p0}\right) \quad (7.7)$$

The slope of the AA curve is determined by the implicit function theorem (see, e.g., Proaño et al., 2005).

$$e'(Y) = -\frac{f_\xi^* r_Y}{-f_\xi^* \varepsilon_e + (f_{W_p} - 1)^* F_{p0}} < 0 \quad (7.8)$$

The AA curve is downward sloping since $f_\xi < 0$, $r_Y > 0$, $\varepsilon_e \leq 0$, $f_{W_p} \in (0, 1)$, and $F_{p0} \geq 0$.

2.4 Case Study

We obtain the adjustment process of the goods-market equilibrium curve

$$\dot{Y} = \beta_Y[C(Y - \delta\bar{K} - \bar{T}) + I(\phi, e) + \bar{G} + NX(Y, \bar{Y}^*, e) - Y] \quad (7.9)$$

and the following dynamics of the financial markets:

$$\dot{e} = \beta_e\left[f\left(r(Y, M_0) - \bar{r}^* - \beta_\varepsilon\left(\frac{e_0}{e} - 1\right), M_0 + B_0 + eF_{p0}\right) - eF_{p0}\right]$$
$$(7.10)$$

Figure 7.3 presents IS–AA diagrams for different values of the average hedging coefficient ϕ (Cases A, B, C, D). In the following, we discuss the characteristics of Cases A, B, C and D as well as the local stability properties.

- Case A: $\phi = 1$
  In this case, no firm is hedged. Consequently, there are only small firms that do not have access to hedging tools. Hence this case corresponds to the case presented in Krugman (2000) and Flaschel and Semmler (2006). The figure shows multiple equilibria, with E_1 representing the 'good equilibrium' with high output Y_1 and low exchange rate e_1, and E_3 represents the 'crisis equilibrium', with low output Y_3 and high exchange rate e_3.

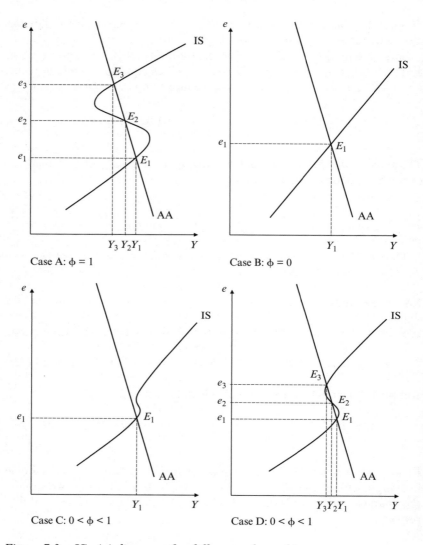

Figure 7.3   IS–AA diagrams for different values of ϕ

● Case B: ϕ = 0

Case B illustrates the situation where all firms are hedged perfectly. With the investment function being independent of the exchange rate, net exports remain the only linkage between Y and e. In the case of a perfectly hedged economy, there is no backward-bending

IS curve and, thus, there are no multiple equilibria. In this framework, a currency crisis cannot occur.
- Cases C and D: $0 < \phi < 1$
Cases C and D present other possible outcomes, depending on the value of ϕ. With decreasing ϕ, the 'bad equilibrium' E_3 moves down the AA curve towards higher values of Y and lower values of e. Hence, in the multiple equilibria case (Case D), the severity of a currency crisis decreases with growing hedging activity. In Case C, the hedging activity is sufficient to avoid multiple equilibria. In this case, a currency crisis does not occur.

2.5 Stability Analysis

In order to study the stability of the system, the Jacobian matrix is derived:

$$J = \begin{bmatrix} \beta_Y[C_Y + NX_Y - 1] & \beta_Y[I_e + NX_e] \\ \beta_e[f_\xi^* r_Y] & \beta_e[-f_\xi^* \varepsilon_e + (f_{W_p} - 1)^* F_{p0}] \end{bmatrix}$$

Considering $f_\xi < 0, r_Y > 0, f_{W_p} \in [0, 1]$ and $\varepsilon_e \leq 0$, we obtain the following signs:

$$J = \begin{bmatrix} - & ? \\ - & - \end{bmatrix}$$

Referring to the four cases mentioned above, it depends on the sign of '?' whether a specific equilibrium $(E_1; E_2; E_3)$ is stable or unstable:

- Case A: $\phi = 1$
$? = \beta_Y[I_e + NX_e]$
If I_e dominates NX_e (E_2), '?' is negative. The determinant and the trace of the Jacobian are both negative $(det(J_{E_2}) < 0, tr(J_{E_2}) < 0)$. Hence E_2 is a saddle point.[6]
If NX_e dominates I_e (E_1, E_3), '?' is positive. Hence $det(J_{(E_{1,3})}) > 0$ and $tr(J_{(E_{1,3})}) < 0$, which gives a stable steady state.
- Case B: $\phi = 0$
Since $I_e = 0$, we get $\beta_Y[NX_e] > 0$.
We have a single equilibrium (E_1) which is stable since $det(J_{(E_1)}) > 0$ and $tr(J_{(E_1)}) < 0$.
- Cases C and D: $0 < \phi < 1$
Case C, the single-equilibrium case, is similar to Case B. At the equilibrium point (E_1), NX_e dominates I_e, the sign of '?' is positive, $det(J_{(E_1)}) > 0$, and $tr(J_{(E_1)}) < 0$. The equilibrium E_1 is stable.

The dynamics of the multiple equilibria, Case D, equal the dynamics of Case A. If I_e dominates $NX_e(E_2)$, we get $det(J_{(E_2)}) < 0$, $tr(J_{(E_2)}) < 0$. Consequently E_2 is unstable. If NX_e dominates I_e (E_1, E_3), then $det(J_{(E_{1,3})}) > 0$ and $tr(J_{(E_{1,3})}) < 0$. Hence the 'good equilibrium' E_1 and the 'crisis equilibrium' E_3 are both stable.

3.   HEDGING COSTS APPROACH

In the previous section, the firms' decisions whether to hedge currency risk or not is given exogenously by assuming that small firms cannot hedge while large firms are able to hedge their currency exposure perfectly. In this section, all firms have the ability to hedge their currency exposure perfectly. Standardized hedging instruments such as currency futures are tradable on organized exchanges and, thus, available to all firms.[7] The decision whether to hedge or not is based on hedging costs and expected losses due to adverse exchange rate movements.

Again, the investment function of firm i is given by $I_i(\theta_i, e)$, where θ_i depends on hedging costs c_h and expected losses $L(e)$:

$$\theta_i = \begin{cases} 0 & \text{if } c_h < L(e) \\ 1 & \text{if } c_h \geq L(e) \end{cases} \tag{7.11}$$

Since the main hedging tools can be traded at low costs, the hedging costs c_h consist almost solely of costs of information and costs of implementing sophisticated risk assessment procedures. In fact, most over-the-counter (OTC) derivatives are 'zero-sum games', which means that no upfront fees are payable. The costs of exchange-traded derivatives do not pose a barrier, either. Taking a futures position costs an initial margin, which is 'seldom more than a small fraction of the costs of the underlying securities, although it does vary from contract to contract' (Chew, 1996, p. 15). Additionally, most OTC derivatives are off-balance-sheet items.[8] Hence the costs connected to OTC transactions do not appear in firms' balance sheets, and costs arising from trading exchange-traded derivatives are neglected because of their small size.

Losses $L(e)$ depend positively on the nominal exchange rate e. The payoff function presented in Figure 7.1 can be interpreted as an inverse loss function. In the case of an appreciation of the domestic currency, the loss function becomes negative, which has to be equated with profit. In this context, feared losses can be taken as a measure of risk aversion among firms. Increasing risk aversion reduces risky business and, thereby, has an overall positive effect on investment.

Table 7.1   Unhedged firm's balance sheet

Assets	Liabilities
pK	eF_f

Table 7.2   Hedged firm's balance sheet

Assets	Liabilities
$pK - c_h$	F_f

The main idea presented in equation (7.11) consists of the assumption that firms will only hedge if the expected loss due to a currency depreciation $L(e)$ exceeds the hedging costs c_h. If firms expect the domestic currency to appreciate, they will not hedge because of hedging costs as well as missed gains due to corresponding losses of the hedge position.[9]

The balance sheets shown in Tables 7.1 and 7.2 illustrate this. The unhedged firm's balance sheet presented in Table 7.1 is that presented in Flaschel and Semmler (2006). Investment depends solely on foreign liabilities and thus on currency developments. However, exchange rates can move in two directions, as shown in Figure 7.1: a depreciation of the domestic currency worsens the balance sheet, while an appreciation has the opposite effect.

Table 7.2 shows a hedged firm's balance sheet. Here, the value of the foreign liabilities is independent of exchange rate movements. Hence there is no loss by a currency depreciation and no gain by an appreciation. The costs for this guaranteed stable value of the liabilities are the hedging costs paid by the firm. The hedging costs reduce the value of the firm's assets, and so it is very important for any firm to calculate potential losses induced by adverse exchange rate movements and to compare them to the hedging costs.

3.1   The Case of *n* Homogeneous Firms

In an economy with n homogeneous firms, with identical hedging costs and loss functions, we have the following investment function:

$$I = \begin{cases} \bar{I} & \text{if } c_h < L(e) \\ I(e) & \text{if } c_h \geq L(e) \end{cases} \tag{7.12}$$

Because of the homogeneity, all firms act equally with respect to their hedging activities. If the expected loss due to a depreciation of the domestic currency exceeds the hedging costs, firms will attempt to hedge their currency exposure perfectly. However, if the hedging costs exceed the expected losses, or if the firms expect an appreciation of the domestic currency that would reduce the value of their liabilities, they will not hedge at all.

Again, the Jacobian is given by

$$J = \begin{bmatrix} \beta_Y[C_Y + NX_Y - 1] & \beta_Y[I_e + NX_e] \\ \beta_e[f_\xi * r_Y] & \beta_e[-f_\xi * \varepsilon_e + (f_{W_p} - 1) * F_{p0}] \end{bmatrix}$$

with

$$I_e = \begin{cases} 0 & \text{if } c_h < L(e) \\ I_e & \text{if } c_h \geq L(e) \end{cases} \tag{7.13}$$

In the case of a perfectly hedged economy, i.e. $I_e = 0$, the signs of the Jacobian are as follows:

$$J = \begin{bmatrix} - & + \\ - & - \end{bmatrix}$$

Here, a currency crisis cannot occur because there is no backward-bending goods-market curve. The single equilibrium is stable, since $det(J) > 0$ and $tr(J) < 0$. However, with $c_h \geq L(e)$, we obtain the multiple-equilibria case, already discussed (Case A in Figure 7.3). In this setting, we can only investigate the cases $\phi = 0$ and $\phi = 1$.

3.2   The Case of *n* Heterogeneous Firms

In this section, we discuss a more general hedging costs approach. Here, hedging costs and loss functions vary among firms. Again, the investment function of firm i is given by $I_i(\theta_i, e)$, where the hedging coefficient θ_i and the exchange rate e enter in a multiplicative form $(\theta_i * e)$, with $\theta_i \in [0, 1]$ for all $i = 1, \ldots, n$. The hedging coefficient θ_i depends on hedging costs $c_{h,i}$ and losses $L_i(e)$ with:[10]

$$\theta_i = \begin{cases} 0 & \text{if } c_{h,i} < L_i(e) \\ 1 & \text{if } c_{h,i} \geq L_i(e) \end{cases} \tag{7.14}$$

Because of firms' heterogeneity and corresponding individual hedging costs $c_{h,i}$ and losses $L_i(e)$, it is possible that firm j hedges its currency exposure, while firm k abstains from hedging. Therefore, there are hedged as well as unhedged firms in the economy. The average hedging coefficient of the economy is

$$\phi = \frac{1}{n} \sum_{i=1}^{n} \theta_i, 0 \leq \phi \leq 1 \tag{7.15}$$

Reducing hedging costs, such as costs of information and costs connected to derivative trading, in general leads to more hedging activity by the individual firm ($\theta_i \nearrow$), and thus to a higher hedging level of the entire economy ($\phi \nearrow$). This in turn reduces the sensitivity of investment to the exchange rate ($I_e \nearrow$). Reducing I_e reduces the backward-bending part of the goods-market curve, and therefore the probability of crisis. Hence, the lower hedging costs ($c_{h,i}$) and the higher feared losses of a devaluation ($L_i(e)$), the more firms will hedge their currency exposure and the less risk there is for the entire economy. Compared to the previous section, the assumption of heterogeneous firms allows us to discuss all cases $0 \leq \phi \leq 1$. Given that a large number of firms hedge, in our model, a currency crisis is ruled out by the fact that the IS curve crosses the AA curve only once (see Case C in Figure 7.3). Increasing risk aversion, providing information as well as risk management techniques and access to risk management instruments such as derivatives, are the key factors for avoiding financial crises.

4.   CONCLUSIONS

The main result of this investigation is that economic stability can be increased by enhancing corporate hedging either by directly simplifying access to hedging instruments (firm size approach) or indirectly by lowering hedging costs, as well as increasing the awareness of specific risks (hedging costs approach). Under the assumption that firms can limit currency risk by hedging, currency depreciations are more manageable and less likely to result in currency and financial crises. In our model, corporate hedging reduces the backward-bending segment of the goods-market curve 'that is key to the possibility of crisis' (Krugman, 1999, p. 6).

Referring to this result, the main duty of officials appears to be the achievement of more transparency and the improvement of information flows. This could be realized by regulating transactions of OTC derivatives, leading to easier access to OTC products and reducing the costs of information, and thus the costs of hedging.

NOTES

*   We would like to thank Ingo Barens for extensive discussions.
1.   Another difference between the two approaches is simply the definition of hedging. In our chapter, hedging activity is always bound to spot market activity, and thus to the risk management of specific capital flows exposed to exchange rate risk. In the investigation of Burnside et al. (2001), banks can even enhance 'their exposure to exchange rate risk via forward markets' (p. 1153). Hence banks use forward markets not only for hedging

activity but also for speculation. However, there is one similarity between these different approaches. In both papers, banks and firms can fully hedge exchange rate risk.

2. For a detailed discussion of the Mundell–Fleming–Tobin model, see Rødseth (2000, ch. 6).

3. However, Géczy et al. (1997, p. 1332) point out that the relationship between firm size and hedging activity might not be that unambiguous. Smaller firms might hedge more because of higher bankruptcy costs and greater information asymmetries. In our simple model, we adopt the mainstream opinion, based on empirical evidence, that there is a positive relationship between firm size and hedging activity (see Pennings and Garcia, 2004, p. 957). The main reasons for this positive relationship are informational economies and economies of scale, as well as access to necessary resources and the potential trading volume of large firms.

4. Perfect hedging possibilities can also be generated using non-linear instruments such as swaps and options. One could also use structured notes, linking foreign currency risk to credit risk. Another approach is the so-called macro derivatives. They combine risks associated with contract-specific variables such as exchange rates, interest rates and counterparty default, as well as more general variables such as GDP (see Schweimayer, 2003). Again, there are many possible hedging strategies, but in this context it is appropriate to use simple linear currency forwards. An example of how to conduct currency hedging using forwards and futures is presented in the appendix.

5. For similar graphical representations of linear hedging strategies, see Grannis and Fitzgerald (1989, p. 102) and Gerke and Bank (1998, p. 444).

6. See the 'Trace-determinant plane' in Hirsch et al. (2004, p. 63).

7. For more details on hedging with currency forwards and futures, see the appendix.

8. Garber (1998, p. 6) points out that the only exception is contracts, where financial flows occur at the time of the trade, for instance, when collateral is demanded by a market maker. For a discussion on off-balance-sheet derivatives, 'shadow transactions' and the resulting problems concerning the balance sheet as a measure of risk and creditworthiness, see Dodd (2000, 2002).

9. See the payoff function in Figure 7.2.

10. Remember that $\theta_i = 0$ corresponds to a perfect hedge, while $\theta_i = 1$ is the unhedged case, respectively.

REFERENCES

Bernanke, B.S., M. Gertler and S. Gilchrist (1996), 'The financial accelerator and the flight to quality', *Review of Economics and Statistics*, **78**, 1–15.

Burnside, C., M. Eichenbaum and S. Rebelo (2001), 'Hedging and financial fragility in fixed exchange rate regimes', *European Economic Review*, **45**, 1151–93.

Chew, L. (1996), *Managing Derivative Risks: The Use and Abuse of Leverage,* Chichester, UK: John Wiley & Sons.

Dodd, R. (2000), 'The role of derivatives in the East Asian financial crisis', Center for Economic Policy Analysis, CEPA Working Paper Series III, 20.

Dodd, R. (2002), 'Derivatives, the shape of international capital flows and the virtues of prudential regulation', World Institute for Development Economic Research, United Nations University, Discussion Paper 93.

Duffie, D. (1989). *Futures Markets*. Englewood Cliffs, NJ: Prentice Hall.

Fender, I. (2000a), 'Corporate hedging: the impact of financial derivatives on the broad credit channel of monetary policy'. BIS Working Papers, 94.

Fender, I. (2000b), 'The impact of corporate risk management on monetary policy transmission: some empirical evidence', BIS Working Papers, 95.

Flaschel, P. and W. Semmler (2006), 'Currency crisis, financial crisis, and large output loss', in C. Chiarella, P. Flaschel, R. Franke and W. Semmler (eds), *Quantitative and Empirical Analysis of Nonlinear Dynamic Macromodels*, Amsterdam: Elsevier, pp. 385–414.

Fung, H.G. and W.K. Leung (1991), 'The use of forward contracts for hedging currency risk', *Journal of International Financial Management and Accounting*, 3, 78–92.

Garber, P.M. (1998), 'Derivatives in international capital flows', National Bureau of Economic Research, NBER Working Paper Series, 6623.

Géczy, C., B.A. Minton and C. Schrand (1997), 'Why firms use currency derivatives', *Journal of Finance*, 52, 1323–54.

Gerke, W. and M. Bank (1998), *Finanzierung: Grundlagen für die Investitions- und Finanzierungsentscheidungen in Unternehmen*, Stuttgart: Kohlhammer.

Goodhart, C. (2000), 'Commentary: crises: the price of globalization?', in Federal Reserve Bank of Kansas City, *Global Economic Integration: Opportunities and Challenges*, New York/Hong Kong, Books for Business, pp. 107–10.

Grannis, S. and S. Fitzgerald (1989), 'Dynamic hedging and the use of derivatives', in C. Stoakes and A. Freeman (eds), *Managing Global Portfolios*, London: Euromoney Publications, pp. 75–97.

Hirsch, M.W., S. Smale and R.L. Devaney (2004), *Differential Equations, Dynamical Systems & an Introduction to Chaos*, 2nd edn, Amsterdam: Elsevier.

Hull, J.C. (2000), *Options, Futures, and other Derivatives*, 4th edn, Upper Saddle River, NJ: Prentice Hall.

Jorion, P. (2001), *Value at Risk: The New Benchmark for Managing Financial Risk*, 2nd edn, New York: McGraw-Hill.

Krugman, P. (1999), 'Analytical afterthoughts on the Asian crisis', mimeo, MIT, Cambridge, MA.

Krugman, P. (2000), 'Crises: the price of globalization?', *Global Economic Integration: Opportunities and Challenges: A Symposium*, Kansas City, KS: Federal Reserve Bank of Kansas City, pp. 75–106.

Mian, S.L. (1996), 'Evidence on corporate hedging policy', *Journal of Financial and Quantitative Analysis*, 31, 419–39.

Neftci, S.N. (2000), *An Introduction to the Mathematics of Financial Derivatives*, 2nd edn, San Diego, CA: Academic Press.

Pennings, J.M.E. and P. Garcia (2004), 'Hedging behavior in small and medium-sized enterprises: the role of unobserved heterogeneity', *Journal of Banking & Finance*, 28, 951–78.

Proaño, C.R., P. Flaschel and W. Semmler (2005), 'Currency and financial crises in emerging market economies in the medium run', *Journal of Economic Asymmetries*, 2, 105–30.

Rødseth, A. (2000), *Open Economy Macroeconomics*, Cambridge: Cambridge University Press.

Schweimayer, G. (2003), *Risikomanagement mit Makroderivaten auf Basis zeitdiskreter stochastischer Prozesse*, Aachen: Shaker Verlag.

APPENDIX: SOME NOTES ON CURRENCY HEDGING

In this appendix, we take a closer look at different hedging strategies using foreign exchange forwards and futures. Since forwards and futures exhibit completely different trading characteristics, this is to be valued highly. As we assume their payoff functions to be identical, the differences in how they are traded become more relevant regarding the different approaches in this chapter.

In the 'firm size approach', we assume that only large firms have access to hedging products. Furthermore, large firms hedge their currency exposure perfectly. These characteristics fit custom-made over-the-counter (OTC) products such as forwards.[1] Moreover, hedging costs do not play any role or, as Hull (2000, p. 59) puts it: 'The value of a forward contract at the time it is first entered into is zero.'

The 'hedging costs approach' gives all firms the possibility to hedge. This approach is better applicable to hedging products traded on organized exchanges such as futures markets. Getting access to futures is much easier than getting access to OTC products. However, trading futures costs an initial margin.

The problem with futures hedging is that it does not necessarily lead to perfect hedges. In this section we show that, using a very simple numerical example, under simplified assumptions, the futures hedging strategy is at least asymptotically perfect. We also show at the end of this section that currency forwards and futures play a dominant role among currency derivatives and that, nowadays, derivative products are available in many emerging markets, too.

A.1   Setting up a Simple Scenario

We begin the explanation of currency hedging with a simple scenario. A European firm borrows \$1 000 000 in $t = 0$ from a US bank and sells the dollars for euros immediately. In $t = 1$, the firm has to buy \$1 100 000, the amount received plus interest ($i = 10$ per cent), to repay the debt. If the exchange rate is constant over the time horizon ($e_{t=0} = e_{t=1}$), the firm repays exactly the expected debt value, i.e. borrowed amount plus interest. If the domestic currency depreciates, the price of the dollar per euro increases ($e_{t=0} < e_{t=1}$), which results in an increased debt value in terms of the domestic currency.

Figure 7A.1 shows the debt value in terms of the domestic currency (€) in the case of a stable exchange rate ($e_{t=0} = e_{t=1} = 1^{€}/s$) and in the case of a depreciation of the domestic currency ($e_{t=0} = 1^{€}/s < e_{t=1} = 1.5^{€}/s$). In the

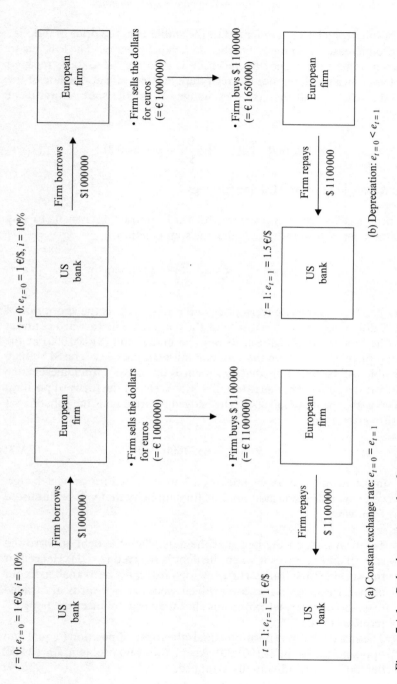

Figure 7A.1   Debt denominated in foreign currency

157

case of the depreciation, compared to the stable one, the price of a dollar per euro increases, leading to a higher debt value in euros. The loss due to the steep domestic currency depreciation is the debt value to be repayed in dollars times the difference between the exchange rate at the date of the spot contract $e_{t=0}$ and the actual exchange rate at the spot commitment date $e_{t=1}$:

$$\$1\,100\,000 * \left(1\frac{€}{\$} - 1.5\frac{€}{\$}\right) = €{-}550\,000 \qquad (7A.1)$$

A.2   A Simple Forward Hedging Strategy

The firm has to enter into a long forward contract in $t = 0$, to buy $\$1\,100\,000$ in $t = 1$, in order to hedge the spot position:

$$\$1\,100\,000 * \left(1.5\frac{€}{\$} - 1\frac{€}{\$}\right) = €550\,000 \qquad (7A.2)$$

where $e_{t=0} = 1€/\$$ is the delivery price and $e_{t=1} = 1.5€/\$$ is the spot price of the US dollar per euro at maturity of the contract. The forward contract gives the holder the obligation to buy the underlying ($\$1\,100\,000$) at the delivery price $e_{t=0} = 1€/\$$ on the spot commitment date $e_{t=1}$. The $\$1\,100\,000$ receivable will be sold immediately for euros on the spot foreign exchange market at the spot exchange rate $e_{t=1} = 1.5€/\$$. Hence the forward position ends up with a profit (€550 000). The hedged return equals the sum of spot and forward returns:

$$€{-}550\,000 + €550\,000 = 0 \qquad (7A.3)$$

The simple hedging strategy presented here results in a perfect hedge. However, we made some assumptions for simplicity that will be discussed in the following:

- The firm puts on the hedge at the date when the debt is borrowed ($t = 0$) and removes it when the debt is repaid ($t = 1$). Hence, for this specific time frame, currency forwards must be available. In our model, this does not cause problems because forwards are traded over the counter, which means that they exactly meet the hedgers' requirements.
- The size of the spot position equals the forward position ('equal and opposite' position: $\$1\,100\,000$). Again, this is no problem, since OTC derivatives are individually arranged.

A.3 A Simple Futures Hedging Strategy

Futures hedging is not as simple as hedging with forwards, and, on average, it does not lead to a perfect hedge. The reason for this is that futures are standardized products, traded on organized exchanges and thus, generally, do not exactly meet the hedgers' requirements. If the size and the timing of the futures position are not equal to the spot commitment, it is almost impossible to eliminate completely the currency risk. In this case, an 'equal and opposite' hedge is not available and the hedger has to compute the risk-minimizing hedging position[2]

$$h = -Q * \beta \qquad (7A.4)$$

with Q the size of the spot commitment and β the hedging coefficient

$$\beta = \frac{\text{cov}(f_{t=1}, s_{t=1})}{\text{var}(f_{t=1})}$$

$$= \frac{\text{covariance of futures price change with spot price change}}{\text{variance of futures price change}} \qquad (7A.5)$$

As already mentioned, there are two main problems when hedging with futures: the timing and the size of the hedging position. First, we examine the timing problem. An arbitrage-free environment requires that spot prices equal futures prices at delivery ($s_{t=1} = f_{t=1}$) if the spot commitment date coincides with the futures delivery date ($t = 1$). Hence we can write equation (7A.5) as (see Duffie, 1989, p. 207)

$$\beta = \frac{\text{cov}(f_{t=1}, s_{t=1})}{\text{var}(f_{t=1})} = \frac{\text{var}(f_{t=1})}{\text{var}(f_{t=1})} = 1 \qquad (7A.6)$$

In this case we, again, obtain an 'equal and opposite' strategy:

$$h = -Q * \beta = -Q \qquad (7A.7)$$

If we further assume that prices in spot and futures markets are perfectly correlated, equation (7A.6) holds for all points in time t. Hence it is not necessary that futures delivery date equals spot commitment date to achieve a perfect hedge. In the case that the futures position matures after the spot commitment date, the hedger offsets the position before maturity in $t = 1$. On the other hand, if the horizon of the futures position is too short, the hedger can 'roll over' the contract and, again, offset the position in $t = 1$.

The second problem is the size of the futures position. In our numerical example above, the hedging position has a total value of $1 100 000. However, futures that exactly deliver $1 100 000 are, on average, not available on the futures exchange. Instead, smaller futures contracts are traded, e.g. delivering $10 000. In this case, our hedging position consists of

$$h = \$1\,100\,000 = \$10\,000 * 110 \text{ contracts} \qquad (7A.8)$$

The firm takes a futures position of 110 contracts.

Now, consider the case where only futures delivering $15 000 are available. Here, the optimal hedging position is

$$h = \$15\,000 * 73 \text{ contracts} = \$1\,095\,000 \neq \$1\,100\,000 \qquad (7A.9)$$

This hedging strategy does not lead to an 'equal and opposite' hedge. However, 99.54 per cent of the spot position is hedged with this strategy, which is very close to a perfect hedge. Hence we can argue that, with a growing variety of futures contracts available, hedging strategies of firms become asymptotically perfect.

A.4 Empirical Facts

Figure 7A.2 illustrates the size of foreign exchange derivatives markets and the key role played by currency forwards and futures. The amounts outstanding, presented in Figure 7A.2, are gross market values of the OTC derivatives, i.e. forwards and forex (foreign exchange) swaps, currency swaps and OTC options, and notional principal of exchange-traded futures and options.

Table 7A.1 shows that today derivatives products are also available in many emerging markets. Most of the exchanges presented in Table 7A.1 were founded in the 1990s.

NOTES

1. In this chapter, perfect hedges are 'equal and opposite' hedges. Perfect hedges can generally be achieved in many ways. Jorion (2001, p. 12) points out that 'The breadth of coverage against risks is astonishing. Hedging with derivatives is similar to purchasing insurance.' In their empirical paper, Fung and Leung (1991, p. 89) state: 'The result implies that financial managers of multinational firms can avoid spending time and resources to estimate the optimal hedge ratio but simply adopt the naive (one-to-one) strategy when using forward markets for hedging currency risk.' In the context of the simple model used in this chapter, we will only discuss the 'naive' hedging strategy.
2. For a detailed look at futures hedging, see Duffie (1989, ch. 7).

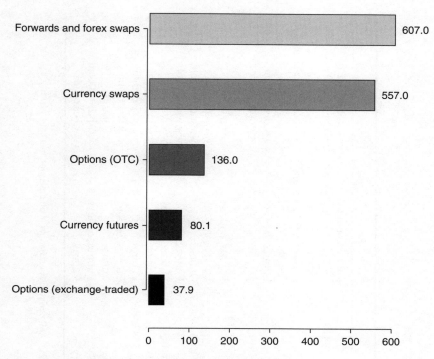

Data source: *BIS Quarterly Review*, September 2004.

*Figure 7A.2   Amounts outstanding of foreign exchange derivatives
(December 2003; in billions of US dollars)*

Table 7A.1 Derivatives exchanges in emerging markets

Country	Name and year of formation	Products	www
Argentina	Bolsa de Comercio de Rosario (ROFEX)	Futures, options	www.rofex.com.ar
Brazil	Bolsa de Mercadorias & Futuros (BM&F), 1985	Futures, options, swaps, forwards	www.bmf.com.br
Chile	Bolsa de Santiago, 1990/1994	Futures (1990), options (1994)	www.bolsadesantiago.com
China	Dalian Commodity Exchange, 1993	Futures, forwards	www.dce.com.cn
	Zhengzhou Commodity Exchange (ZCE), 1990		www.czce.com.cn
	Shanghai Futures Exchange		
Israel	Tel-Aviv Stock Exchange (Tase), 1993	Futures, options	www.tase.co.il
Korea	Korean Stock Exchange (KSE), 1996	Futures, options	www.kse.or.kr
Mexico	Mexican Derivatives Exchange (MexDer), 1994	Options	www.mexder.com
Poland	WGT, 1999	Futures, options	www.wgt.com.pl
Romania	Romanian Commodities Exchange (BRM), 1998	Futures, options	www.brm.ro
Russia	Moscow Interbank Currency Exchange (MICEX), 1994	Futures	www.micex.com
South Africa	South African Futures Exchange (SAFEX), 1987/1995	Futures	www.safex.co.za
Thailand	Thailand Futures Exchange (TFEX)	Futures, options	www.tfex.co.th
Czech Republic	Prague Stock Exchange (PSE), 2001	Futures	www.pse.cz
Hungary	Budapest Commodity Exchange (BCE), 1989	Futures, options	www.bce-bat.com
Indonesia	Surabaya Stock Exchange, 2001	Futures	www.bes.co.id

Note: The aim of this presentation is not to give a complete overview of all derivatives exchanges in all emerging markets worldwide.

PART III

The Public Sector and the Future of the
Welfare State

8. Public debt and public spending in Germany: the last 40 years

Alfred Greiner and Norbert Schütt

1. INTRODUCTION

In 2005, the German government violated the 3 per cent deficit criterion of the Maastricht criterion for the fourth time. Meanwhile, German government debt also clearly exceeded 60 per cent of GDP, which is the upper bound for the debt ratio of euro area countries.

Although these numbers are somewhat arbitrary and there may be better indicators in order to answer the question of whether given deficit and debt ratios pose problems from an economic point of view, these numbers can nevertheless be justified. This can be done by arguing that they serve to limit excessive public sector borrowing, which may give rise to severe economic problems.

An important aspect in this context is the question of whether governments remain solvent. While the answer to this question usually does not pose a problem for private households because the latter have finite lifetimes, this does not hold for governments, since governments do not have a natural final period. Instead, they are usually assumed to live infinitely, which causes some problems. Nevertheless, there are studies that suggest answers as to whether fiscal policies are sustainable.

Such analyses are indeed important since they yield a picture of how strong the burden for future generations will be, resulting from today's debt policy. During his academic life, Horst Hanusch has been interested in the dynamic evolution of economies. So, major fields of his research agenda have focused on the explanation of innovations and industry evolution, the behaviour of financial markets, and the impact public finance can have on the future state of economies. Therefore we present with this chapter, written in honour of Horst Hanusch's 65th birthday, a contribution to the field of public finance, in particular, the way in which public debt may affect the future of market economies.

The rest of our contribution is organized as follows. In the next section, we analyse the behaviour of public debt in Germany. There, we first make some theoretical considerations as to the relationship of the primary surplus–GDP ratio and the debt–GDP ratio, and the question of whether a given fiscal policy is sustainable. Next, we empirically estimate this relationship through penalized spline smoothing. In section 2, we study the evolution of public spending in Germany. Section 3 concludes.

2.   PUBLIC DEBT

Before we analyse the evolution of public debt in Germany and, in particular, the question of whether it is sustainable, we present some brief theoretical considerations.

2.1   Some Theoretical Considerations on Public Debt and Sustainability

In economic theory, it is usually postulated that governments cannot play Ponzi games. This means the government must stick to its intertemporal budget constraint, stating that a given level of public debt in real terms must equal expected future primary surpluses.[1]

Neglecting stochastic effects and assuming a constant interest rate, the intertemporal budget constraint can be written as

$$B(0) = \int_{0}^{\infty} e^{-r\tau} S(\tau)\,d\tau \tag{8.1}$$

with r the interest rate, $B(0)$ public debt at time zero, and S the primary surplus. Equivalent to equation (8.1) is the following equation

$$\lim_{t \to \infty} e^{-rt} B(t) = 0 \tag{8.2}$$

with $B(t)$ public debt at time t, so that the present value of public debt converges to zero for $t \to \infty$.

From (8.2), one realizes that the interest rate plays an important role when this equation is tested with time-series methods. Bohn (1995, 1998) argues that estimating (8.2) requires strong assumptions because it involves an expectation about states in the future that are difficult to obtain from a single set of time-series data, and because assumptions concerning the discount rate must be made.

Therefore Bohn (1995, 1998) proposes a different test, which does not require assumptions about the interest rate. He suggests testing whether the primary surplus is a positive linear function of the debt ratio. In order to see that such a policy guarantees sustainability of public debt, we assume that the government sets the primary surplus to GDP ratio according to the following rule:

$$\frac{PS(t)}{Y(t)} = \frac{T(t) - G(t)}{Y(t)} = \alpha + \beta(t)\left(\frac{B(t)}{Y(t)}\right) \tag{8.3}$$

with $PS(t)$ the primary surplus at time t, $T(t)$ tax revenue, $G(t)$ public spending, $Y(t)$ GDP, and α a constant that can be negative or positive. α is a systematic component that determines how the level of the primary deficit reacts to variations in GDP (it can also be interpreted as other (constant) economic variables which affect the surplus ratio). $\beta(t)$ shows how the primary surplus–GDP ratio reacts to variations in the debt–GPD ratio and can be termed a reaction coefficient. Note that β is a function of time, which we assume to be twice differentiable.

The evolution of public debt is described by

$$\dot{B}(t) = rB(t) - S(t) \tag{8.4}$$

Inserting (8.3) in (8.4), integrating, and multiplying both sides by e^{-rt} in order to get the present value yields

$$e^{-rt}B(t) = e^{-\int_0^t \beta(\tau)d\tau}\left(B(0) - \alpha Y(0)\int_0^t e^{\int_0^\tau \beta(\mu)d\mu - (r-\gamma)\tau}d\tau\right) \tag{8.5}$$

with γ the growth rate of GDP, which is assumed to be constant.

To gain additional insight, we define the following terms

$$\int_0^t \beta(\tau)d\tau \equiv C_1(t), \int_0^\tau \beta(\mu)d\mu \equiv C_1(\tau), (r - \gamma)\tau \equiv C_2(\tau) > 0$$

such that the second term on the right-hand side in (8.5) can be written as

$$\frac{\int_0^t e^{C_1(\tau)}e^{-C_2(\tau)}d\tau}{e^{C_1(t)}} \equiv D(t),$$

where we have normalized $\alpha Y(0) \equiv 1$:

If $\int_0^\infty e^{C_1(\tau)}e^{-C_2(\tau)}d\tau$ remains bounded, $\lim_{t\to\infty}C_1(t) = \infty$ guarantees that D converges to zero. $\lim_{t\to\infty}C_1(t) = \infty$ means that the reaction coefficient $\beta(t)$ is positive on average for $t \in [0, \infty)$. Boundedness of $\int_0^\infty e^{C_1(\tau)}e^{-C_2(\tau)}d\tau$

is given for $\lim_{t\to\infty}(C_1(t) - C_2(t)) = -\infty$. If $\lim_{t\to\infty}\int_0^t e^{C_1(\tau)}e^{-C_2(\tau)}d\tau = \infty$, applying l'Hôpital gives the limit of D as

$$\lim_{t\to\infty}D(t) = \lim_{t\to\infty}\frac{e^{-C_2(t)}}{\beta(t)}$$

For $(r - \gamma)t = C_2(t) > 0$, D converges to zero in the limit if $\beta(t)$ does not decline exponentially. Now, assume that $\beta(t)$ declines exponentially. This would imply that $\lim_{t\to\infty}C_1(t) = \lim_{t\to\infty}\int_0^t \beta(\tau)d\tau < \infty$ holds. Consequently, if $\lim_{t\to\infty}C_1(t) = \infty$ holds, $\beta(t)$ cannot decline exponentially, and D converges to zero, too.

Thus we have shown that a positive coefficient of $\beta(t)$ on average, which implies that $\lim_{t\to\infty}\int_0^t\beta(t)dt = \infty$ holds, is sufficient for sustainability of a given fiscal policy. Before we go on, we note that in a dynamically efficient deterministic economy $r - \gamma$ is positive. For Germany, this can also be observed empirically. For example, the difference between the interest rate and the growth rate of GDP from 1960 to 2003 was about 1 per cent.

In the next section, we empirically test how the primary surplus reacts to variations in public debt in Germany with data from 1960 to 2003.

3.   EMPIRICAL EVIDENCE

The previous section demonstrated that a positive, at least linear, rise of the primary surplus–GDP ratio as the debt ratio rises gives strong evidence for sustainability of a given fiscal policy. In this section, we estimate the correlation between the primary surplus and the debt ratio, assuming a time-varying coefficient and, then, we test whether the relation between the primary surplus and public debt is non-linear. As to the estimation strategy, we apply penalized spline smoothing, which is more flexible than OLS (ordinary least squares) estimation. Before we present the estimation outcome, we give a brief introduction to penalized spline smoothing.

3.1   Spline Smoothing and Penalized Splines

Assume that we have n data points for the dependent variable y, which is explained by the independent variable x. Thus we have observations (y_i, x_i), $i = 1,\ldots, n$, and the regression model we want to estimate is

$$y_i = f(x_i) + \varepsilon_i, \ \varepsilon_t\sim\text{iid}(0, \sigma^2). \tag{8.6}$$

$f(\cdot)$ is an unknown function that is not specified further, except that we require $f(\cdot)$ to be continuous and sufficiently differentiable. The idea behind spline estimation, then, is to find the function $f(x)$ such that the following minimization problem is solved (cf. Hastie and Tibshirani, 1993):

$$\min_{f(\cdot)} \left\{ \sum_{i=1}^{n} (y_i - f(x_i))^2 + \lambda \int (f''(x))^2 dx \right\} \qquad (8.7)$$

Equation (8.7) shows that the function to be minimized consists of two components: first, the deviation of the fitted function from the observed values should be minimized, which as usual gives the goodness of fit. Second, complex functions are penalized by the second term in (8.7), measured by the second-order derivative.

Reinsch (1967) demonstrated that $f = (f(x_1), \ldots, f(x_n))$ in (8.7) can be written as $f = C\alpha$, with C as cubic spline basis and α the spline coefficient. Thus, (8.7) can be rewritten in the following form:

$$\min_{\alpha} \|y - C\alpha\|^2 + \lambda \alpha^T H \alpha \qquad (8.8)$$

with $\| \cdot \|^2$ the usual Euclidian norm and H a penalty matrix.[2] The term λ in (8.7) and (8.8) is a smoothing parameter, which controls the trade-off between closely matching the data and having a linear model. For $\lambda \to \infty$, the minimization of (8.8) gives a linear fit, whereas letting $\lambda \to 0$ gives a wiggly function.

These considerations demonstrate that the choice of λ plays an important role in the estimation. In principle, λ can be set by hand, but it is also possible to choose λ through the data. One possibility to do so is to resort to cross-validation. Cross-validation works as follows: leave out one observation and fit the model to the rest of the data. Then, compute the squared difference between the observation point that was left out and the value for this observation predicted by the estimated model. This procedure is repeated for each data point in the data set and the following cross-validation sum of squares is computed:

$$CV(\lambda) = (1/n) \sum_{i=1}^{n} (y_i - \hat{f}_{-i,\lambda}(x_i))^2 \qquad (8.9)$$

with $\hat{f}_{-i,\lambda}(x_i)$ the estimate for $f(xi)$ based on data points (x_j, y_j), $j = 1, \ldots, i - 1, i + 1, \ldots, n$, and computed with the smoothing parameter λ: The minimization of $CV(\lambda)$ with respect to λ then gives a data-driven value for λ: In practical applications, one replaces the cross-validation criterion by the generalized cross-validation (GCV) criterion which is easier to compute (for details see Hastie and Tibshirani, 1993).

One problem associated with solving (8.8) is that the spline basis C

grows with the size of the sample. So, for large samples, the smoothing spline estimation would lead to the problem of inverting an $n \times n$ matrix, where n gives the size of the sample. A modification to smoothing spline estimation results by reformulating (8.8) such that $f = D\alpha$, with D a high-dimensional basis function (conventionally, D is 10 to 40 dimensional). The difference with respect to smoothing splines is that the number of basis functions is fixed and does not grow with the number of observations.

To fit a model, the spline coefficients are penalized in the same way as in (8.8), with an appropriate penalty matrix H giving the minimization problem:

$$\min_{\alpha} \|y - D\alpha\|^2 + \lambda \alpha^T H \alpha \qquad (8.10)$$

This approach is referred to as penalized spline smoothing (see Greiner, forthcoming, and for more details, Ruppert et al., 2003).

Writing the objective in (8.10) as

$$(y - D\alpha)^T(y - D\alpha) + \lambda \alpha^T H \alpha = y^T y - 2\alpha^T D^T y + \alpha^T [D^T D + \lambda H]\alpha \qquad (8.11)$$

and minimizing by differentiating with respect to α and setting the result equal to zero, gives $\hat{\alpha} = (D^T D + \lambda H)^{-1} D^T y$.

The fitted function, then, is obtained as

$$\hat{f}(x) = A(\lambda)y, \text{ with } A(\lambda) = D(D^T D + \lambda H)^{-1} D^T. \qquad (8.12)$$

The matrix $A(\lambda)$ is called the smoothing matrix and the trace of this matrix is the estimated degrees of freedom of the model. This reflects the degree of complexity of the fitted model. For $\lambda \to \infty$ the trace of $H(\lambda)$ equals 1, giving a linear fit, while for $\lambda = 0$ the trace of $H(0)$ is $p + 1$; with p as dimension of the matrix D. Setting $\lambda = 0$ implies that the curvature is not punished and, consequently, yields a very wiggly function.[3]

Our considerations above dealt with a model where the dependent variable y was a function of one explanatory variable x, as modelled in (8.6). One extension is obtained when we generalize the assumption of normality and write the equation as

$$g(\mu) = f(x) \qquad (8.13)$$

with $\mu = E(y|x)$ the expected value, $g(\cdot)$ a monotonic and differentiable link function which is known, and y belonging to an exponential family distribution. Another extension is obtained by allowing y to depend on more than one explanatory variable, for example x and z, in a non-linear way. This gives rise to a generalized additive model (GAM), which can be written as follows:

$$g(\mu) = f(x) + h(z) \qquad (8.14)$$

where $\mu = E(y|x, z)$ is again the expected value and $f(\cdot)$ and $h(\cdot)$ are unknown but smooth functions, which are to be estimated from empirical data.

With more than one function, the estimation of the model can be done by using a backfitting strategy. This means that all terms are kept fixed except for the smooth, which is fitted by following smoothing as described above. One then circles over the different smooth components by fitting just one of the smooth functions. For further details, we again refer to Hastie and Tibshirani (1993). The major advantage of the additive model is that the curse of dimensionality, stating that the required sample size grows exponentially with the dimension of the fitted function, can be avoided.

Of course, one can also fit a semi-parametric model, i.e. a model that consists of a parametric and of a non-parametric part. For example, such a model could be written as

$$g(\mu) = f(x) + \beta z \qquad (8.15)$$

where β is the parameter and $f(\cdot)$ is the non-linear function to be estimated.

Another type of model, the varying coefficient model (see Hastie and Tibshirani, 1993), is obtained when metrically scaled and nominal variables are used as explanatory variables. However, we shall not go into the details of this class of models. In statistics, much work has been devoted to find efficient ways to fit those models, as well as models (8.14) and (8.15) (see, e.g., Kauermann and Tutz, 2000; Wood, 2003).

3.2 A Model with a Time-varying Coefficient

As outlined above, the main idea in testing for sustainability is to estimate the following equation:

$$ps(t) = \beta(t)b(t) + \alpha^T \mathbf{Z}(t) + \varepsilon(t) \qquad (8.16)$$

where $ps(t)$ and $b(t)$ is the primary surplus-GDP and the debt ratio, respectively, $\mathbf{Z}(t)$ is a vector that consists of the number 1 and of other factors

Table 8.1   Estimates for equation (8.17)

	Coeff.	Std. error (*t*-stat.)	Pr (> |*t*|)
Constant	−0.04	0.02 (−1.56)	0.13
$b(t)$	0.17	0.1 (1.72)	0.09
$Soc(t)$	0.39	0.39 (4.68)	$4.68 \cdot 10^{-5}$
$r(t)$	0.13	0.19 (0.68)	0.5
$s(t)$	edf: 5.54	F: 8.21	*p*-value: $2.5 \cdot 10^{-6}$
R^2(adj.)		0.62	
DW		2.02	

related to the primary surplus, and $\varepsilon(t)$ is an error term that is i.i.d. (independent and identically distributed) $N(0, \sigma^2)$.

As concerns the other variables contained in $\mathbf{Z(t)}$, which are assumed to affect the primary surplus, we include the real long-term interest rate ($r(t)$) and the social surplus ratio (Soc).[4]

Summarizing our discussion, the equation to be estimated is as follows:

$$ps(t) = \alpha_0 + \beta(t)b(t) + \alpha_1 Soc(t) + \alpha_2 r(t) + \varepsilon(t) \qquad (8.17)$$

where $ps(t)$ is the primary surplus ratio. We should like to point out that the reaction coefficient is assumed to vary over time. The other coefficients, however, are constant. We make this assumption because pre-estimations have shown that there is no evidence for time dependency of these parameters.[5]

The estimated coefficient for $b(t)$ in equation (8.17) gives the mean of that coefficient over the whole period, and $s(t)$ gives the deviation from that mean depending on time. Table 8.1 shows that the mean of the reaction coefficient $\bar{\beta}$ is positive and statistically significant at the 10 per cent level. Estimating (8.17) without the variable $r(t)$, the significance of the coefficient $\bar{\beta}$ rises to 5 per cent. Thus our estimation confirms results obtained by estimations with different exogenous variables and with a slightly different equation, where the debt ratio of the previous period $b(t-1)$ was used as exogenous variable (cf. Greiner et al., 2006). That is, the average of the reaction coefficient in Germany is positive over the period 1960–2003. The social surplus ratio has a significantly positive effect on the primary surplus, as was to be expected, while the interest rate is not statistically significant. The term edf in Table 8.1 gives the estimated degrees of freedom of the smooth term and the higher the number, the stronger the evidence for non-linearities. Further, the Durbin–Watson test statistic (DW) does not indicate that the residuals are correlated.

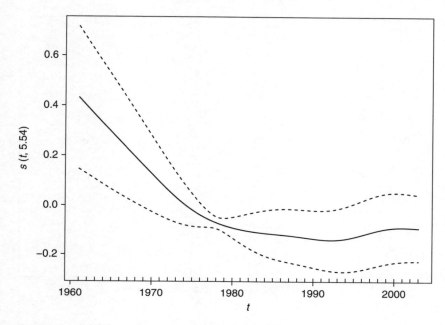

Figure 8.1   Time-varying component s(t) *giving the deviation from the mean value* $\bar{\beta}$

Further, Table 8.1 demonstrates that the time-varying smooth term $s(t)$ is significant, implying that the reaction coefficient has not been constant. In Figure 8.1, we depict the graph of the estimated $s(t)$.

Figure 8.1 shows that the reaction coefficient declines over time. It should be noted that the reaction coefficient $\beta(t)$ is given by the mean, $\bar{\beta}$, plus the the smooth component, $s(t)$, i.e. $\beta(t) = (\bar{\beta} + s(t))$.

So, we can conclude that, over time, the government had less scope for its spending, leading it to put less importance on the question of sustainability of public debt. Nevertheless, it should be noted that $\beta(t)$ remains strictly positive over the whole period. Further, it seems that the negative trend was curtailed in the mid-1990s. Thus the overall conclusion we can draw from our estimations made up to now is that Germany has pursued a sustainable fiscal policy over the last 40 years.

3.3   A Semi-parametric Model

In the last section, we estimated (8.17), where we assumed a linear relationship between the primary surplus ratio and the debt ratio. An important question, however, is whether this relationship can be characterized

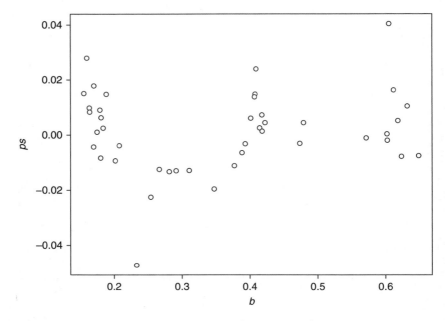

Figure 8.2   Debt ratio and primary surplus ratio from 1960 to 2003

by a linear function or whether it is non-linear. For example, if it were convex, this would imply that the primary surplus increases, the higher the debt ratio. In this case, a given fiscal policy should be sustainable because higher debt ratios imply higher primary surpluses. However, if the relationship was concave, sustainability is not necessarily given, because the primary surplus ratio reacts less than linearly to increases in the debt ratio.

Therefore we want to estimate a semi-parametric model in this subsection, where the primary surplus depends in a non-linear way on the debt ratio and linearly on the other variables. Before presenting the estimation result, we first take a look at the data. Figure 8.2 gives the debt ratio and primary surplus ratio from 1960 to 2003. The picture suggests that the response of the primary surplus ratio indeed becomes larger, the higher the debt ratio.

In order to gain more insight, we estimate a semi-parametric equation, where the debt ratio enters the equation non-linearly while both the social surplus ratio and the interest rate enter the equation in a linear way. The equation to be estimated, then, is written as follows:

$$ps(t) = \alpha_0 + s(b(t)) + \alpha_1 Soc(t) + \alpha_2 r(t) + \varepsilon(t) \qquad (8.18)$$

Table 8.2   Estimates for equation (8.18)

	Coeff.	Std. error (*t*-stat.)	Pr (> |*t*|)
Constant	−0.01	0.01 (−1.34)	0.19
Soc(*t*)	0.39	0.23 (1.74)	0.09
r(*t*)	0.32	0.18 (1.73)	0.09
s(*b*(*t*))	edf: 4.74	F: 4.75	*p*-value: $3.6 \cdot 10^{-4}$
R^2(adj.)		0.45	
DW		1.43	

The estimation result is shown in Table 8.2.

Table 8.2 shows that both the social surplus ratio and the real interest rate have a positive effect on the primary surplus ratio, but are only statistically significant at the 10 per cent level. Thus we get the same results with respect to the social surplus ratio as in the linear model. A higher social surplus goes along with a higher primary surplus. The positive effect of the real interest rate can be explained by the fact that periods with high interest rates characterize periods of high growth, implying high primary surpluses.

But Table 8.2 also shows that the R^2(adj.) in the semi-parametric model is clearly smaller than in the linear model, with a time-dependent coefficient. Thus the linear model with a time-dependent coefficient explains a larger share of the variance than the semi-parametric model. The Durbin–Watson test statistic suggests that the residuals of the estimation are correlated, in contrast to the estimation of the last subsection.

As concerns the effect of the debt ratio on the primary surplus, we see from Table 8.2 that the assumption of a non-linear relationship is statistically significant. Figure 8.3 shows the estimated function.

Figure 8.3 suggests that the response of the primary surplus ratio to the debt ratio first declines as the debt ratio is small. Only when a certain threshold is reached does a higher debt ratio go along with higher primary surpluses, although, for very large values of the debt ratio, the relationship seems to become negative again. It should be noted that the function is normalized, so that its mean is equal to zero. In order to compare the results of the semi-parametric model with those of the linear model, we give a picture of the primary surplus ratio over the time period we consider. Figure 8.4 shows the graph.

Figure 8.4 shows that the primary surplus ratio declined fairly steadily up to the mid-1970s. This decline is reflected in the downward trend of the reaction coefficient $\beta(t)$ in the linear model and also in the negative relation

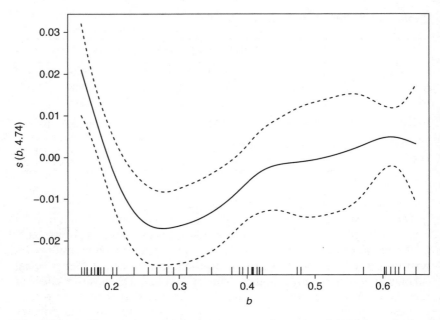

Figure 8.3   The primary surplus ratio ps as a function of the debt ratio b

between the primary surplus ratio and the debt ratio in the semi-parametric model. Only in the early 1980s did the primary surplus become positive again, which shows up as the point where the relation between the primary surplus ratio and the debt ratio becomes positive in the semi-parametric model. In the linear model, the decline in the reaction coefficient continues but becomes smaller before it is halted in the mid-1990s. In early 2000, however, a decline in the reaction of the primary surplus to higher debt can be observed for both the linear and the semi-parametric model.

4.   DETERMINANTS OF THE PRIMARY SURPLUS

In the last section, we saw that the primary surplus–GDP ratio rises as a response to an increase in the public debt–GDP ratio. But, assuming a linear model, the coefficient determining the magnitude has declined over time. Nevertheless, the reaction was positive on average, suggesting that the path of public debt was sustainable. In this section, we intend to shed some light on the question of how the government succeeded in bringing about a rise in the primary surplus ratio.

First, one could assume that the discussed evolution of the primary

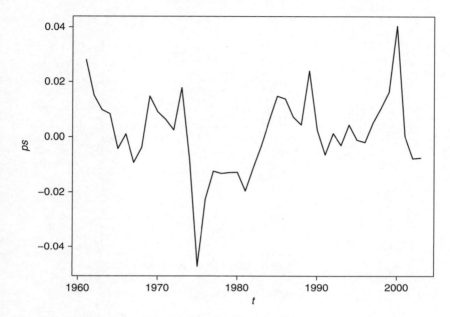

Figure 8.4   Evolution of the primary surplus ratio over time

surplus in Germany is the result of increasing tax revenue–GDP ratios. In order to check this, we consider the period from 1976 to 2003. In 1976, Germany generated for the first time a positive net debt,[6] measured as government net financial liabilities. In addition to this, most of the welfare state enlargement managed by the coalition of social democrats and liberals was completed by 1976.

Figure 8.5 shows the evolution of the tax revenue–GDP ratio from 1976 to 2003. The tax revenue–GDP ratio[7] was 0.3610 in 1976 and 0.3550 in 2003, with a maximum of 0.3750, a minimum of 0.3540, and an average of 0.3671. The line within the illustration is the result of a simple linear regression with respect to time and a constant.[8] The figure suggests that the tax ratio declined over time. Because of its negative slope, we can conclude that the above-mentioned evolution of the primary surplus in Germany is not the result of higher tax revenue–GDP ratios.

Therefore the government must have reduced any kind of public expenditure. We shall concentrate our analysis on three types of expenditure, which are of specific interest for the well-being of a country. These are public expenditures for education (focus: human capital formation); public expenditures for R&D (knowledge capital), and public investment in infrastructure (public capital).

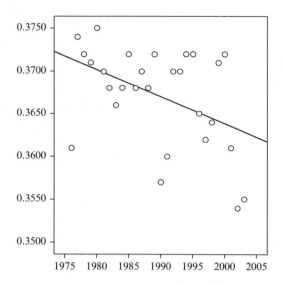

Figure 8.5   The tax revenue–GDP ratio from 1976 to 2003

Concerning education and R&D, OECD data[9] for both variables are only available for the period 1991–2003. In that period, the public expenditure on education–GDP ratio was 0.0428 on average (min. 0.0406; max. 0.0450), whereas the average value of the public expenditure on R&D–GDP ratio was 0.0034 (min. 0.0033; max. 0.0035). Based on these findings, we can state that these two ratios were more or less stable over this phase.

Regarding public investment, measured as government fixed capital formation,[10] we again consider the period 1976–2003. Figure 8.6 shows the evolution of the public investment–GDP ratio over that period.

The curve-fit is again the result of a simple linear regression with respect to time and a constant. All in all, the ratio experienced a dramatic slowdown over time. In 1976 the initial value was 0.0401, whereas the final value in 2003 was 0.0162, which was about 40 per cent of the initial value.

On the one hand, the fiscal policy of the German government is sustainable in the sense of the model discussed. On the other hand, the significant reduction of the public investment–GDP ratio is problematic concerning the future development of the German economy. Furthermore, public infrastructure could also serve as a collateral for public debt.

Using the theory of political economics, the result seems to be reasonable, because there is no important lobby group fighting against budget cuts on public investment. Moreover, the German government is only obliged

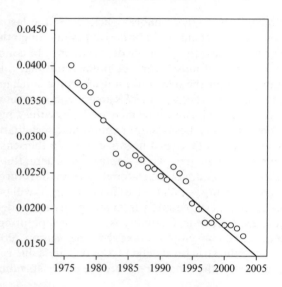

Figure 8.6   The public investment–GDP ratio from 1976 to 2003

to ensure according to the constitution that the annual gross public investment exceeds an increase in public net debt.

5.   CONCLUSION

In this chapter we have studied German debt policy over the time period from 1960 to 2003. The starting point of our analysis was the observation that a positive linear response of the primary surplus ratio to the debt ratio gives strong evidence for sustainability of a given debt policy. Thus, if governments raise the primary surplus in the future at least linearly as public debt rises, governments remain solvent, which is intuitively plausible. It must be pointed out that this theory should replace the Ricardian equivalence theorem because it is more general. So, if a government intends to raise the primary surplus, there are three possibilities.

First, the government can raise taxes, which is roughly the Ricardian equivalence principle. Second, it can reduce other types of public spending in order to increase the primary surplus. Third, there may be an increase in the primary surplus without raising taxes or without reducing spending when GDP growth rate rises, leading to higher tax revenues and, thus, to higher primary surpluses.

As to the empirical results, our estimations suggest that German governments have pursued sustainable policies over the last 40 years. It should be noted that this result could be derived even though the debt ratio increased over time. Hence an increasing debt ratio may be compatible with sustainability. However, it must clearly be pointed out that this cannot go on forever, implying that the debt ratio must become constant sooner or later, or decline. This holds because there is an upper bound for the surplus– GDP ratio beyond which it cannot be increased. Once this upper bound is reached, the debt ratio must be constant to guarantee sustainability.

We have also seen that there is a negative trend in the sense that, over time, governments have put less weight on stabilizing debt. But it should be stressed that this result cannot be taken for granted in the future. This holds because, with a fast-ageing population, as in Germany, it will become more and more difficult to react adequately to higher government debt. Further, the most recent experience in Germany is very disappointing. Although the government raised consumption taxes by 3 per cent in 2007, it did not succeed in reducing the structural deficit to zero. This is due to politicians' unwillingness or/and to their inability to reduce public spending.

NOTES

1. Strictly speaking, it should be public net debt, that is gross debt minus government assets, which equals future surpluses.
2. In Wood and Augustin (2002), for example, it is demonstrated in detail how this matrix can be constructed.
3. We do not discuss questions of statistical inference. For a description of how to obtain the variance associated with the smooth term, see e.g., Wood and Augustin (2002) or Hastie and Tibshirani (1993).
4. $Soc(t)$ is computed by subtracting social benefits paid by government from the social security contributions received by government.
5. All estimations were performed using the mgcv package, version 1.3–7, in R, version 2.2.0 (cf. Wood, 2001). The data are from OECD *Economic Outlook Statistics and Projections*, June 2003.
6. See *OECD Economic Outlook Statistics and Projections*.
7. The data are from the OECD database: Revenue Statistics of OECD Member Countries.
8. The curve-fits were generated using the SPSS-package, version 12.0.
9. The education data are from the OECD database: National Accounts, IV; and the R&D data are from the OECD Research and Development Statistics.
10. See *OECD Economic Outlook Statistics and Projections*.

REFERENCES

Bohn, H. (1995), 'The sustainability of budget deficits in a stochastic economy', *Journal of Money, Credit, and Banking*, **27** (1), 257–71.

Bohn, H. (1998), 'The behaviour of U.S. public debt and deficits', *Quarterly Journal of Economics*, **113**, 949–63.
Greiner, A. (forthcoming) 'Estimating penalized spline regressions: theory and application to economics', *Applied Economics Letters*.
Greiner, A., U. Köller and W. Semmler (2006), 'Testing sustainability of German fiscal policy: evidence for the period 1960–2003', *Empirica*, **33** (2–3), 127–40.
Hastie, T.J. and R.J. Tibshirani (1993), 'Varying coefficient models', *Journal of the Royal Statistical Society, Series B*, **55**, 757–96.
Kauermann, G. and G. Tutz (2000), 'Local likelihood estimation in varying coefficient models including additive bias correction', *Journal of Nonparametric Statistics*, **12**, 343–71.
Reinsch, C.H. (1967), 'Smoothing by spline functions', *Numerische Mathematik*, **10**, 177–83.
Ruppert, R., M.P. Wand and R.J. Carroll (2003), *Semiparametric Regression*, Cambridge: Cambridge University Press.
Wood, S.N. (2001), 'mgcv: GAM's and generalized ridge regression for R', *R News*, **1** (2), 20–25.
Wood, S.N. (2003), 'Thin plate regression splines', *Journal of the Royal Statistical Society, Series B*, **65**, 95–114.
Wood, S.N. and N.H. Augustin (2002), 'GAMs with integrated model selection using penalized regression splines and applications to environmental modelling', Working Paper, University of Bath http://www.maths.bath.ac.uk/~sw283/simon/papers/wagam.pdf (a slightly different version is published in Ecological Modelling, **157**, 157–77).

9. Biofuels, innovations and endogenous growth

Thomas Kuhn and Michael Pickhardt

1. INTRODUCTION

In the European Union (EU), about 99 per cent of the transport sector's energy demand is covered by petroleum oil products, which represents 67 per cent of final oil demand (European Commission, 2001, pp. 16 and 36). Yet limited stocks of non-renewable fossil fuels as well as temporarily limited production and distribution capacities, coupled with increasing fuel demand, are bound to lead to sharp increases in fossil fuel prices and to more price volatility in the near future. But in a globalized economy, which naturally depends on the smooth functioning of the transport sector, such price developments and the associated adjustment processes may have a severely negative impact on economic growth. Moreover, as fossil fuel stocks in the EU and other developed countries contribute an ever-decreasing share to local fossil fuel demand, growing import dependence and the associated risks may represent another important obstacle to future economic growth. Finally, current growth rates in virtually all countries may not be sustainable with fossil fuels, because fossil fuels contribute a substantially larger share to pollution and global warming (for details see, e.g., Pahl, 2005, pp. 56–60).

Hence, for the foreseeable future, sustainable growth rates necessarily require a massive substitution process in which fossil fuels are gradually replaced by biofuels or hydrogen. To this extent, growth-orientated policy schemes as well as future energy policy must be, in large part, concerned with transportation fuel issues (Pickhardt, 2005, p. 497). Yet, given current technologies and knowledge, this substitution process critically depends on innovations and, thus, on investment in R&D.

This chapter aims at modelling this substitution process by incorporating both a non-renewable resource (petroleum-based fuels) and a renewable resource (biofuel feedstock such as sugar cane, corn [maize] or rapeseed), both of which can serve for producing transport fuels, into a conventional Romer-type endogenous growth model. The chapter proceeds as follows. In the next section, we provide some background on biofuels and introduce the way in which we model the difference between petroleum-based fuels and biofuels. In section 3, we present our modelling approach and the social planner solution of the model. The main results of the chapter, the Keynes–Ramsey rule and the Hotelling rules for the renewable and non-renewable resources, are discussed in section 4. The final section offers an agenda for further research on the issue.

2. SOME BACKGROUND ON BIOFUELS

In recent years, many countries have launched initiatives to support a more widespread use of biofuels. In the EU, this process is based on the biofuel directive 2003/30/EC and the energy tax directive 2003/96/EC. In article 2, the former defines biofuel as 'liquid or gaseous fuel for transport produced from biomass' and provides a list of products that should at least be considered biofuels. This list includes, among others, bioethanol, biodiesel, biogas, biomethanol, biohydrogen and pure vegetable oil. Moreover, article 3 of the biofuel directive calls on member states to ensure that a minimum proportion of biofuels is placed on their markets and gives as a reference target value 2 per cent, calculated on the basis of energy content, of all transport fuels by 31 December 2005, and 5.75 per cent by 31 December 2010. To achieve these targets, member states may apply for an exemption or a reduced rate of taxation for biofuels according to article 16 of the energy tax directive.

As the two most popular biofuels are biodiesel and bioethanol, the following two subsections provide some background on these biofuel types. The third subsection then summarizes the advantages and disadvantages of biofuels and briefly reflects on innovations required for an ongoing substitution of petroleum-based fuels, with a view to motivate the modelling of biofuels and innovations in section 3.

2.1 Biodiesel

Biodiesel (i.e. methyl-esters or ethyl-esters) can be used as a partial substitute for petroleum-based diesel in the range of up to 5 per cent with no engine modifications, but any higher percentage share of biodiesel or the use of pure biodiesel requires such modifications. For example, in Germany, which is currently the world's largest producer and consumer, biodiesel has been available since the late 1980s; until the end of 2003, only pure biodiesel (B100) was sold (Verband Deutscher Biodieselhersteller, 2007; Pahl, 2005, p. 167). Yet, based on the biofuel directive of the EU, B5

Table 9.1   Biodiesel production capacities in thousand tons

	2003	2004	2005	2006
Germany	1025	1088	1903	2681
France	500	502	532	775
Italy	420	419	827	857
UK	5	15	129	445

Source: European Biodiesel Board.

Table 9.2   Biodiesel production capacities and consumption in Germany in thousand tons

	1998	1999	2000	2001	2002	2003	2004	2005	2006
Production capacities	NA	NA	249	668	953	1109	1200	2012	3200*
Consumption	100	130	340	450	550	810	1180	1976	2500*

Note: * Denotes estimates and NA denotes not available.

Source: Verband Deutscher Biodieselhersteller.

biodiesel (which is petroleum-based diesel that contains up to 5 per cent of biodiesel) can be sold without notification and since January 2007 all diesel sold at the pump must by law be B5 biodiesel (Biokraftstoffquotengesetz, which requires 4.4 per cent of biodiesel). However, in 2006, about 60 per cent of the entire biodiesel production was still sold as pure biodiesel (B100) and biodiesel had a 7 per cent share of the German diesel market (Verband Deutscher Biodieselhersteller, 2007). The high share of pure biodiesel (B100) distinguishes the German market from virtually all other markets, where biodiesel is predominantly sold as B2 or B5 blend.

Table 9.1 gives an overview with respect to production capacities in European countries that lead in biodiesel production. Table 9.2 shows the development of production capacities and consumption in Germany.

Biodiesel has a number of environmental benefits. In comparison with petroleum-based diesel, biodiesel may reduce CO_2 emissions in a range of 40 to 80 per cent (Umweltbundesamt, 2006; Peters and Frondel, 2006, p. 13), emissions of particulate matter and soot by up to 50 per cent, emissions of unburned hydrocarbons by up to 80 per cent and may reduce emissions of carbon monoxide (Verband Deutscher Biodieselhersteller, 2007; Tat and van Gerpen, 2002, p. 33). Further, in contrast to petroleum-based diesel, biodiesel is extremely low in sulphur, biodegradable in just 21 days, and non-toxic. This notwithstanding, Greenpeace and others have pointed out that the emission of cancer-causing particulates is virtually the same for biodiesel and petroleum-based diesel, that the emission of oxides of nitrogen (NO_x) is higher for biodiesel, and that an increasing use of biodiesel actually raises the ethical question of food versus fuel production (Greenpeace Redaktion, 2006).

In fact, biodiesel is produced from oil-producing crops such as rape-seed (canola), sunflower, soybean, maize (sweet corn), coconut, peanut, jatropha, mustard, safflower and palm oil, but can be produced also from algae, animal fat or frying oils that have been used in the food chain (Pahl, 2005, pp. 46–54). In Europe, however, biodiesel is predominantly produced from rapeseed. For example, about 1.5 million hectares are currently used for growing rapeseed in Germany, which represents roughly 13 per cent of Germany's arable land (Stern, 2007, p. 27). As noted, in 2006 biodiesel had a market share of about 7 per cent. These figures, together with those of Table 10.2, already indicate that current biodiesel production technology is not sufficient for satisfying present German diesel demand with homegrown crops. Similar ratios apply for many other countries, and crop rotation issues and the avoidance of monocultures would make such ratios even worse.

Hence the substitution of petroleum-based diesel with biodiesel can be achieved in the foreseeable future only if substantial progress is made at all stages of the biodiesel production process and in reducing transportation fuel demand as such, for example, through energy efficiency improvements. In other words, outstanding product and process innovations are required.

2.2 Bioethanol

Bioethanol may serve as a substitute for petroleum-based gasoline in vehicles powered by an Otto engine or as a kerosene substitute in plane turbines. Currently bioethanol is predominantly used as a partial substitute, usually in mixtures of E2, E5, E10, E25 and E85, because pure bioethanol (E100) may react with rubber and plastics and, therefore, requires substantial engine modifications. Unmodified engines can use E2, E5 or E10 without any problems. However, the latest generation of flexible fuel vehicles (FFV), particularly popular in Brazil, can operate with any mixture of bioethanol and petroleum-based gasoline of up to E100. In fact, Brazil is currently the world's largest producer, consumer and exporter of bioethanol – in 2005, Brazil produced 12.7 million tons of bioethanol, which represented roughly 36 per cent of world production (Landwirtschaftliche Biokraftstoffe e.V., 2007). Yet this picture might

Table 9.3   Bioethanol production in million tons

	2004	2005	2006
Brazil	11.57	12.67	NA
USA	10.17	11.7	16.1
EU	0.42	0.73	1.24
Spain	NA	0.237	0.32
Germany	0.02	0.13	0.34

Note: NA denotes not available from the same source.

Source: Landwirtschaftliche Biokraftstoffe e.V. (2007).

change dramatically over the next few years because of biofuel initiatives such as the biofuel directive of the EU and similar programmes in the USA and elsewhere, which are expected to lead to high growth rates in the world production of bioethanol. This notwithstanding, bioethanol production in the EU is still at a comparatively low level, with Spain and Germany being leading producers. Table 9.3 provides an overview. Also, it follows from a comparison of Tables 9.1 and 9.3 that bioethanol is currently the leading biofuel.

Like biodiesel, bioethanol has various environmental benefits, which includes a reduction of CO_2 emissions by up to 80 per cent. Yet it is worth keeping in mind that, for all biofuels, negative external effects associated with intensive crop production, due to a high application rate of fertilizers and agrochemicals, soil erosion or excessive water and groundwater use, might overwhelm such benefits.

Bioethanol can be produced from any sugar or starch crop, e.g. sugar cane, sweet corn (maize) and sugar beet in the former case, and barley, oat, wheat, rice and potatoes in the latter. However, another potential feedstock is lignocellulosic biomass, which includes agricultural residues (corn stover, crop strow, sugar cane bagasse), herbaceous crops (alfalfa, switchgrass), short rotation woody crops (eucalyptus), forestry residues, wastepaper and other biowaste (Kim and Dale, 2005, p. 427). Due to regional climate and soil particularities, bioethanol is exclusively produced from sugar cane in Brazil, predominantly from corn (maize) in the USA, and from wheat and sugar beets in the EU. Lignocellulosic biomass is not yet used on an industrial scale, but has by far the largest potential – based on current figures and technologies, Kim and Dale (2004) estimate that the world potential bioethanol production from crop residues and wasted crops is 491 GL (gigalitres) per year (i.e. 387.89 million tons per year), which would cover some 32 per cent of global gasoline consumption.

Again, these figures make it clear that substantial product and process innovations are needed in order to substitute fully biofuels for petroleum-based fuels.

2.3 Modelling Biofuels and Innovations

The preceding subsections have made it clear that the substitution of petroleum-based fuels by biofuels may have various benefits, but may also be associated with some negative effects. In particular, biofuel advantages and disadvantages over pretroleum-based fuels can be summarized as follows:

(a) *Fewer CO_2 emissions*:   Biofuels may reduce CO_2 emissions by up to 80 per cent, depending on how the by-products are used, how much fossil fuel energy is used in the production chain, and how much N_2O is emitted from feedstock fields. (N_2O is also known as laughing gas, a greenhouse gas that causes 300 times more damage than CO_2; see Umweltbundesamt, 2006.) Note, however, that, over time, fossil fuels may be replaced at an increasing rate by biofuels, so that the CO_2 reduction may approach the 80 per cent level. Yet agrochemical innovations are required to reduce N_2O emissions, which in turn may help to push the reduction level beyond 80 per cent.

(b) *Less pollution*:   Biofuels, in particular biodiesel, may reduce the emission of some pollutants such as unburned hydrocarbons or carbon monoxide. Further, it is worth noting that, over the last decades, diesel engines have been optimized based on the use of petroleum-based diesel. Optimizing diesel engines based on the use of biodiesel may, therefore, help to further reduce the emission of pollutants – Tat and van Gerpen (2002, p. 34) argue that 'the different physical characteristics of biodiesel are causing changes in the way the engine uses the fuel and these changes result in more NO_x emissions'. Hence engineering advances in engine technology may help to overcome higher NO_x emissions currently associated with the use of biodiesel. Advances in filter technology may help to further reduce the emission of pollutants.

(c) *Less import dependence*:   With biofuels, all oil-importing countries can reduce their need to import oil. In some cases, where consumption is low and availability of arable land is high, oil imports may be reduced close to zero, even with current technologies. Moreover, in principle, international trade in biofuels should be associated with less uncertainty, because the number of biofuel-exporting countries should over time be much higher than the number of oil-exporting countries.

(d) *Less environmental risk during transportation and use*:   Biodiesel is biodegradable in just 21 days. Hence any leaking would cause almost no environmental damage. This is particularly important with respect to transportation because accidents with loads of petroleum-diesel or even crude oil may cause severe environmental damage, as recent history has shown. Moreover, with biofuels, the need for long-distance transportation of fuels would be substantially reduced, because a higher share is produced close to demand (see (c)), which in turn helps to reduce the potential risk of environmental damage.

(e) *More competition in fuel markets*:   Biofuels are predominantly produced by the agriculture and sugar industries and not by the petrochemical and oil industries. Therefore the number of players in transport fuel markets may increase with an increasing use of biofuels. This fact alone could lead to more competition in fuel markets. But to ensure the full benefits of more competitive fuel markets, government regulation may still be necessary. The biofuel directive of the EU, which ensures the compulsory sale of B5 and E2 or E5 blends at public pump stations, is one such example. In the foreseeable future, making the sale of B100 or E85 and flexible fuel vehicles compulsory might be other options.

(f) *Negative external effects due to more agrochemicals*:   An increasing use of biofuels may lead to more intensive agriculture regarding biofuel feedstocks. With current technologies, this would generate negative external effects, for example, due to a high application rate of agrochemicals or excessive water and groundwater use. Hence any extension of the use of biofuels calls for an environmentally friendly form of agriculture and this may not be feasible without further investment in agriculture-related research, including bioengineering.

(g) *Ethical concerns over fuel versus food production*:   Essentially, ethical concerns over fuel versus food production come down to the following question: is it ethically acceptable that some arable land is used for fuel production when this land could be used alternatively for food production either to overcome starvation or to extend the present size of the population? This is a puzzling question that is not easy to answer. At present, however, the circumstances are such that this question is posed in a mitigated form, where the increasing use of biofuels contributes to price increases for some food products. In general, such food price increases and ethical conflicts over fuel versus food production can be avoided over time only if: (i) lignocellulosic biomass is used for biofuel production; (ii) wasteland is transformed into arable land for biofuel production; and finally (iii) plants that grow in water rather than on land, such as algae, are used as feedstock for biofuel production. Again, any of these possible options would require a massive research effort because current technology is simply insufficient.

Hence, at least the aforementioned aspects (a) to (g) should be incorporated when biofuels are modelled. To keep things simple, however, we choose an aggregate measure of these seven aspects as a first approximation. In particular, we assume that the environmental net effect of substituting biofuels for petroleum-based fuels is always positive. This is achieved by assuming that the use of petroleum-based fuels always creates negative external effects, whereas the use of biofuels causes fewer external effects.

3. ENDOGENOUS GROWTH WITH FUEL RESOURCE SECTORS

Following Pittel et al. (2005), a conventional Romer-type endogenous growth model (e.g. see Aghion and Howitt, 1998, pp. 35–9) is extended to incorporate simultaneously a non-renewable resource (fossil fuels) and a renewable resource (biofuels). In addition, transport fuel produced from the renewable resource is modelled as causing less environmental damage than fuel produced from non-renewable fossil resources.

3.1 The Model

Our model comprises a household sector, various production sectors, a research sector and the environment. We consider a representative household to maximize discounted lifetime utility u:

$$u = \int_0^\infty u(C, E)\, e^{-\rho t} dt \qquad (9.1)$$

where C denotes consumption, E reflects the state of the environment, and ρ is the rate of time preference. The usual assumptions for the first- and second-order derivatives of u with respect to C and E hold, that is, $u_C > 0$, $u_{CC} < 0$ and $u_E < 0$, $u_{EE} > 0$. Further, for the sake of simplicity, u may be assumed to be separable in C and E. In the utility function (9.1), negative external effects associated with the use of non-renewable

resources as described in the preceeding section are explicitly incorporated, as long as they damage the environment. We shall come back to this
point later in more detail.

On the production side of the economy, we consider a final-goods
sector, an intermediates sector, as well as a knowledge sector. Final production is given by

$$Y = F(L, K, X) \qquad (9.2)$$

where output Y is produced from capital K, labour L, and intermediates
X. The intermediate input might be considered as an index of an endogenous number of differentiated goods produced from fossil fuels Z and
biofuels R, which are taken as substitutes:

$$X = G(Z, R)H \qquad (9.3)$$

The variable H reflects the stock of public knowledge, which is the engine
for growth in this model. The evolution of the knowledge stock takes
place along past experience, which may continuously be enhanced through
novel innovations made in the knowledge sector. The production function
for knowledge reads

$$\dot{H} = h(1 - L)H \qquad (9.4)$$

The amount of labour employed in the knowledge or research sector is
given by $1 - L$ when total labour endowment in the economy is set to 1,
and $h(1 - L)$ gives the labour productivity in this sector.

Next we introduce the resource stocks:

$$\dot{S} = -Z \qquad (9.5)$$

$$\dot{A} = \eta_A \cdot A - R \qquad (9.6)$$

where S denotes the stock of exhaustible fossil resources Z and A is the
stock of renewable resources R. Non-renewable resources are extracted
from a given, known stock, S, at no cost, where $\dot{S}$ describes the evolution
of the stock over time. Renewable resources are extracted from the stock
A, which by assumption regenerates at the constant rate η_A, so that $\dot{A}$
again describes the evolution of the stock.

Let us now discuss how the extraction of resources, both non-renewable
and renewable, affects environmental quality. As already motivated, we
may assume that fossil fuels always damage the environment more than

biofuels. Hence, in a first approximation, we may need to consider just the net effect, which in some sense is given by the environmental disadvantage of fossil fuels over biofuels. In this case, the following measure of environmental quality E (first proposed by Aghion and Howitt, 1998, ch. 5) might be useful:

$$\dot{E} = -Z - \eta_E E, \quad E < 0 \tag{9.7}$$

The state of the environment is taken to deteriorate along with the extraction of fossil fuels (in contrast to the extraction of biofuels). Further, η_E gives the maximal potential rate of regeneration, where E is defined to be non-positive everywhere. As a result, environmental quality cannot grow without bound, but is limited to zero, which reflects the virgin state of nature. Therefore environmental quality might be considered to measure the difference between the virgin state of nature and the actual state.

Further, concerning the issue of sustainability, growth will be considered sustainable if the optimal path obeys a constraint of the following form:

$$E_{\min} \leq \dot{E} < 0 \tag{9.8}$$

$E_{\min}$ is a critical threshold below which the state of the environment must not fall at any point in time. This implies that the 'pollution intensity' of resource extraction must not go beyond the regeneration capacity of the environment to rule out a process of permanent environmental degradation.

Finally, the equilibrium condition for the capital market has to be met, where we abstract from the depreciation of capital:

$$\dot{K} = Y - C \tag{9.9}$$

4. OPTIMAL GROWTH PATH

In this section, we shall derive the social planner solution to the problem of optimal growth, followed by a preliminary discussion of some implications for the optimal extraction of resources.

The present-value Hamiltonian is

$$H = u(C,E)e^{-\rho t} + \pi(Y - C) + \psi Hh(1 - L)$$

$$+ \theta(\eta_A A - R) - \lambda Z + \mu(-Z - \eta_E E) \tag{9.10}$$

where π denotes the shadow price of capital, ψ is the shadow price of the stock of knowledge, θ is the shadow price of the biofuel stock, λ is the shadow price of fossil fuels, and μ is the shadow price of the environmental stock. The first-order conditions for the control variables C, L, R and Z, respectively, are:

$$C: u_C e^{-\rho t} - \pi = 0 \tag{9.11}$$

$$L: \pi Y_L - \psi h_{1-L} H = 0 \tag{9.12}$$

$$R: \pi Y_R - \theta = 0 \tag{9.13}$$

$$Z: \pi Y_Z - \lambda - \mu = 0 \tag{9.14}$$

First-order conditions for the state variables K, H, S, A and E, respectively, are:

$$K: \dot{\pi} Y_K = -\dot{\pi} \tag{9.15}$$

$$H: \psi h(1 - L) + \pi Y_X - X_H = -\dot{\psi} \tag{9.16}$$

$$S: 0 = -\dot{\lambda} \tag{9.17}$$

$$A: \theta \eta_A = -\dot{\theta} \tag{9.18}$$

$$E: -\eta_E \mu + u_E e^{-\rho t} = -\dot{\mu} \tag{9.19}$$

Next, for $t \to \infty$, in the limit, the transversality conditions are:

$$\pi_t K_t = 0 \tag{9.20}$$

$$\psi_t H_t = 0 \tag{9.21}$$

$$\lambda_t S_t = 0 \tag{9.22}$$

$$\theta_t A_t = 0 \tag{9.23}$$

$$\mu_t E = 0 \tag{9.24}$$

To give an interpretation to the first-order conditions, let us concentrate on those terms in (9.10) to (9.19) that are not quite familiar from standard growth theory. In particular, equations (9.13) and (9.14) mean that the shadow prices of fossil and biofuels, respectively, have to equal the marginal value of the respective input in the accumulation of capital (which in turn is equal to the value of consumption foregone, measured in utility terms). However, while the shadow price of biofuels does not reflect any environmental degradation, the shadow price of fossil fuels does by taking the shadow value of the environment μ into account. Or, in other words, the shadow value of fossil fuels is lower than its marginal value product in final goods production because of environmental degradation, which reduces the value of fossil fuels by μ.

Furthermore, some important implications follow from the first-order conditions for the state variables and the transversality conditions:

$$-\frac{\dot{\pi}}{\pi} = Y_K \qquad (9.25)$$

$$-\frac{\dot{\lambda}}{\lambda} = 0 \Rightarrow \lambda \; const \qquad (9.26)$$

$$-\frac{\dot{\theta}}{\theta} = \eta_A \qquad (9.27)$$

$$-\frac{\dot{\mu}}{\mu} = -\eta_E + \frac{u_E}{\mu}e^{-\rho t} \qquad (9.28)$$

The shadow value of capital is given by the marginal productivity of capital in final production, which has to be constant along the balanced path. That in turn requires allocating labour between knowledge production and final production such that increasing knowledge can always compensate for the decreasing marginal productivity of the fuel resource inputs. This issue, however, is not the main focus of our chapter.

The implications with respect to the shadow values of the resource inputs deserve more attention. As far as fossil fuels are concerned, the shadow value is constant over time, and so it is socially optimal to completely exhaust the given stock. Concerning biofuels, the shadow value grows at a (negative) rate, which is given by the regeneration rate of the stock. Finally, the shadow value of the environmental stock moves with the regeneration rate less the discounted disutility generated by environmental damage.

5.   DISCUSSION

In this section, we provide a discussion of the Keynes–Ramsey rule and the Hotelling rules for the optimal extraction of renewable and non-renewable resources, respectively. In particular, we would like to emphasize the conditions to be met with respect to the substitution of biofuels for fossil fuels in order to assure sustainable growth.

The Keynes–Ramsey rule for the accumulation of capital turns out to be fairly standard:

$$Y_K = \varphi - \frac{\dot{u}_c}{u_C} \tag{9.29}$$

As usual, the Keynes–Ramsey rule states that the marginal productivity of capital is to be set equal to the rate of discount, less the growth rate in the marginal utility of consumption (which is negative). In other words, the marginal value of capital used in production must be equal to the opportunity cost of capital accumulation (which is the foregone utility from consumption). Hence consumption can grow over time only if the marginal productivity of capital is above the rate of discount.

The Hotelling rules for the extraction of natural resources are given by:

$$g_{Y_R} = \frac{\dot{Y}_R}{Y_R} = Y_K - \eta_A = Y_K + g_\theta < Y_K \tag{9.30}$$

$$\frac{\dot{Y}_Z}{Y_Z} = Y_K + g_{\lambda+\mu} \tag{9.31}$$

where

$$g_{\lambda+\mu} = \frac{(\lambda \dot{+} \mu)}{(\lambda + \mu)} = \frac{\eta_E \mu - u_E e^{-\varphi t}}{u_C e^{-\varphi t} Y_Z} > 0 \tag{9.32}$$

The Hotelling rules (9.30) and (9.31) for biofuels and fossil fuels, respectively, generally show that the growth rate of the social return of the resource (in real terms) must be equal to the physical rate of return to capital. However, the social returns of fossil and biofuels differ substantially by the second terms of the left-hand sides of the equations above. While the social return of biofuels has to grow at a rate below the growth rate of the physical return, the social return of fossil fuels has to grow at a rate above the growth rate of the physical return.

The former result is true due to the regeneration capacity of the stock of biofuels, which leads to a lower shadow value of the stock at any point in time. The latter result holds due to the environmental damage caused by the extraction and use of fossil fuels. In a sense, fossil fuels have to earn a return that is above the physical rate of return to capital because the (negative) change in the value of the environmental stock over time has to be taken into account. Therefore the true change in the shadow value of fossil fuels is not given by g_λ, which is constant, but by $g_{\lambda+\mu}$. It is in turn composed of the change in the shadow values of the resource and the environmental stock.

Combining (9.30) and (9.31) and rearranging yields:

$$\frac{\dot{Y}_R}{Y_R} - \frac{\dot{Y}_Z}{Y_Z} = \overset{<0}{\underset{\theta}{g}} - \overset{>0}{\underset{\mu+\lambda}{g}} < 0 \Rightarrow g_{Y_Z} - g_{Y_R} > 0 \qquad (9.33)$$

While, at any point in time, the more biofuels are extracted the larger is the regeneration capacity, the extraction of fossil fuels must be slowed down due to its impact on environmental quality. Moreover, it is shown that biofuels must substitute for fossil fuels to ensure sustainable growth.

6. CONCLUSIONS

In this chapter, it has been emphasized that in most countries the markets for transportation fuels are dominated by non-renewable fossil fuel products such as gasoline and petroleum diesel. Yet limited stocks of non-renewable fossil fuels as well as limited production and distribution capacities, coupled with increasing demand, are bound to lead to sharp increases in fossil fuel prices in the near future. This development may be reinforced by the fact that fossil fuels, in comparison to biofuels, contribute a substantially larger share to pollution and global warming. Consequently, alternative fuels such as renewable biofuels (i.e. biodiesel, bioethanol) or hydrogen may become economically more attractive, and, moreover, may serve as a means to maintain sustainable growth.

The aim of the chapter, therefore, has been to address the role of biofuels for sustainable growth. A conventional Romer-type endogenous growth model has been extended by incorporating a non-renewable and a renewable resource, which can both serve in the production of transport fuels. In addition, transport fuel produced from the renewable resource has been modelled as causing less environmental damage than fuel produced from non-renewable fossil resources.

Innovations that enhance the energy efficiency of transport are necessary to move along the optimal growth path of the economy. Moreover, it can be shown that the growing stock of knowledge must be accompanied by an ongoing substitution process in production and transport, where biofuels replace fossil fuels. This is the only means in our model to ensure sustainability of growth in the sense of a non-degrading environmental quality, and might be considered as the main contribution of the chapter.

Nevertheless, there is of course scope for future research, in particular with respect to the decentralization and microfoundation of the model as well as with respect to the analysis of the transitional dynamics and the food versus the energy substitution process.

REFERENCES

Aghion, P. and P. Howitt (1998), *Endogenous Growth Theory*, Cambridge, MA: MIT Press.

Directive 2003/30/EC of the European Parliament and of the Council of the European Union, *Official Journal of the European Union*, 17.05.2003, pp. L123/42–L123/46.

Directive 2003/96/EC of the Council of the European Union, *Official Journal of the European Union*, 31.10.2003, pp. L283/51–L283/70.

European Biodiesel Board (2007), *Statistics*, available online at http://www.ebb-eu.org.

European Commisson (2001), *Green Paper – Towards a European Strategy for the Security of Energy Supply*, Luxembourg: Office for Official Publications of the European Communities.

Greenpeace Redaktion (2006), *Biodiesel: Mogelpackung auf Kosten der Umwelt*, available online at http://www.greenpeace.de.

Kim, S. and B.E. Dale (2004), 'Global potential bioethanol production from wasted crops and crop residues', *Biomass and Bioenergy*, **26**, 361–75.

Kim, S. and B.E. Dale (2005), 'Life cycle assessment of various cropping systems utilized for producing biofuels: bioethanol and biodiesel', *Biomass and Bioenergy*, **29**, 426–39.

Landwirtschaftliche Biokraftstoffe e.V. (2007), available at http://www.bdbe.de.

Pahl, G. (2005), *Biodiesel – Growing a New Energy Economy*, White River Junction, VT: Chelsea Green Publishing.

Peters, J. and M. Frondel (2006), 'Biodiesel: a new Oildorado?', Working Paper, Rheinisch-Westfälisches Institut für Wirtschaftsforschung (RWI Essen), Essen, Germany.

Pickhardt, M. (2005), 'Energy policy', in M. Peter van der Hoek (ed.), *Handbook of Public Administration and Policy in the European Union*, New York: CRC Press (Taylor & Francis), pp. 489–500.

Pittel, K., Amigues, J.-P. and T. Kuhn (2005), 'Long-run growth and recycling: a material balance approach', INRA Working Paper, University of Toulouse.

Stern (2007), *Biosprit vom Acker*, **8**, S. 162.

Tat, M.E. and J.H. van Gerpen (2002), 'The speed of sound and bulk modulus of alkyl esters and their blends with diesel fuel', *Landbauforschung*, Special Issue, **239**, 33–8.

Umweltbundesamt (2006), *Biodiesel*, available online at http://www.umweltbundesamt.de.

Verband Deutscher Biodieselhersteller (2007), *Alles über Biodiesel*, available online at http://www.biokraftstoffverband.de

10. Paretian welfare theory and European competition policy

Arnold Heertje

1. INTRODUCTION

Paretian welfare theory relates the subjective and formal character of welfare, which consumers derive from the satisfaction of wants, to the allocation of scarce resources. In fact, it is a theory of allocation that describes a technically feasible allocation, with the property that each consumer maximizes his utility, given the level of utility of all the other consumers. As Paretian welfare theory considers the welfare of the citizens exclusively from the point of view of their individual preferences as consumers, a Pareto optimum also implies optimal social welfare. With another distribution of income, we face another Pareto optimal allocation. Pareto optimality is defined independently of the distribution of income and of the institutional structure of the mechanism of allocation. This insight confirms Hennipman's view that Pareto optimality is an 'analytical tool' and does not imply a value judgement (Hennipman, 1995, p. 59).

A Banach space is an abstract, rich, robust and, above all, simple mathematical structure to represent an economy with consumers, producers, means of production and consumer goods. The number of goods may be infinite. Consumer goods are depicted as bundles of characteristics upon which utility functions are defined. Important characteristics are location and time of the availability of goods. Utility functions differ from consumer to consumer, profit functions from producer to producer. Besides present generations of consumers and producers, future generations may be distinguished. The welfare of future generations of consumers may be brought within the scope of Paretian welfare theory through the hypothesis that, nowadays, consumers identify themselves with their children, their grandchildren and so on. Uncertainty and incomplete information can be taken care of. Under all conditions, a Pareto-optimal allocation can be determined.

2. RICARDO, MARX AND SRAFFA

The analytical scope of Pareto optimality may be deepened even further. To look at price systems as continuous, linear functionals on a Banach space of goods leaves us with different interpretations. Economic theory often argues in terms of perfect competition. This market form produces a vector of given market prices for consumers and producers. However, if we consider our abstract scheme as a point of departure, the linear functional may be conceived as the representation of reproduction prices. These prices have the property of reproducing the production processes of the producers. They are equal to the costs of reproduction of the goods and they prepare the ground for the Marxian scheme of reproduction.

An interesting aspect of this view is that the academic debate between neoclassicals and neo-Ricardians or neo-Sraffians boils down to the choice of the positive, linear functional on the goods space. From this point of view, Ricardo, who in his *Principles* used both market prices and natural or reproduction prices, may be considered a classical economist, walking in a dual Banach space of linear functionals and choosing the proper specification compatible with his interpretation of the economic process.

3. PARETO OPTIMALITY AND REALITY

The impression may emerge that Pareto optimality is a nice theoretical construct without practical relevance. For several reasons, the actual allocation may differ from the Pareto-optimal allocation that reflects the preferences of the consumers. The analysis of the causes of the distinction between actual and Pareto optimal allocation benefits from the concept of Pareto optimality as a frame of reference. But there is more. If a politician decides to base economic policy on the achievement of Pareto optimality, its practical relevance is beyond doubt. Such behaviour is not in contradiction with Pareto optimality as an analytical tool in economic theory. Let me illustrate this for European competition policy. I confront this policy with Paretian welfare theory and ask, 'What is the proper task of competition policy?' European legislation and the literature display a wide variety of criteria, considerations and opinions. We are in need of clarification.

4. THE TREATY OF ROME

A perusal of Articles 81–90 of the Treaty of Rome on the rules for competition between companies and state aid reveals that restrictions on competition are gauged principally by their impact on economic and technological development, notably on production, sale, prices, investment, innovation and regional underdevelopment; that is, on a heterogeneous collection of factors without any consistent rationale or internal ranking. The decisive objective of European competition policy is not defending the interests of today's and tomorrow's consumers. Under Article 81(3), provisions that restrict competition between companies may be declared inapplicable in the event of growth, improvement in the distribution of goods and technical progress, 'while allowing consumers a fair share of the resulting benefit'. Article 82 refers in passing to 'consumers' as the victims in the event of abuse of a dominant position, without making it clear whether it means final consumers. Article 87 on state aid refers to individual consumers (European Union, 2003, pp. 64–8).

Given the nature of the legal basis for policy, it is understandable that there is considerable confusion within the European Commission and in the literature as to the purpose of competition policy. As early as 1966, Hennipman noted that international competition policy had developed 'into an extremely opaque and complex structure. There are considerable differences between one country and another (including the European Communities)' (Hennipman, 1966, p. 380). Hennipman's observation is as pertinent now as it was then. In implementing policy, civil servants and politicians lay emphasis first on one and then on another economic viewpoint, not infrequently on the basis of their own opinions and preferences.

5. LITERATURE

In the recent literature, Motta's detailed book is significant (Motta, 2004). It provides a broad overview of the theory and practice of competition policy in both the USA and Europe. However, the welfare-theory-related approach to the topic is extremely weak. Motta takes the sum of the consumer surplus and companies' total profits as the benchmark for welfare (Motta, 2004). This is a strange monetary benchmark for assessing dominant positions on the market, as the different components have contradictory features.

Motta then refers to the concept of consumer welfare by equating it – erroneously – with the consumer surplus. He notes that he finds it difficult to determine whether 'competition authorities and courts favour in practice a consumer welfare or total welfare objective' (Motta, 2004, p. 19). He then argues, without any further explanation, that it makes no difference whether one takes consumer welfare or total welfare as the benchmark.

This is a bizarre opinion, as consumers and producers have conflicting interests in monopolistic market situations. Motta opts for total welfare as the benchmark for assessing dominant positions on the market, and, in so doing, he limits the concept of consumer welfare to the impact on prices of the exercise of power by producers. His argument lacks a solid basis, as he fails to take account of the impact on consumers' welfare of non-price competition, such as quality, service, freedom of choice and product innovation, let alone the interests of future generations of consumers. Confusion is total when Motta states that consumer welfare is not one of the guidelines for competition policy as 'consumer policy by definition does not take into account the gains made by the firms' (Motta, 2004, p. 21). If the European Commissioner for Competition is obliged to start taking account of negative effects on the profitability of companies in her policy, she may as well step down.

6. EUROPEAN COMPETITION POLICY

The reason Paretian welfare theory is of great practical significance has to do with establishing order in fragmented competition policy at both the national and the European levels. My hypothesis is that the ultimate purpose of competition policy is to enhance the welfare of today's and tomorrow's consumers and to achieve Pareto improvements.

I go one step further by venturing to suppose that the current European Commissioner for Competition, Ms N. Kroes, has decided to make the Pareto optimum the benchmark for her policy, as is suggested by her public utterances. For a politician, this action does not conflict with the analytical character of the Pareto optimum. It simply means that the measures taken by the European Commission in the competition field will be subjected to a decisive test: whether or not they improve the position of consumers. This view of competition policy means that other considerations, such as growth, have no significance in themselves. Growth is justified by the fact that it enables consumers to satisfy their needs. This is necessarily the case, as competition policy tackles companies that have dominant positions, while at the same time maintaining such dominant positions through a positive growth effect.

If the Pareto optimum is the ultimate objective of European competition policy for today's and tomorrow's European consumers, the promotion of innovation is incorporated into that objective by identifying its impact on consumer welfare. Product innovations resulting from fundamental and applied research provide for consumers' anticipated needs. In the case of process innovations, the issue is whether these are directly relevant to consumers' utility functions, or whether they serve only to boost companies' profitability (because potential price decreases are not passed on to consumers, for instance).

The qualitative aspects of employment may also be brought within the purview of Paretian welfare theory by viewing labour not merely as a factor of production, but also as a consumer good. Employees are increasingly developing preferences with regard to the work they do, as though they were purchasing a consumer good. In this way, they indicate with whom, where and for what periods and how long they want to work. If one accepts this view of labor as a consumer good, competition policy can be used to improve the quality of work in the eyes of the employee or consumer.

For all sorts of reasons, the use of scarce means of production at a given income distribution differs in reality from the Pareto optimum, which links allocation with the satisfaction of consumers' needs through the production of goods and services, the conservation of the natural and cultural heritage, and work.

Competition policy comes into play where the Pareto optimum does not arise naturally, owing to the dominant positions of companies or nationalistic behaviour by sovereign states. The hypothesis that European competition policy takes the Pareto optimum as its norm implies that competition and state aid are viewed exclusively in terms of consumers' interests. This view serves to clarify decision making. Other considerations, such as employment, growth and innovation, are secondary, rather than of equal importance, to the objective of meeting the needs of consumers. They are gauged in relation to this objective, which is put into practice by observing the impact of competition on the quality on price of goods and services. Our hypothesis reflects the normative statement of Adam Smith in the third edition of the *Wealth of Nations:* 'Consumption is the sole end of production' (Smith, 1784, p. 584).

We have reached this simple conclusion by making a virtue of the one-sidedness of the Paretian view – only consumers count in the allocation game – an approach that is very much at variance with economic theory, which discounts the Pareto optimum as unrealistic.

REFERENCES

European Union (2003), *Consolidated Treaties*, Luxembourg, European Communities.
Hennipman, P. (1966), De taak van de mededingingspolitiek, *De Economist*, **114**, 379–417.

Hennipman, P. (1995), 'Pareto optimality: value judgment or analytical tool?', in Donald Walker, Arnold Heertje and Hans van den Doel (eds), *Welfare Economics and the Theory of Economic Policy*, Aldershot, UK and Brookfield, USA: Edward Elgar, pp. 59–86.

Motta, M. (2004), *Competition Policy, Theory and Practice*, Cambridge: Cambridge University Press.

Smith, A. (1784), *An Inquiry into the Nature and Causes of the Wealth of Nations, II,* London: W. Strahan and T. Cadell.

11.   French industrial policy

Alain Alcouffe and Christiane Alcouffe

HISTORICAL OVERVIEW

The French claim precedence in inventing the concept of industrial policy, which can be traced back to Jean-Baptiste Colbert, Louis XIV's famous minister. Henceforth national economics, the idea that 'national economic strength is measured by productive capacity and that productive capacity can be increased by state aid,' (Clough, 1939, p. 8) permeated French political and economic life. The ambition of 'Colbertism', as such policies went on to be labelled, was to attain full employment, to stave off mass poverty, and to strengthen national industrial champions necessary for national supremacy.

FROM THE FIRST INDUSTRIAL REVOLUTION TO THE SECOND WORLD WAR

In the nineteenth century, Colbert's ambitions were revived by the Saint-Simonian ideology adopted by Napoleon III in his effort to boost French industry. Unlike mercantilism, however, Saint-Simonianism advocated free trade and is usually credited with having sustained the major industrial spurt of the century. Later on, under the parliamentary regime established after the Franco-Prussian War of 1870–71, relations between industrialists and politicians became more intricate. The Depression of the 1890s reintroduced the claim for protection and tariffs, while the fear of socialism restrained the growth of firms and the concentration of workers.

By the beginning of the twentieth century, all industries of the Second Industrial Revolution were in place: steel, electricity, petrol, railways, telegraph, chemistry, automobiles, aeronautics. These sectors innovated at a sustained rhythm between 1900 and 1930, with an average growth of 5 per cent per annum, which was triple that of the rest of the economy (Lévy-Leboyer, 1991). In the other industrialized countries, this technological change led to the emergence of 'corporate capitalism', marked by the rise of large companies, substituting the 'visible hand' of managers for the 'invisible hand' of market coordination (Chandler, 1990). Industrial organization did not experience a boom comparable to that of other big industrialized countries (the USA, Germany and the UK), which surpassed France in terms of economic growth. Structural dispersal and decentralization still dominated the industrial landscape, so that France at the end of the 1920s was characterized by 'la poussière industrielle' (industrial proliferation) (Dormois, 1999, p. 63). The Popular Front was the first manifestation of the public service elite's new-found commitment to 'planism' and strategic government intervention. For the first time, US industry was presented as a model to emulate and many 'young Turks' of rationalization crossed the Atlantic for inspiration. But Leon Blum's New Deal amounted to the multiplication of trade and industry subsidies by a factor of nine. An Act passed in the summer of 1936 prescribed temporary financial assistance to businesses in difficulty to fend off closures.

Nevertheless, it is difficult to find a coherent vision of economic development throughout these policies and, by and large, up to the eve of the Second World War, such a vision is hard to sustain, as it is sometimes believed abroad that France had been dirigiste or 'Colbertist' since Louis XIV's times. Through three republics and two empires, the regime was only mildly interventionist (Meisel, 2004). French governments largely adhered to a liberal doctrine and the interventionist policies generally provoked hostile reactions from intellectuals as well as from businessmen. These limits to state intervention were due to a conviction of state impotence in the fields of economics. The predominant doctrines among economists considered economic 'laws' as 'natural' and rejected government interference (Alcouffe, 1999).

But this deference to economic laws did not include respect for competition and its benefits. On the contrary, economic rationalization in France took the form of establishing capital-intensive links among companies with complementary activities (insider finance networks) and cartels among competitors, rather than of concentrating activities through corporate mergers. The country witnessed a double concentration of power: in capital markets (equity investments, holdings, subsidiaries) and in product markets (agreements, cartels, syndicates).

In 1945, France's prewar finance and economic institutions were seen as incapable of rising to the challenge of modernization, and also as largely responsible for the debacle of the previous 15 years and for France's lag.

THE PLAN COMMISSION

Positive externalities are associated with this institution in France during the 'Glorious Thirty' ('Trente Glorieuses'[1]). It is worth presenting a brief history of the Commissariat Général du Plan (CGP) and its inventor, Jean Monnet. Monnet was, first, about the only Frenchman who understood something about US affairs,[2] and second, about the only European banker who was pro-industrialist in his worldview. In exile after France's occupation by the Nazis, he launched himself, using his various connections, into the middle of US and UK government circles, calling for a specific policy. rather than just extrapolating from the usual schemes. Roosevelt used him as an 'inspirer', a rabble-rouser in the US state bureaucracies. Monnet wrote in his Mémoirs:

> Mustering all my strength, I contributed to the coming into being of this unstoppable war machine. Its motive was simple: The stubborn will of a small group of men, united around the bearer of an unprecedented power and responsibility, himself supported by the vast majority of the public. (Monnet, 1976, p. 189)

John Maynard Keynes told French banker Emmanuel Monick:

> Roosevelt was presented with a plan to build airplanes that every American technician found to be miraculous or far too much. Monnet was the only one who dared to think it was not enough. The President rallied to his views. This key decision has probably shortened the duration of the war by a year. (Monick, 1970, quoted in Monnet, 1976, pp. 211–12)

Monnet, as soon as he arrived in France in 1944, stressed the need for 'indicative planning', to break with the routine, to promote pioneering technologies, and to create a national drive to achieve reconstruction, modernization, and an increase in the living standards of all. He conceived, following the Roosevelt model, a team of about 30 people to direct the French administration, and to organize a collective effort around modernization committees, composed of representatives of the administration, experts, employers, trade unionists, and executives, to muster all the forces of the nation around a liberated France. He proposed to de Gaulle to take full responsibility for this initiative (the 'Plan'), on the condition that he be directly connected to the then-president of the Council, the head of the French executive. When de Gaulle left office in January 1946, Monnet imposed his full powers on all the weak French politicians, and centralized the state economic policies around him. The first three French Plans were a total success, and the basis of the French economy was re-established. A key point is that, to finance the investments in the Plan without discontinuity or inflation, Monnet created a 'fond de modernisation et d'équipement' (a fund for national modernization and equipment), and this fund, thanks to Monnet's intervention, was given the equivalent of the sums corresponding to the Marshall Plan funds. Later Monnet would comment that, in the UK, the Marshall Aid credits, instead of being used to restore or to modernize industry, as was the rule in France and in Germany, were used to restore UK financial power, according to the perverse system of foreign investments. The weakness and backwardness of UK industry were caused by just that, and they kept accumulating over time.

It is, therefore, clear that it was with the US methods of the New Deal system that Europe was salvaged from the rubble of the Second World War and the backwardness of most of its elites. Even more interestingly, Monnet thought that if French industrialists were to proceed by the old methods, disaster would soon loom. So he told his team: 'Let's send them to the United States'. And he had his friends organize the famous 'productivity missions', through which hundreds of French industrialists came to the USA to learn how the Americans worked.

Monnet's close collaborator, Jean Fourastié, stressed the importance for European elites of acknowledging the part played by productivity in economic affairs.

> The idea was very well received, quickly and everywhere. We all noticed that there was something paradoxical that our European treatises on economic science would ignore the concepts of productivity and technological progress. Economic science, as it was taught in France – but the situation was the same in all Europe – ignored such notions. (Cheminade, 2008)

The planning commission offered: (a) an interface between policy makers and the private economic and financial actors invited to take part in designing five-year indicative plans; (b) data collection on the real economy and the construction of statistical indicators to inform and to evaluate policies, and (c) an independent research centre at the heart of the public debate solely concerned with growth and the coordination of actors over the medium and long term. The think-tanks benefited from the improvement of econometric tools, and the sixth plan (1970–75) could boast of the use of 1600 equations integrating 4000 exogenous parameters in a model of the French economy, labelled 'Fifi' (physical–financial model). But following advocates such as Fourastié as well as observers (Hall, 1986), the key contribution was the coordination of growth forecasts and the creation of a climate of confidence favourable to investment, giving to economic agents a common outlook of reasonable growth projections, thus reducing uncertainty (Massé, 1965). The Plan was less effective in its exhibited missions than in helping social actors to accept social change, and finally facilitating social change itself (Hall, 1986).

The data collected by Maddison (2001) for the annual growth rates between 1955 and 1974 (Table 11.1) are quite impressive and explain the long-lasting reverence that surrounded the CGP. France, which had

Table 11.1   Post-war economic growth: four miracles and two laggards

	1955–68	1968–73
Japan	9.5	8.9
France	5.1	5.6
Germany	4.9	4.6
Italy	6.3	3.9
USA	3.9	3.5
UK	2.8	3.4

Source: Maddison (2001).

lagged behind the other industrialized countries since the first Industrial Revolution, was just below Japan.[3]

THE HISTORIC LARGE-SCALE PROGRAMMES: AN OVERVIEW

But during the postwar period, planism was not the only feature that differentiated France from other countries in Western Europe.[4] These 'golden' years are also important because of the *grands programmes* that were launched then and that still affect the French economy. The concept of large-scale programmes has long been at the heart of French industrial policy. Whether it be Concorde, the TGV (high-speed train), civil nuclear energy or Minitel, a sizeable amount of public funds have been invested in order to create new objects, yielding important technological advances. Table 11.2 presents the different large-scale programmes that have been launched between 1962 and 1989. The table highlights important successes, such as Airbus,[5] civil nuclear energy and the components programme. On the other hand, the computing programme is considered a failure. In this last case, it appears that the public authorities financed for too long a programme whose difficulties were obvious. As the first section showed, the success of previous large-scale programmes contributed largely to defining French industrial assets in high technology. France continues to support these large-scale programmes. Table 11.3 presents some current ones.

Dormois (1999) links the *grands programmes* to the Fifth Plan (1966–70). It inaugurated a new approach to 'proactive' industrial policy, defining activities of special significance to French industrial development in which the government intended to build up national champions capable of competing on a par with world leaders.

Table 11.2   The large-scale programmes (1962–89)

Programme	Launch date	Technological breakthrough	Principal industrial group	Amount invested
Concorde	1962	Electric flight controls	Aérospatiale	€3.8 billion between 1970 and 1990
Computing	1966	Digitalization	UNIDATA, Bull	€8 billion of support for Bull*
Telecommunications	1968	Digital commutator		Not available
Civil nuclear energy	1968	Nuclear subsector	CEA, EDF	Not available
Airbus	1969	Motorization, steering, maintenance, costs	Aérospatiale, Airbus	€3 billion of repayable advances for Aérospatiale from 1971 to 1997 (all programmes)
Space research	1973	Ariane	Aérospatiale, Air liquide	Not available
Reactors	1973	Airbus motorization	CFMSG	Not available
TGV (high-speed train)	1974	Doubling of commercial speed	Alsthom, SNCF	€2.1 billion of public investment for the launch of the first TGV line
Minitel	1978	Telematics	France Telecom	€1.2 billion of investments for PTTs
Components	1989	Miniaturization	Thomson, then STMicroelectronics	Not available

Note: * The so-called 'Plan calcul' funded not only Bull (later Honey-well Bull) but several other firms including European ones such as Philips and Siemens: see Cohen (1992).

Sources: Direction de la prévision et de l'analyse economique (DPAE); Court of Accounts (Cour des Comptes) (adapted from Cohen, 1992 and Beffa, 2005).

The selected activities had to be nurtured on French soil thanks to a privileged diet of monopoly exemptions, public orders, fat operating subsidies, preferential tariffs, and public R&D financing before facing foreign competition. (Ibid., p. 85)

There is no general evaluation of the *grands programmes* direct effects and, if we are to believe Dormois:

Table 11.3   Different current large-scale technological programmes

Programme	Activities	Means of public support	French public budget
Nuclear energy	3rd generation reactor: EPR Participation in the international programme ITER for nuclear fusion	Public research (CEA) and aid for AREVA	~ €550 million of public research spending (2003), €30 million of public funding for private R&D (essentially AREVA)
Space research	Terrestrial observation (Envisat, Calipso, Champ, GMES, etc.) Space observation: Cluster, Mars Express telecommunications: Galileo Space flight: Ariane V and ISS	Public research (CNES, ESA) partially outsourced	Budget €1.7 billion, of which €0.6 billion for the ESA (2003), €150 million of public funding of private R&D
Aeronautics	Development of new commercial aeroplanes (A 380, A 350, A 300-0G)	Repayable advances to Airbus	Repayable advance of €1.2 billion for the A 380 (2004–) Request for repayable advance of €1 billion for the A 350

Sources: CNES; Chambolle and Méaux (2004); CEA; MINEFI.

Because measuring the costs and benefits of industrial policy is so hard – not to mention the lack of adequate information because of intricate accounting procedures – it is difficult to issue a substantiated verdict on the issue. Like so many policies, it resembles the 'curate's egg': some parts of it are excellent. (Ibid., p. 92)

Their institutional consequences are better documented (e.g. ibid., p. 85), as their schemes were very characteristic, as exemplified by the Minitel telephone programme, which was a spin-off, but also by the aerospace programme, of which Airbus is the most famous part, once celebrated as a great success for French industrial policy and European cooperation, and now under fire.

THE MINITEL CASE

An Initiative of the DGT

One of the principal characteristics of the French telematics project is that it was started at the initiative of the government, through the

National Telecommunications Administration (Direction Générale des Télécommunications – DGT). The project got under way in the late 1970s. Two major events had an impact on the period and on the French economy at the time, namely the oil crisis, which affected all industrialized nations, and the telecommunications overhaul plan. The project originated with an idea summarized in the 1978 Nora–Minc report to French president Valéry Giscard d'Estaing (Nora and Minc, 1978). The French president was concerned about the recession that industrialized countries were going through, and was looking for new areas in which French industry could have a competitive edge, and new ways to enhance its competitiveness. The report suggested that the solution could be found in the service sector and promising future technologies (telephony, computers, telematics), which would be the sources of growth and competitiveness for years to come. The report pointed out the lead enjoyed by the USA in computer technology and electronics, noted the success of new experiments conducted by the CNET on a new videotex system known as Télétel, and expanded on an idea first voiced by Gérard Théry, the head of the DGT at the time, of a Plan Télématique, as part of the Telecommunications Plan then in progress.

The Telecommunications Plan was launched in 1974. At the time, Gérard Théry had noted that the French telecommunications system was probably one of the most inefficient, unsophisticated and underdeveloped in all the industrialized countries. By 1974, there was a telephone in only 12 per cent of all French homes. The head of France Télécom submitted a plan to the government, aimed at creating 14 million new lines over a seven-year period. The project was accepted, with the DGT becoming the main agency and coordinator for the telecommunications sector. The National Industrial Agency (Division des Affaires Industrielles – DAI), which was in charge of specifying, jointly with the CNET, the technical features and standards of the new network, set down with suppliers certain objectives in terms of standards, compatibility and low-cost equipment. The project was highly successful. By the middle of the next decade, France had caught up. Between 1981 and 1989, the proportion of homes with telephones rose from 74 per cent to 95 per cent. Seventy per cent of the network was digital. The first stage had been completed. The DGT moved on to the next challenge, which consisted of developing new on-line services.

A Political, Economic and Social Project

Backed by a public-sector company, the project called for services that would 'contribute to improving democracy and citizenship'. They would have to be accessible to the entire population, serve everyone's needs, and provide as much public and commercial information as possible. The system was also expected to create an incentive for all to become more familiar with computers and telematics, so as to prevent the development of 'a two-tier information society, consisting of those with access to it and those without'. Furthermore, the system had to be upgradable, so as to incorporate services with more added value. It also had to make a profit. After a few tries, the Télétel was given its public start in 1983. Between 1983 and 1991, 5 million terminals (the Minitels[6]) were distributed free of charge throughout France. By 1989, 38.2 per cent of all residents of France had a Minitel at work or at home, giving them access to more than 12 000 services. As of 1997, the number of services had more than doubled since 1989, accounting for more than 110 million hours of usage yearly.

According to Thomas J. Housel and William Davidson, France's success was due, first of all, to the structure and regulation of the telecommunications sector, and to a deliberate approach favouring the development of projects with a positive long-term return on investment: 'France's co-ordinated policy and regulation afforded an environment conducive to taking risks with new technology implementations that required long-term return on investment.' (Housel and Davidson, 1991, p. 42).

The success of France's data-transmission system had to do in part with the fact that, at the time the Minitel came out, a modern and productive infrastructure existed that could offer a wide range of sophisticated services that were relatively easy to use. Unfortunately, the Minitel did not hold on to its technological lead, so that today the system has been overtaken by the advances of the Internet. In 1983, the Minitel was the most sophisticated data-transmission system available and it remained so until the advent of browsing systems developed for the Internet in the early 1990s.

The Minitel was the first instrument that combined a computer with a telephone and, as such, it became dominant in its field from the mid-1980s. Thanks to the Télétel system, firms could develop their own servers and bulletin boards, and use them for in-house, external and business communications, and for relations with customers and suppliers. Confidentiality of data is ensured by the fact that this is a closed network (not accessible from the outside), which requires access codes or passwords. This is one reason why the Minitel is more popular than the Internet in France, with both consumers and business. In France, 95 per cent of firms with more than 500 employees and 80 per cent of all businesses use the Minitel.

The 'Kiosque' system provides for secure billing and ease of access. Users of the service are charged for calls from their Minitel to the server as well as various rates for using services. Billing is included with invoices for telephone service. France Télécom collects all payments and turns over portions to service providers. 'This billing system, which requires no password or subscription, exists nowhere else in the world; it makes things simpler for users (a single bill) as well as for service providers, who need not concern themselves with collecting payment.' (Rincé, 1990, p. 103).

The service offered by the Minitel requires a cooperative effort on the part of three players, namely France Télécom, the service provider and the supplier of the medium. France Télécom acts as both the carrier responsible for the quality of transmissions and the network's overall manager. It looks after the finances of the system by setting rate levels, giving out codes, collecting fees and redistributing payments. Service providers create the sites and are liable for their content. Those supplying the medium are the servers, which act as the interface between the services and the networks. Clear boundaries have enabled each participant to develop an expanding market with capital investments under their control (Rincé, 1990, p. 102).

All industrial projects targeting new markets are initially faced with problems caused by the lack of both supply and demand. It is not sufficient for a market to develop just to promote new technology. Problems caused by the lack of demand and supply can be long lasting and ultimately lead to the success of less ambitious but more accessible competing projects (those more akin to past practices and customs, or less costly). That is why the videotex development policy had as its objective to break this cycle and to generate a 'network effect', by making equipment available to the broadest population, developing public services, using cross-subsidies to reduce the cost of certain services and assisting new-project developers. As the network faced no competition, France Télécom was able to cross-subsidize various types of services and customers, but mainly between telecommunications and telematic services. According to Housel and Davidson (1991), the Minitel project would never have come to life in the absence of subsidies from the telecommunications side. Because of cross-subsidizing, the DGT was able to set rates based not on the financial performance of the project, but on the market penetration and development objectives adopted. The absence of competitors had another impact. Since France Télécom started its project in an environment where no network service existed (in France, the Internet was not yet accessible in 1983), it benefited from the broadest possible development base.

OVERALL PRODUCTIVITY

For the French government, the Minitel is considered a success because the project is not evaluated on the basis of pure financial return, but on that of 'overall productivity' standards, including short-term and long-term positive economic and social externalities. In 1989 a dispute arose between an inspector general and the then Minister for PTT and space, Paul Quilès. The inspector's report claimed that the Minitel project was not breaking even. Paul Quilès answered by first stating that 'the system must be evaluated not just on the basis of its immediate income but on that of the income it generates for the rest of the economy', and secondly that 'the productivity of this system can be measured only over the long run'; and finally that 'it is very hard to assess the social benefits from special services for the handicapped, free information, distant education, etc. from a standpoint of financial profitability alone'. By adding up the income generated by the entire Transpac system (€100 million), the increase in revenue by firms manufacturing the technology, software and terminals required by the system; and the growth in VAT generated by the system, the Minister came up with a total added value generated by the project of about €800 million in 1988 (Housel and Davidson, 1991).

In 1994, the expansion of the Minitel system in France started to decline. There was a decline, first, in the total number of Minitel-compatible terminals, and second and more importantly, in calls to the Kiosques. Furthermore, the Internet started catching up with the Minitel. Following considerable growth in the number of Minitels in France, which continued until 1985, the annual growth rate began to fall and, although Minitels were being replaced by newer models, from 1990 it continued to decline at an even faster rate. However, it would appear that from 1990 to 1994, this stagnation in the number of Minitels was compensated by the growth in the number of Minitel emulation boards, which enable a PC to access the Minitel.

A Final Appraisal

As successful as the widespread acceptance of the Minitel was, it effectively set a new technological standard that was not open to competitors. This locked in a technology that failed to keep up with other technological developments such as packet-switching protocols (e.g. TCP/IP) and protocols that are broadly interoperable across a wide variety of communication service providers with other network providers. Consequently, the system and some of the services it supports may now be at an economic disadvantage *vis-à-vis* other network systems not based on proprietary technology.

One lesson that may be drawn from this is that *de facto* standards set by market acceptance may be superior to *de jure* standards set by the government or private entities. Although the Internet protocol, TCP/IP, was, like

the Minitel, formally developed as a cooperative effort between government and industry, it was a non-proprietary, open system. Thus the lesson
to be drawn does not involve how standards are set. Rather, the question
is whether standards will be open to use by competitors. To achieve widespread adoption and interoperability, systems must be truly open.

More generally, if we are to remember that Minitel was only a part of
a large-scale programme devoted to telecommunications, we could draw
some interesting lessons from this experience. Its launch took place in a
context in which France suffered very poor telephone infrastructures and
full employment was threatened by the first oil shock. The rationale of
the programme was twofold. On the one hand, France was eager to modernize its technologies and productive capacity, while on the other hand,
countercyclical public spending and support to full employment were
present. To reach this goal, a typically Colbertist organization was built.
Under the supervision of a *grand corps* (telecom engineers) organized in
the DGT, a mobilization of the relevant stakeholders (including a public
research centre and industrialists) was realized. While the programme was
proposed as early as 1968, it was actually launched in 1974 – President
Giscard was the only statesman whose ideological background was linked
to French economic liberalism. Two important issues have to be kept in
mind:

1. the choice of digital time-division switching instead of the US ana-
    logue space-division switching,[7] which ensured French industrialists a
    technological lead;
2. the central part played by DGT, which monitored its suppliers
    through the R&D realized by the CNET research centres and/or by
    R&D contracts, and fostered industrial organization and competi-
    tion.

Large French firms, such as Matra, Alcatel and Sagem, which were to
be important industrial players in the telecoms fields, received the initial
impetus and benefit of these programmes to develop and reach an efficient
size. The DGT itself was to become France Telecom in 1988, an autono-
mous provider of a public service, and, eventually, one of the world's
leading telecommunications carriers, with over 118.6 million customers as
of 31 March 2004, and its performance supports comparisons with other
historical counterparts. The results in terms of well-qualified jobs, domestic work charge, spatial development (Brittany) are certainly important
achievements.

For Minitel itself, the most recent report 1999 from the Cour des
Comptes, which was always very sceptical if not hostile to the procedures

of this *LSP*, confirms the economic success of the programme for public service.

Nevertheless, some drawbacks must be mentioned:

- costs have not been well evaluated in the commutation transformation;
- in a situation of monopoly, the administration uses the price of telecoms without taking into account the demand side, whereas the monopoly rent financed different programmes and became an alternative to taxes;
- at the dawn of globalization, DGT and later France Télécom were unable to imagine the development of videotex to the right level and made Minitel so French that it was difficult to expand abroad so that, eventually, it was surpassed by the more international scope of the Internet.

AIRBUS IN COMPETITION TODAY[8]

If we are to analyse the factors that have made Airbus a success for the firm and an example of large European transnational projects (in contrast to Concorde, high-definition TV etc.), neither a thorough cost–benefit analysis nor a definite welfare evaluation for Europe or the world is really possible. The purpose here is to identify some determinants of success for very large international projects.

The European aircraft producer Airbus was established in 1970 as the 'GIE Airbus Industrie' consortium of the French Aérospatiale and the German Messerschmidt–Bölkow–Blohm (MBB) companies, each holding an initial stake of 50 per cent. The consortium was enlarged in 1971 by the Spanish Construcciones Aeronauticas SA (CASA) company and in 1979 by British Aerospace (BAe). Since then and until 2000 the French and the German shares amounted to 38 per cent each, the British share 20 per cent and the Spanish share 4 per cent. In 2000, the European Aeronautic, Defence and Space Company (EADS) was created by merging Aérospatiale Matra SA of France, Daimler Chrysler Aerospace AG of Germany and CASA of Spain. Airbus SAS (a simplified joint stock company incorporated under French law) was formed as a joint venture of EADS (with an 80 per cent stake) and BAE Systems (with 20 per cent). It employs some 57000 people of over 80 nationalities. Design and production sites are grouped into four wholly owned subsidiaries: Airbus France, Airbus Deutschland, Airbus España and Airbus UK. The two assembly plants of Airbus are in Toulouse and in Hamburg.

With a turnover in 2006 around €26 billion, more than 8019 aircraft ordered by international customers, 1184 aircraft orders for 2007 and a total of 4938 deliveries, Airbus is a world leader in the civil air transport marketplace and represents approximatively 45 per cent market share and more than 51 per cent of all outstanding orders.

However, this success is mitigated today as there is an uncertain future for the very large A380 aircraft and fierce competition between the future A350 and Boeing's 787 Dreamliner.

According to Airbus's 2006–25 global market forecast, more than 70 per cent of all aircraft delivered in the next 20 years will be single-aisle types with seating for 100–220 passengers (successful A320 category), representing more than 15 300 aircraft or 42 per cent by value of all passenger aircraft deliveries.

The mid-market twin-aisle passenger aircraft requirement will continue to grow strongly, with an estimated 5300 new airliners in this category being delivered in the next two decades. This would account for about 42 per cent of the total value of all passenger aircraft delivered. The A310 (that was never a good seller) and the future A350 are in this segment.

In the very large aircraft sector, Airbus anticipates a demand for 1660 aircraft (20 per cent of total sales value). In addition, there would be a demand for some 400 freighters sized in this very large aircraft category. But this forecast is strongly questioned and Boeing forecasts a much smaller figure. The issue therefore is whether Airbus will break even with the A380.

So the future of Airbus's commercial position against Boeing depends on its wide-body jets. Its position in this market segment is worrying. Both plane makers aim at fuel economy and eco-friendliness, and boast one-piece composite fuselage sections. The much-vaunted use of composite materials, which account for almost half of the Dreamliner's structure, may make the plane lighter, more fuel-efficient and quieter, but it is also untried technology. This is the first time a wide body has been made out of composite barrels. Boeing's 787 Dreamliner aircraft (250-passenger capacity) represents a serious challenge to Airbus. Launched over two and a half years ago, this long-range, middle-market jet has secured over 450 orders from some of the world's most prestigious carriers. Airbus's position in this high-profit-margin market is not nearly as auspicious. Airbus has launched the A350 as its response to the 787 but it won't take to the skies until 2013, while Boeing's 787 Dreamliner orders will begin being delivered in 2010.

After a year of delivery delays and withdrawn orders, Airbus must restore its customers' confidence and, although the 2007 new orders are impressive, they mostly come from loyal buyers, not new customers.

As a consequence of the duopoly situation, fierce competition has developed between Airbus and Boeing. An outgrowth of this competition was the mutual accusations of unfair practices, in particular through government subsidization. Both sides have claimed a decision from the World Trade Organization, where the cases are still pending.

Aerospace Industry Facts

Civil aircraft manufacturing is a business characterized by special features that must be considered when analysing the Airbus case:

- The aerospace industry is faced with high development costs, hence the question of funding and when to reach the break-even point or 'neutral point' arises.
- Aircraft is a complex product: in an average plane, there are over 4 million parts, most of them of a 'high-tech' nature.
- Contracts with suppliers usually extend over long time spans, as a plane is in operation for 10 to 30 years and large quantities are produced (many types of aircraft sell over 500 units).
- The number of significant suppliers is rather small, and they may well deliver to either one of the major competitors.
- Production activities depend on cyclical demand conditions that cause long-term funding problems.

Airbus Competitive Advantages

We first review the Airbus competitive advantages (1) in the management of the supply chain and mastering the costs, and (2) in innovation. Data and examples presented chiefly relate to the Toulouse area, which houses the largest of the Airbus production facilities, with more than 10000 employees. The Toulouse area is characterized by a number of factors that contribute to form a cluster-like production environment: the nearness of production facilitates material exchanges, and knowledge communication allows firms to work together. For instance, over a quarter of the engineers permanently working at the Airbus Research Department are on the payroll of suppliers/subcontractors. This allows them to play a substantial role in the decision-making process for the product design. As they know exactly their firm's competencies, they can transmit the information to Airbus and insist on the development of convergent technical choices there and/or conversely can encourage their firm to develop convergent competencies. Other relevant elements that contributed to the evolving cluster of producers and subcontractors in the aerospace industry concern state aid and regional support for investments in the physical infrastructure. Recent local examples are the development of the 220-hectare Aeroconstellation site of the A380 assembly line, the enlargement of roads between Langon (Bordeaux) and Toulouse to make way for the large parts of fuselage transported by trucks, and local airport development. Of similar importance have been the educational and training resources in Toulouse (two examples: 75 per cent of the French aerospace engineers are trained in local schools; public research is specialized in the aerospace field: CERT, ONERA, CEAT, LAAS, CNES and CNRS laboratories, just to mention a few, employ 6430 researchers).

Competitive advantage in the management of the supply chain and mastering the costs

Parts and goods bought outside the organization make up approximately 70 to 75 per cent of the cost of planes. Airbus has traditionally given suppliers the responsibility for sub-assembly and complete systems rather than individual parts that require in-house assembly. Suppliers are empowered with great responsibility and transparency, and are therefore required to establish and maintain full trust with regard to all stages of the production planning process. A notable sign that purchasing is considered of utmost strategic importance as a source of competitiveness is the permanent efforts to restructure these functions. There are over 1200 procurement personnel in Airbus today, in multinational teams. One way to increase the efficiency of purchasing has been to work with cross-functional teams in which the many trades, cultures and nationalities involved in research, development and manufacturing of planes could express their different points of view and contribute to optimal choices. The functional experts retain their identification with their functional area and report the experience acquired to their functional colleagues, ensuring diffusion of broader knowledge in the organization. At the end of the 1980s, most Airbus subcontracting was due to in-house capacity shortages, and subcontractors were considered mere underlings. The beginning of the 1990s saw the implementation of EDI (electronic data interchange) and the development of a hierarchical organization of suppliers, integration of first-tier and major suppliers in EDI Greenloop (1992), and rationalization with the effect of reducing the number of major suppliers from 700 (1993) to fewer 130. Greenloop was much more than a circle of suppliers exchanging electronic data about orders and invoices. It was a community sharing information about activity levels, education, training, organization, the first steps of supplier development still at work today. Airbus keeps close commercial relationships with over 1500 main suppliers all over the world. Even if Boeing and Airbus share many a supplier for rather similar intermediate products, different ways of handling the relationship may result in significant cost differences.

Airbus uses the concept of 'ownership cost', which considers purchases not only on the basis of price, but on all aspects of the acquisition, including quality, supplier risk, integration into the supply chain and total impact throughout the economic life of an aircraft. Airbus has systematically sought improvements in the operation of the supply chain through standardization, reduction of unnecessary customization, innovative financing, lead-time reduction and risk sharing. The design of contracts plays an essential part in the attempt to strike the right balance between long-term relationship and the consequent lack of competition. Lean manufacturing is the motto, which at Airbus is understood to contribute to sustainable competitiveness over a longer period. When orders for new planes decline during a business cycle, Airbus attempts to keep up the activities of suppliers, sharing with them the consequences of declining orders, and the less dependent suppliers see their orders cut over-proportionately. This strategy seemed to have paid off during the long slump of the years 1991–95, when Airbus gained market shares from Boeing, by keeping employed its skilled workforce and suppliers, ready to face recovery in demand. Labour productivity seems to be favourable in Europe. In terms of deliveries in 2003, Airbus data show an 8 per cent higher output than Boeing using 18 per cent less human resources (Deloitte, 2004). But relative workforce costs, as all other costs, depend on the value of the euro versus the US dollar.

Power 8 aims at the reduction of the Airbus supply cost base. It will also contribute to the reshaping and consolidation of the supply base and building of a network of strong risk-sharing partners to tier 1 suppliers, while streamlining the logistics organization (from 80 to eight logistic centres).

Competitive advantages in innovation

The product breakdown in major modules and systems and repartition over the different French, German, British and Spanish plants is central as it retains internally the core competencies with respect to design and development, and production activities of critical airframe components. Boeing is following quite a different strategy for the 787, outsourcing more and more of its work, even detailed design and engineering. Airbus, by contrast, only outsources what it does not consider to be a core competency. 'Core business' activities include overall aircraft and cabin architecture, systems integration, as well as the design, assembly, installation, equipping, customization and testing of major and complex components or manufacturing of new technology parts.

With respect to product innovation, Airbus has a long record of technological 'firsts', e.g. fly-by-wire, an electronically managed flight control system. One of the main Airbus innovations and therefore a competitive advantage in design is 'commonality'. In Airbus terms, 'commonality' means a set of common characteristics across several types of aircraft which permit cost-saving standardization of aircraft handling. Commonality is a unique feature of Airbus's new generation of jetliners, developed on the basis of the fly-by-wire system in the late 1980s. As a result, ten aircraft models, ranging from the small A318 through to the largest A380, feature very similar flight decks and handling characteristics. In many cases, such as the entire single-aisle A320 family, the aircraft share the same pilot-type rating, which enables pilots to fly any of them with a single licence endorsement. The benefits of commonality for operators include a much shorter training time for pilots when transitioning from one Airbus fly-by-wire type to another; and it offers schedule planners a high level of flexibility as aircraft of different mission capabilities, such as the A320 and the A330, can be operated and maintained by the same teams as a single aircraft fleet. Offering airlines increased cost-efficiency, it has become one of the keys to Airbus's success.

In design, commonality allows a much shorter time for engineers to transition from one type to another. Airbus can invest in an improved process, test it on one product and then apply it immediately to the family and thereby amortize its costs. Commonality also leads to significant savings through streamlined maintenance procedures and reduced spare parts holdings, with common parts accounting for as much as 95 per cent within the single-aisle family, for example.

Airbus Disadvantages

Managing production across the four partner countries

Although production of components is dispersed over the four partner countries, Airbus has remained a relatively integrated company, mastering the supply of critical airframe components. To be successful, this decomposition of work between different business units must ensure that all components and subsystems interface exactly, so that final assembly can be reduced to just joining the components. Overall assembly in the aircraft industry represents about 20 per cent of production time. With the sub-assembly system by sites adopted by Airbus (wings in the UK, rear fuselage in Germany, central fuselage in Pays de Loire, etc.), final assembly is reduced to 4 per cent of the total time. But the pieces of the jigsaw have to fit accurately. Mutual understanding and unified methods are of utmost importance. Since 2000, Airbus has been busy unifying the different cultures and experiences of the national entities, with some success.

This is the main (alleged at least) cause of the A380 delays. Besides production organizational issues, there is a more worrying concern affecting corporate restructuring – the persistent dispute about leadership between the Germans and French – and beyond the 'unanimous approval' of Power 8 restructuration, claiming 'Airbus will introduce a fully integrated and transnational organisation to support the implementation of Power 8 and the establishment of the new business model' (Airbus, 2007), some conflicts may remain unresolved (see Uterwedde, 2004).

Design and engineering

Airbus has strong intellectual R&D assets and skills but sometimes gets carried away with developing inventive and new technically complex solutions, sometimes regardless of cost. This may be due to engineering staff who are more technique-oriented than market-oriented. 'The core objective [of Power 8] is to make Airbus more efficient and competitive, so as to produce the most advanced and profitable products, and *to serve its customers better in the future*' (ibid.; our emphasis). Other objectives are to reduce cycle time of new aircraft development from 7.5 to 6 years (Boeing develops faster: 5 years) and to improve productivity in engineering activity by 15 per cent. Commonality is also a source of vulnerability: an integrated product line makes major changes very costly and so may handicap innovation.

Financial terms

Airbus has invested billions in the A380 programme, delays have pumped cash. Power 8 will allow Airbus to devote its resources to core activities and eliminate inefficiencies within its current structure. The programme aims at a full industrial integration of Airbus by establishing a new industrial organization with transnational Centres of Excellence replacing the existing national structures. A large part of the cost savings will be achieved through reducing the total Airbus overhead workforce (including temporary and on-site supplier workforce) by 10 000. For the competitive position of Airbus *vis-à-vis* Boeing, exchange rates are of course of particular importance ('We cannot continue to produce at our current Euro costs and sell at Boeing's dollar prices'). It should be borne in mind, however, that many major components come from outside Europe (e.g. engines from the USA). On an average, US parts total 40 per cent of the cost of an Airbus aircraft.

Airbus aims to introduce a fully integrated and transnational organization to support the establishment of the new business model. But this may mean outsourcing work from European plants to competitive subcontractors. Suppliers fear that Airbus, in the cost-saving process, may delocate part of its procurement. This would modify the boundaries of the 'extended enterprise' as it has been organized up to now, and probably means a change of organizational model. It may be that the difficulties (as real as they have been) caused by A380 delays and French/German differences have been alleged to facilitate and influence the change of model.

Both experiences have fuelled the debates over French industrial decline and its possible remedies.

RENEWAL OF FRENCH INDUSTRIAL POLICY

The French Doctrine on Industry and Industrial Policy

The place of industry in the French economy has been a matter of consistent public concern during the last half-century. J. Fourastié, who played a part in the modernization of the French economy, stressed the importance of productivity and technical progress in economic growth. With an approach similar to that of Colin Clark or Simon Kuznets, he showed that technical progress very quickly enhanced productivity in agriculture and industry, whereas the evolution was very slow in services (Figure 11.1). He consequently forecasted

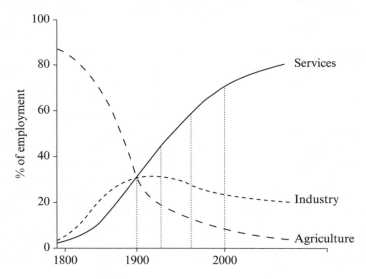

Source: Fourastié ([1949] 1979), p. 148.

Figure 11.1   Employment distribution over time along the three-sector hypothesis

a dramatic evolution of employment, with an overwhelming importance of services. In addition, he advocated a reduction of work time in order to avoid mass employment as a consequence of technical progress.

This link between technical progress, employment and social structure remained an important feature in the debates on industrial policy and, more generally, on economic policy. The large-scale programmes could be replaced in this framework. As France engaged in European construction, it seemed important to keep French industry alive *vis-à-vis* the other industrialized countries, even if everybody knew that technical progress would reduce employment in these sectors. Unfortunately, at the beginning of the 1980s, the more representative sectors of the traditional industries (textiles, coal and metallurgy) were in very bad shape. The first government appointed by President Mitterrand after his victory in 1981 undertook a large programme of nationalization of the banking and credit sectors, and the indebted industrial firms in basic sectors. As a consequence of the scattered ownership of French firms, the state through these nationalizations inherited control of a large part of the French economy. As Élie Cohen (2003) put it:

> Until the great U-turn of 1983, the French state controlled prices, investment flows, monetary rates, exchange rates, a big chunk of the financial system, even the Bank of France, as well as regulatory bodies like COB or Conseil de la Concurrence. Through credit controls, specialized credit channels and interest rates subsidies, the state essentially substituted itself for financial markets in the allocation of resources to the various sectors of the economy. In this type of capitalism, there is a market for goods and services (although it may be subject to state intervention), but hardly for factors of production.

But very quickly, the complete centralization of the economy reached its limits as the constraints put into place by foreign exchanges were felt. The French government had to acknowledge that it could no longer implement the voluntarist industrial policy it had dreamed about. Indeed, during the 1970s, the French government had to safeguard some sectors (*créneaux*) in which French firms seemed to enjoy serious advantages. After 1981, as the industrial policy did not achieve the expected results, a more ambitious programme was developed, designed to develop and sustain vertically integrated sectors chosen for their supposed strategic importance. But it was difficult to delimit these sectors inspired by the economic theory of production *à la* Leontief, and it was impossible to adjust specific measures for them, whereas the failures of quantitative planism were obvious everywhere. Consequently, the government was compelled to restructure the nationalized sector, reshaping firms according to their competencies and rejecting the conglomerate tendency which had prevailed previously.

Table 11.4   State shareholding

	1999	2000	2001	2002	2003
31 December 2003	1657	1594	1569	1623	1447
First rank	99	97	96	100	99
Employment (%)	5.30	5.10	5.10	5	5.20
First rank/ total public sector (%)	86.50	84.70	84.60	85	84.30

Source: www.minefi.gouv.fr/vie. publique-Etat actionnaire.

The following government, sustained by right or left majorities, chose to privatize as many firms as possible in order to reduce the debt and limit the scope of industrial policy.

By the end of 2003, the public sector was reduced to a mere 5 per cent of the total employment (see Table 11.4) and, while the number of firms partially owned by the state is impressive, the French legal structure of firms, which gives a legal existence to many subsidiaries, must be taken into account. Indeed, hundreds of firms account for nearly 85 per cent of the public sector, which would be reduced in the coming months with the privatization of EDF and GDF. This reduced state shareholding does not mean that it is better managed and it could be helpful to implement a strategic industrial policy. On the contrary, the management of the remaining firms is fiercely criticized in a recent report of the parliament, which denounces 'the omnipresence of the government allied to a lack of strategy'.

Moreover, if the large industrial French firms behave pretty well compared to other global firms, their anchorage in the French economy is more and more dubious. For example, if we look at the top ten French firms included in the 500 largest industrial firms, we can see that no more than 40 per cent of their employment is in France (Table 11.5).

It is interesting to note that, among these ten firms, two are public utilities (for the time being state owned), whereas Renault was nationalized after 1945 and four others were nationalized in 1981 (five if we include Aventis, which was formed from the Rhône-Poulenc pharma branch). Eventually, only the two family-owned firms (Michelin and Peugeot) were never part of the public sector.

The national character of French firms is also questionable if we consider the shareholders. Simultaneously, the ownership of the largest French firms has been increasingly scattered around the world, so that a great number of former national champions have more than 50 per cent of their stock held by foreigners. For the 40 largest listed firms (the CAC 40 index), the official estimate by the Banque de France is 44.4 per cent.

Table 11.5   Globalization of large French firms

	Sales	Profit	Employees (world)	Employees (France)
Among the first hundred				
Total Fina Elf	102 540	5 941	121 469	53 440
PSA Peugeot Citroën	54 436	1 690	198 600	123 700
Électricité de France	48 359	481	171 995	115 100
Suez	46 090	−863	198 750	60 550
Between 101 and 200				
Renault	36 336	1 956	132 351	78 000
Saint-Gobain	30 274	1 040	172 357	49 980
Between 201 and 500				
Alstom	21 351	−1 381	109 671	26 320
Aventis	20 622	2 091	78 099	Not available
Alcatel	16 547	4 745	75 940	25 000
Michelin	15 645	614	126 285	26 305

Source: SESSI (2003–04).

Among these 40 top firms (they change from one year to another), 33 were continuously in the CAC40, and for these 33 the official reports state that over half have the majority of their stock in foreign hands.[9] Élie Cohen (2003) concludes a review of these figures, asserting:

> Wide-ranging liberalization and large scale privatization against the background of weak institutional investors have thus brought French-style capitalism to an abrupt end. Resistance to liberalization does exist, but concentrates on issues relating to competition in the transport, postal service and electricity sectors, which are dominated by state-owned monopolies.

The conclusion seems too far-fetched: French corporate governance is still characterized by very dense networking of boards and special careers of directors (which include for 41 among the first 100 an initial stage in a Ministry).

On the contrary, it seems that industrial policy is becoming more and more crucial in economic and political debates. During the last few years, the discussion was fuelled by a growing concern about European integration (the Maastricht Treaty) and globalization. As Maclean et al. (2001, p. 313) put it:

> In few countries has the phenomenon of globalisation been as widely debated as in France. Here, globalisation has become synonymous with danger, first

and foremost in the form of délocalisations, where multinational companies move production sites to low-wage countries in pursuit of lower costs and greater flexibility in hiring and firing, a problem highlighted in 1993 when Jean Arthuis warned of the inevitability of companies chasing hourly labour rates of one French franc (0.15€) in China as against FF50 (7.63€) at home. When the electrical goods manufacturer Hoover moved production sites from Lyon to Dundee in 1994, there was a predictable public outcry in France; but Hoover was an American multinational, with no instinctive loyalty to Lyon or France. The problem is that some French companies have followed suit. In 1996, for example, SGS Thomson decamped to Casablanca in Morocco, enticed by a low-cost, high-quality, flexible and French-speaking workforce.

This concern, which is repeatedly found not only among politicians but also among industrialists,[10] is very far from the mild appreciation we find in European circles, as the following statement proves:

> Such a process of industrial change [relative deindustrialization] is, generally, beneficial if it is properly anticipated, identified and fostered. It should not be confused with absolute deindustrialisation. The latter, a much more alarming prospect, would imply industrial decline characterised by consecutive reductions in employment, output and productivity growth, and exacerbated by a trade deficit. By definition, such a development can only be identified with certainty over the long term. The available data do not allow us to conclude that such a phenomenon exists in the EU. (European Commission, 2004)

Some milestones of the controversies can be identified: in 2000, Prime Minister L. Jospin was supplied with a report by E. Cohen and J. Lorenzi (Cohen and Lorenzi, 2000). The authors examined the theoretical foundations as well as the feasibility of industrial policies in Europe. Their lengthy discussion did not lead to clear-cut conclusions, but they suggested that European industrial policies would be difficult to implement, as the Maastricht Treaty enhanced the part played by competition policy so that any industrial policy is at risk of being discarded as conflicting with the latter. Moreover, as strategic trade needs a powerful government able to conceive and implement strategies, it does not fit the European situation. Consequently they were reduced to defending the case for innovation and R&D policies. Three years later, Bernard Carayon, a member of the parliament, was to present a report to the new prime minister, J.P. Raffarin, devoted to economic intelligence. Bernard Carayon presented himself as a guardian of the French national interests and judged the situation to be very dangerous: he maintained that strategic thinking if anything is embryonic and unrelated to politicians' decisions. He gave as proof the yearly list of key technologies, which is elaborated by the Ministry of Industry without any consultation with other ministries and without any followup. Consequently, the French government never defined the strategic industries from the point of view of sovereignty, employment, influence, or the pertinent technologies or the 'swot' (strengths, weaknesses, opportunities and threats) of the French firms operating in these industries.

In this poor situation, Carayon found only two positive initiatives: the first stems from the Ministry of Defence, which has begun to think about technological dependence with the Ministry of Finance and Industry.[11] The second is due to the agency for the diffusion of technological information, which has undertaken to scrutinize the sovereignty technologies and the risk of French *décrochage* (decoupling).

Eventually, Carayon presented a proactive industrial policy under the cover of economic intelligence. He concluded that, first, a survey should be undertaken, defining priorities for research and innovation and key sectors, and eliciting partnerships. For him, such an exercise in the past allowed the realization of Concorde, the TGV, Ariane and Airbus.[12]

> If it is possible to identify technological items as symbolic, the prospective about the development of strategic domains, as information technology, environment, or nanotechnologies should demonstrate where are not only the dependencies, but also the opportunities, possibly not so symbolic but equally important. (Carayon, 2003, p. 25)

Bernard Carayon's plea for interventionism is that of a deputy belonging to the majority, but we can find echoes in a statement by the Socialist Party. Introducing the proceedings of a conference devoted to industrial policies, Henry Weber writes (2004, p. 5):

> We need an economic and political voluntarism with policies and tools which don't exist now but which are absolutely necessary. The liberalist ideology is today totally contradictory with our needs and that could be understood also by people belonging to the right wing. Just note how the right could have realised voluntarist policies after Liberation, in the 1950s and 1960s, when the authoritarian modernizers (Gaullist or Bonapartist) ruled.
>
> Among the defensive policies, we can mention the improvement of our stronghold especially for France: aeronautics, transport, telecoms, industries based on computer science including nuclear energy. Vis-à-vis this last issue, we should not follow the German example and reduce our investment. We have also to consider 'deterrent' policies as proposed by John Kerry. We should retaliate against firms which delocate; this retaliation should be used to subsidise the employees and the industrial areas which suffer from these delocalizations.

Among the positive policies, Weber offers 'the creation of "ecosystem" between research, universities, and production Silicon Valley or Route 108 "à la française"'. It is striking to note the convergence of Weber's and Blanc's (2004) recommendations.

This convergence confirms the judgement of Russell Carlberg (2001, p. 135):

> The French elite believes in the French government's competence to shape markets, and to direct both the economy and even society as a whole, in broad terms. The French invention of the Minitel, a computer terminal connected to the telephone that was widely available in French homes in the 1980s, is a prime example of the *dirigiste* tradition at work.

Nevertheless, we find advocates of the two arguments: one is very sceptical about the feasibility of industrial policies in the age of European integration and globalization, and the second argues, against the 'end of history', that defence and sovereignty still matter.[13] Both strands nevertheless join in stressing the importance of forecasting and R&D.[14] This convergence is also to be found *vis-à-vis* the location of industries.

PROPOSALS BY LEVET AND DATAR

Two reports are worth mentioning here. The first is devoted to subsidies and the part they could play in industrial policy. With Levet (2003), the idea of public subsidies remains obscure, even for the relevant stakeholders. This situation is not unrelated to the lack of knowledge about subsidizing at different levels – local, regional, national. 'There is no exhaustive census.' The opacity begins with the budget documents related to subsides by the government, whereas there is no specific rule at the regional level. Consequently, the regional authorities are left without any idea of the consequences of subsidizing on regional development.

This situation is a matter of concern, as the amount of subsidizing is far from negligible (around €15 billion, 1 per cent of French GDP for the sole national subsidies, which are regulated by European rules). The survey published by Levet does not show a large difference between aid to industrial firms in France and in Europe (2003, p. 15) (see Table 11.6).

Consequently, Levet proposes two improvements for the French system. First, he suggests gathering yearly reliable data to be discussed in parliament, an improvement of the budget documents, an enhancement of the resources devoted to this topic at the regional level in order to evaluate the efficiency of subsidies, and benchmarking in order to diffuse the best practices.

Then he deals with the goals of the system and joins the proponents of strategic thinking:

- forecasting exercises on the productive system, the needs of firms, and subsidizing procedures, taking into account the varieties of businesses;

Table 11.6   Comparing subsidies in France and Europe (2001)

		France	EU-15
% GDP	1992–94	1.2	1.5
	1995–97	1.46	1.43
	1997–99	1.38	1.16
Euros/employee	1992–94	641	631
	1995–97	790	656
	1997–99	772	563
% budget	1992–94	–	–
	1995–97	2.64	2.82
	1997–99	2.55	2.4

- defining national and European perspectives and priorities for the great markets of the future;
- improving the attractiveness of territories.

Interestingly enough, Levet introduces a distinction between competencies and technologies, and suggests that technological policies should be reoriented from their traditional track, focused on technologies, towards a positive attitude *vis-à-vis* learning and the development of competencies. He suggests that the environment should be made friendlier for cooperation and cooperative projects, and stresses that SMEs (small and medium-sized enterprises) should be more involved in networks and cooperation. Consequently, subsidizing should be reoriented from an individual basis to a project logic, which will mean groups of firms aiming to cooperate.

DATAR (2004) has elaborated some of these suggestions in its last report on 'competition poles'. It suggests implementing a regional European policy devoted to industry and territories. This policy should aim at the realization of networking for competencies and innovation throughout Europe, beginning with France, Germany and Austria, where some interest is to be found. This should enable an enhancement of the concentration of means necessary to cope with the great US poles. DATAR quotes the first transborder projects developed in biotechnology (Medicon Valley between Denmark and Sweden, BioValley Alsace–Fribourg–Basel). The ambition of such policies should be to realize, at the cluster level, the same achievements as were attained for great global firms such as EADS,[15] creating true industrial partnerships between European firms and networks.

DATAR also shares the nostalgia of large-scale programmes and suggests that networking could be organized around such programmes, as was the case around Ariane. Such programmes could be launched not only in high-tech industries but also in more traditional ones, where there are specific European competencies and know-how (luxury goods, cars, clothing).

As Cohen (2003) put it:

> One can argue that the French, who had tacitly accepted the liberal program of 1983 for Europe's sake, on the condition that this Europe would deliver growth and safeguard welfare benefits, are on the way to concluding that the objectives have not been met.

Cohen illustrates through two cases the disappointment of the French *vis-à-vis* the Commission policy, especially the EDF and the Alstom cases. In the EDF case, it is well known that the French are very sceptical about the liberalization when they look at the US electricity market and compare its performance to that of the French monopoly. Moreover, generations of French economists have theorized the welfare conditions required in order to regulate optimally such a natural monopoly and are consequently very reluctant to replace an efficient organizational design with a liberal model that has not proved its superiority theoretically or practically.[16] Anyway, the complaints of the Commission against EDF, where the shortcomings of the liberalization process are obvious, cannot but nurture euro-scepticism. The same holds in the Alstom case. Alstom is basically the collateral victim of the strategy carried out by Serge Tchuruk (CEO of Alcatel) in order to replace the shareholder-value model of corporate governance. Eventually, the strategy followed by its shareholders weakened a company dealing with capital goods and put it near bankruptcy. The initial rejection of the rescue plan for Alstom by the Commission and later the concession sought in exchange illustrate the potential conflict between a rigid competition policy and an impotent policy.

In both cases, it is easy to understand why the nostalgia of French industrial policy could flourish. It pervades all reports and debates, including the Beffa Report (Beffa, 2005). As it is the more ambitious and has begun to be implemented, it is worth presenting it at length.

THE IMPOSSIBLE REVIVAL OF INDUSTRIAL POLICY

After President Chirac's re-election, industrial policy had returned to the forefront of political debate. Two reports have recently dealt with the issue. Drafted at the behest of President Chirac by Jean-Louis Beffa, chair of the Saint-Gobain glass company, and assisted by a task force of 12 people, including industrialists, experts and two trade unionists, the Beffa

Report appeared as a plea for industry. The authors note first that 'even if the weight of the services sector is increasing in the economy, a solid industrial sector is necessary to the equilibrium of the balance of trade and the growth of the economy' (ibid.). Furthermore, the opposition between services and industry has become almost meaningless. The development of the service sector is essentially driven by services to firms, which are growing far faster than services to individuals (Brière et al., 2004). Therefore the development of industry and of services must be conceived as complementary and not as substitutable. More generally, industry remains one of the principal motors of economic activity in terms of value added and employment. It exercises a powerful tractor effect on the entire spectrum of economic activities, most notably through intermediary consumption: for €1 of production, industry consumes €0.7 of intermediary products, as opposed to €0.4 consumed by the services sector (DATAR, 2004). Thus the importance of industry must be evaluated using a boundary matching the scale of its real economic impact, in which case industry represents nearly 41 per cent of French GDP and 51 per cent of market labour in 1998 (Postel-Vinay, 2000). Furthermore, industry possesses a strong structuring influence on the diffusion of technological innovation throughout the entire economy, and, by extension, on its global productivity.

In any case, as noted in the report, France remains a big industrial power. It is the fifth industrial country in the world in terms of exports (DATAR, 2004). Over the past 30 years, French industry has experienced a phase of profound transformation accompanied by an efficient modernization of its productive capability. Industrial employment, strictly defined, is certainly in decline, but the share of manufacturing industry in the volume of total added value over the last 20 years is stable (Fontagné, 2004).

The good shape of French industrial capacity is based on a certain number of sectors in which France possesses first-rate firms and where it preserves its strengths and assets better, in relative terms, than do its neighbours. These sectors are, for example, the chemical and steel industries, the cement and glass industries, the aeronautic and automotive sectors, and the railway infrastructure sector. French industry has been able to rely on high-quality research in numerous fields. In a recent study undertaken by OST and DATAR (2004), within Europe, France holds second place in technological fields in terms of scientific publications and registered patents. In Europe, France lies in third place in scientific fields, after Germany and the UK (Czarnitzki et al., 2002). Research potential in France is of exceptional quality and is grounded, in the main, on public research: in 2001, 50 per cent of research personnel worked in the public sector. It is essential both to strengthen the public research capacity, and to construct or improve the interfaces between public research and the industrial universe. These summary recommendations, however, do not suffice to remedy the apathy affecting industrial dynamics in France: a precise statement of the causes of its attenuation is necessary.

Signs of Decoupling in the Industrial Domain

The diagnosis of the decline of industry in France was widely shared (Fontagné, 2004; Académie des Technologies, 2004; Levet, 2003). The global lag of French industry is perceptible in employment creation, in the contribution to value added, and in the contribution to the balance of trade. This tendency does not result from a move towards services, because, in this area, France lags relative to other industrial countries. It is also the result of weak French R&D effort, which appears related, not to any lack within the individual sectors of the economy, but to an overly strong specialization in low-technology industries.

Therefore, in order for France's technological position to improve, its industrial specialization must evolve.

The contribution of French industry to the creation of value added in the manufacturing industries of OECD countries exhibits a decreasing trend. To appreciate the evolution of French industry, one needs to compare the value added of French industry with that of other developed countries. A clear declining trend is observable, which highlights the deficit or lag in the value addition of French industry relative to the industries of other large OECD countries. The weighting of the USA in the total added value of manufacturing industries has increased: it rose from 33.5 per cent in 1991 to 37.2 per cent in 1999.

The worrying figures in respect of French industry are the result of an industrial specialization that is strong in 'old economic' sectors and weak in new or high-technology industries. French industry possesses global leaders in a large number of sectors, for example primary materials, cement and glass, aeronautics, agri-food, luxury goods and railway infrastructure. However, French industry has few leading firms at the international level in the high-technology sectors that represent strong growth markets. There are some happy exceptions, but these do not suffice to reverse the global trend.

Using the grouping into four categories designed by the OECD, several studies show that France's specialization is weak in high technologies. France's mediocre industrial specialization in high technology is also observable at the level of employment. The level of French employment in high-technology industries is weak relative to other OECD countries. According to Fontagné (2004), the contribution to the trade balance, also called the 'revealed comparative advantage', of these high-technology industries exhibits a break in the recent trend, which means that France has experienced a clear erosion of the competitiveness of its high-technology products on the international plane.

The sources of inadequacy in industrial specialization and the difficulties of high technology in France are located in its weak R&D effort. Comparison by industry type of the universe of countries shows that, for a given type, France does not undertake less R&D than other countries. Its weak innovation effort is related to its industrial specialization in low-technology industries, which, structurally, engage in little R&D. Therefore the goal should be a reorientation of France's industrial specialization in order to improve its position.

Diversity of Structures of Public Support for Industrial Innovation

As Levet (2003) notes, it is difficult to present public aid to firms in all dimensions. Nevertheless, the data of the office of statistics on research enable one to distinguish six structures of public aid for industrial innovation. These structures finance 14 per cent of research undertaken by firms in 2002, or €3.1 billion. This figure underestimates public aid because the aid coming from local authorities, such as the repayment of local corporate tax, is not taken into account.

In 2002, the breakdown of public aid for these six types of financing was as follows:

1. Defence financing represents €1.5 billion. It has decreased since the beginning of the 1990s and tends to be focused on purely military applications developed by a limited number of very large firms, with little fall-out in the civil area.[17]
2. Large-scale programmes of the 1970s and 1980s continue to receive financial support, in aeronautics, space research, nuclear energy and the micro and nano-electronics sectors, which constitute the continuation of the old components plan, with subsidies (€575 million) and *ad hoc* aid (repayable advances for Airbus, regional aid for the Crolles project). The only recent programme involves micro and nano-electronics. The Ministry of the Interior supports this field particularly. Thus the DIGITP devotes 80 per cent of its €158 million of R&D aid to the nano-technology sector. Sixty million euros are devoted to the Crolles II project, and €60 million to different thematic networks (clusters) such as MEDEA+, PIDEA+ and EURIMUS II, which form part of the Eureka project.
3. Ministerial actions (€200 million), outside large-scale programmes, are of greater benefit to SMEs and are characterized by geographic

and sectoral sprinklings: the distribution of the budgets for the principal initiatives across a multitude of fields (16 RRIT, 19 CNRT, Eureka etc.), the dispersion of skill centres (7 oncology poles, 8 genetics poles).

4.   The funding of ANVAR is directed towards SMEs and works according to a subsidy system (€80 million) and repayable advances (€190 million, with a 60 per cent repayment rate).

5.   Research tax credits (€489 million) favour the SMEs in the main, because of its ceiling. It is due to reach €1 billion in 2008.

6.   Finally, France benefited from approximately 10 per cent of the financing for the 5th European R&D Framework Programme (ER&DFP), of which 45 per cent went to firms (€122 million in the framework of the 5th ER&DFP). European funding of firms is again on the rise following an increase in the budget of the ER&DFP (+17 per cent from the 5th to the 6th ER&DFP) and an increasing focus on development (integrated projects) and SMEs.

Public aid related to defence and historic large-scale programmes – the aeronautics, space research, nuclear energy, and the nano-electronics sectors – represents nearly 80 per cent of all public aid devoted to innovation. This is not to suggest that these sectors receive too much aid, but to point out the weakness of resources available in other sectors.

The weakness of the contribution to the R&D funding of firms employing more than 50 salaried workers is damaging to any industrial redeployment towards high-technology industries. In order for internationally competitive firms creating a high number of jobs in the high-technology sectors to emerge, large firms must be constructed capable of confronting international competition. This can happen either through the transformation of medium-sized firms into larger firms, or through a process of technological differentiation within large firms. France's industrial policy does not promote these two processes, since it finances little R&D in firms having more than 500 salaried employees outside the historic large-scale programmes. The rise to power of research tax credits, which were capped at €8 million per firm per year in 2004, has the mechanical effect of increasing aid relative to small firms.

There is a common belief that small firms, grouped in clusters facilitating the circulation of information, lead efforts at innovation. This notion is certainly not without foundation. However, the role of large firms at the hub of these clusters is often important. Agrawal and Cockburn (2002) adduce some evidence tending to confirm, in the USA, the role of large firms within these clusters, where small high-technology firms are particularly active in R&D. These hub firms are large enterprises with significant volumes of R&D spending. The authors advance the idea that the role of these firms is to create the externalities of demand from which small firms profit. Another explanation is that large firms play the role of coordinator and guarantor, underwriting the specific investments of small firms.

The signs of industrial decoupling in France coincide with a policy marked by a dispersion of means outside defence and the 'historic' large-scale programmes. This policy is in stark contrast to that of countries pursuing targeted industrial policies in new technologies of high industrial potential. Therefore a more focused industrial policy seems necessary.

The Case of State Interventionism According to the Beffa Proposal

Whether in the domains of nano-electronics, biotechnology, or fuel cells, for example, there exists significant potential for innovations of large magnitude possessing every chance of changing future living conditions and creating important technological externalities (Kopp, 2003–04). These new perspectives necessitate high levels of investment and gestation periods of several years. It is difficult for firms to invest against horizons that are so remote. Numerous macroeconomic risks exist, involving exchange rates, financial fluctuations, and energy price fluctuations, against which firms can only partially insure. Consequently, the state has a role to play in promoting industrial investment in projects that contain significant technological risk. This role is all the more vital when projects are risky, the amounts of investment significant, and the technological externalities great.

The state alone can contribute to the financing of large risky projects: it should play the role of guarantor and incentive provider, diversifying the risks across different projects. There may be different modes of state support for long-term innovative projects. Either the state itself undertakes the launch of new projects, as was the case in the historic large-scale programmes, or it can contribute to reducing the risks to which firms are exposed. It can provide stable and incentivizing finance or enable the existence of a public market. The modalities of insurance and incentivization of private agents can therefore take different forms, the goal being to increase strongly investments in projects capable of changing France's technological specialization.

The second function of the mobilizing programmes is to enable the coordination of private and public agents around a production project. This function should allow the resolution of certain defects of coordination among industrialists, subcontractors and public research agents.

Research agents, both public and private, agree on the necessity of transfer of knowledge and methods of fundamental research into applied or purpose-oriented domains; this transfer helps the valorization of the public research effort (États Généraux de la Recherche, 2005). One function of the mobilizing programmes might be to contribute to ensuring coordination between knowledge and processes elaborated within public research and private resources around a production project. This role of coordination and mobilization is very important in other countries, notably in Japan. It is necessary in France, where interfaces are rare and interactions are not always successful. It is important to emphasize that the coordination of public and private research must happen without subordinating one to the other, and in full respect of their respective logics.

- The first justification relates to problems of coordination and information dissemination among all the agents that bedevil the industrial analysis of technologies. The fine-tuning of large-scale industrial innovation requires the coordination of the skills of different firms and different public research agents. An institutional framework is most often necessary in order to guarantee this coordination.
- The second justification is the existence of externalities, that is, global outcomes related to research into new technologies that are not taken into account by firms. R&D efforts have secondary outcomes that are difficult to forecast, but that increase the productivity of numerous industries.
- The third justification is the existence of very heavy initial costs, long-term horizon, and high risks of R&D activities.

Financial markets are not efficient in enabling the financing of such projects under these conditions, because the risks cannot be hedged over the time horizons involved.

These justifications are well known in economic analysis (Rodrik, 2004; European Commission, 2004c; Krugman and Obstfeld, 1995, ch. 12). Moreover, the argument about the inefficiency of financial markets for long-term financing is widely developed in the economic literature (Allen and Gale, 1997 and more generally Shleifer, 2000 and Boyer et al., 2004). The three effects highlighted above induce underinvestment in long-term projects with high R&D intensity. The state must therefore play an incentivizing role.

Answering the Criticisms of Targeted Industrial Policies

The nature of the information available to determine priority sectors and type of intervention lies at the heart of the first series of arguments against industrial policy. The amounts in play are very significant and it can be difficult to affirm that the industrial gain is greater than the opportunity cost of the public money invested, that is, the social use of that sum employed for other purposes.

The state may misjudge its actions and support projects that the evolution of demand does not validate, whereas firms would never have thrown themselves into such investments. The state might just as well give unfounded industrial advantages to certain firms, causing a damaging distortion of competition, by creating monopolies of uncertain industrial dynamism.

A second line of critical arguments against targeted industrial policies points to the political agenda of the state. The state may, for purely political ends, support for too long an industrial project whose failure appears manifest, as the case of Bull shows. Alternatively, it may stop the financing of socially profitable but as yet incomplete projects, for short-term budgetary reasons. Even if the state can envisage useful economically targeted interventions, state management of industrial projects can lessen their interest.

These criticisms of state sectoral intervention do not invalidate industrial policy in general. They are often used in order to justify the putting in place of 'horizontal' aid benefiting certain agents, for example, small firms or innovative firms, without determining the focus of industries. Theoretical arguments and international comparisons show that focused aid is not always wrong, either theoretically or empirically: heavily industrialized countries do not exclusively favour horizontal aid. In the case of a country the size of France, where economies of scale are weaker than in Japan and *a fortiori* in the USA, resource autarchy and relative independence from foreign investment bolster the choice of an industrial policy oriented towards innovation. Criticisms of targeted aid often simply summarize the lessons of failed industrial policies in different countries. Therefore the proposals of this report will take these points of view into account when determining the modes of intervention of an effective industrial policy that is consistent with these objectives.

Re-evaluating the Concept of Large-scale Industrial Programmes

In order to contribute to the strengthening of industrial specialization in France, industrial policy must once again take on its functions of incentivization and coordination. These functions had as their previous frameworks the large-scale industrial programmes launched by the state. The historic large-scale programmes cannot be conceived today as they were in the past. They were founded on the coordination of public research, public firm and public contract (order placement). This coordination made possible the convergence of long-term industrial and research efforts around a 'demonstration model', destined for a public client (Minitel, Concorde, TGV etc.). The regulatory and competitive context of that epoch allowed a policy of constituting national champions, born out of political will alone.

The coordination of these three types of agents has been called into question by the internationalization of the economy and the desire of public authorities to position themselves within a properly European space. Exposure to the EU orients the set of recommendations of the present report. On the side of public research, it is imperative to respect the autonomy required for the elaboration of knowledge and to create at the same time an interface capable of mobilizing the knowledge necessary for private research. On the side of public demand, an important role can be played in supporting industrial projects. Once there is consent about the technological initiative, the use of public demand should be clearly defined and economically justified. High-definition analogue television, launched at the European level, is an example of the failure of a public technological choice due to non-existent demand.

Finally, the creation of public firms within the framework of large-scale programmes cannot be entertained, simply because of the increase in international competition. The presence of immediate competitors renders this strategy dangerous and costly.

Reliance on adequate industrial potential appears necessary in order to confront current competition and to define appropriate industrial orientations.

The success of the nano-electronics sector illustrates the correct conduct of a targeted industrial policy. The concentration of resources and geography enabled large firms to associate; these large firms invigorated the local industrial fabric, stimulating a network of SMEs. The public effort made improvement of French industrial specialization possible by creating a global pole in nano-technologies. Thus a firm like STMicroelectronics went from fifteenth place (in terms of market share) in 1987 to global fourth position in 2002. The sites of Crolles and Rousset now attract foreign firms (Motorola and Atmel, in particular, have decided to locate significant R&D departments).

CHARACTERISTICS OF A NEW TARGETED INDUSTRIAL POLICY

The economic analyses presented in preceding sections and the assessment of the historic large-scale programmes lead to the proposal of a programme in the sense of an action plan for a targeted industrial policy.

1. The goal of the programme is to result in a product that both involves private agents and corresponds to expected demand in a European or global market. The choices of the sectors and products should be grounded in an economic justification, in a way that makes clear evaluation of the programme's results possible.
2. The programme should combine R&D efforts leading to a demonstration model in which a strong technical component is present; it must bring solutions to major scientific and technological questions.
3. The programme should bring together private agents right from the elaboration of projects in order to use fully any existing industrial capacities. An industrial project should be based, from the start, on an evaluation of the potential in manpower, production capacities and the research of public and private agents. The potential knock-on effects of the conclusion of the programme, at both the French and global levels, must be taken into consideration when the choices are made.
4. The programme should be organized on a medium to long-term horizon, in order to play the role of guarantor fully. The scale of projects must enable a sustainable contribution to the improvement of French industrial specialization.

The implementation of the programme was foreseen to take the following form:

1. Public aid would guarantee partial funding of R&D expenditure; involvement of potential clients in the programme would make it possible to find a substitute for public order placement in an incipient market when the latter cannot be envisaged.
2. The mobilization and close coordination of different agents should contribute to the clear definition of expected needs: industrialists capable of carrying out projects, partner firms, scientists able to evaluate the technical issues, users, potential clients and representatives of public organizations.
3. Regular evaluation according to criteria defined at the beginning of the project should allow transparent management of public money, making simultaneously possible continuity of funding for projects that are evaluated positively, and the cessation, in agreement with the partners, of programmes that are not reaching their objectives.

These principles differ from those of the 'large-scale programmes', as they were thought of previously. If the importance of public order placement is not actually excluded, it does not play a central role: the existence of potential clients associated with the development of the programme can enable the definition of a private substitute for public demand. The European dimension was, moreover, constitutive of these mobilizing projects. Thus the expression 'mobilizing programmes for industrial innovation' (MPIIs) was used to refer to targeted industrial projects conforming to these principles.

Implemented at the beginning of 2005, the Industrial Innovation Agency (IIA) was supposed to complement the industrial policy tools and to implement the MPIIs. Unfortunately they were soon suspected by the European Commission to be at variance with fair competition whereas it was impossible to organize partnerships with other European countries.[18] After two years of efforts to revive the *Grands programmes*, President Sarkozy's government throw in the sponge.

CONCLUSION

During the ten last years, beginning with the Arthuis Report, concern with respect to industrial policy has grown in France. Probably it is tied with a French tradition that stresses the government role in economic matters and includes specific institutions (*grands corps*) and corporate governance. It is also nurtured by a growing feeling that France sacrifices important assets (social compromise including an interventionist part devoted to the state) against deceptive liberal dreams. The different attempts to reform French industrial policy take into account the European framework and recommend European partnerships at the European level between firms, research centres and policies. It is worth noting also that a great deal of attention is paid to procedures. The traditional command system in which the government decides through its *grands corps* is clearly discarded in favour of incentive frameworks (contracts instead of control).

NOTES

1. This expression was coined by Jean Fourastié by analogy with the Trois Glorieuses – three revolutionary days in 1830 that witnessed the overthrow of Charles X, a reactionary king, and his replacement by a more 'bourgeois' and democratic one, Louis Philippe.
2. On Monnet's strong link to the USA see Monnet (1976), Chapters 14 and 16 and on the role of his many elite American supporters, see Clifford P. Hackett's 'Introduction' (Hackett, 1995).
3. According to other sources, the rate of growth of the French economy in the period between 1952 and 1973 was only slightly lower than those of Germany and Italy. GNP grew at a yearly rate of 5.2 per cent as opposed to 5.6 and 5.7 per cent in Italy and France respectively.

4. French planism is very close to its Dutch counterpart, the first director of which was Jan Tinbergen. The Central Planning Bureau (CPB, Netherlands Bureau for Economic Policy Analysis) is legally based on the 'Law of 21 April 1947'. It stipulates in Article 3: 'The task of the Central Planning Bureau is to accomplish all duties regarding the preparation of a Central Economic Plan that will be settled on a regular basis by the Government, as well as publishing advice on general questions that may occur in regard to the realisation of the Plan. The Central Economic Plan is a well-balanced composition of estimates and procedures with respect to the Dutch Economy. The Central Economic Plan contains among other things sets of figures regarding the future growth of production in the broadest sense, regarding the future height and development of price levels, national income and its components, regarding spending that income and regarding all further variables of importance for good coordination of the economic, social, and financial policy.' *Source*: http://www.cpb.nl/eng/general/org/cpb/wettelijke_basis.html.

5. See the section on the Airbus case below.

6. Minitel is the name used for the terminal linked to the Télétel network. The system, in operation since October 1982, extends to all of France and has expanded as the number of terminals and available services increased. It consists of the switched telephone network RTC (Réseau Téléphonique Commuté) for users and the Transpac network for servers, along with videotex access points to link the two. The Télétel access service acts as the interface between Minitels and the servers in three ways, namely as a telecommunications device, for interaction between users and servers, and as a means of determining the method of payment. With the combination of these techniques, anyone who is connected to the network has access to data transmission, service providers and communication facilities. The Minitel is compatible with other techniques and technologies used in business, such as personal computers, office electronics and other telecommunications devices. It can be used by companies for sales or financial transactions, and as a promotion, telecommunications or information tool.

7. http://www-rocq.inria.fr/qui/Philippe.Deschamp/RETIF/20000922-tout.html#C provides us with a glossary for technical terms.

8. This section uses Airbus internal documents and communications: see the websites section in the References.

9. *Bulletin de la Banque de France*, No. 134, February 2005.

10. See Commission permanente de concertation pour l'industrie (CPCI), *L'industrie française en 2003–2004*.

11. The French doctrine considers that the existence of a competitive and efficient industry is a major asset for any defence policy. It is considered important, as France should have at its disposal an industry that can conceive, realize and maintain army equipment. Its strategic autonomy depends on the control of some key technologies. Besides, the defence industries are important for the national economy, with a turnover of €14 billion and 170 000 employees. But this asset concerns Europe too, as it is well understood that the defence industry can no longer be considered merely in the national framework. Considering the huge outlays made by the USA and the strength of US defence industries and firms, the only possibility for European states to choose their equipment is by the construction of a European defence industry. See appendix.

12. The same nostalgia is to be found in Grignon (2004): 'Your group encourages the European Union to facilitate the creation of champions in the field of industrial programmes, able to reinforce the Union pre-eminence where it enjoys comparative advantage. The goal is to come back to the framework which allowed for achievements like Ariane or Airbus. A political voluntarism with a midterm vision is necessary to launch grand programmes of industrial development in the sunrise economic sectors (biotech, computer, information technology, semi-conductors), as it was done twenty years ago. In order to go ahead determinedly in this way, despite the difficulties of an European union with 25 members, the French German axis could be a motor for such a renewed European industrial policy, which other states could join later. Therefore

the commission is pleased to note the mobilisation on the late May 13 exhibited by the President of the Republic and the Chancellor in order to give birth to the industrial champions Europe is expecting'.

13. Andrew Moravcsik (1998, p. 3), has convincingly argued that De Gaulle's policies were more linked to French economic interests than generally believed: 'De Gaulle's nuclear ambitions, his criticism of the United States, his policy toward the developing world, and his schemes for overcoming the East–West divide may well have been motivated by a visionary geopolitical ideology. His European policy, however, was motivated by the same goals shared by postwar democratic politicians everywhere: generations of elec-toral support and avoidance of disruptive strikes and protests through the promotion of economic welfare and, above all, appeasement of powerful sectoral producer groups.'

14. A. Etchegoyen, new Plan commissioner, wrote that 'State prospective does not mean any radical break in the history of Plan Commission. The future is the matter of Plan, consistently with Jean Monnet's vision'. This position is certainly at variance with the low commitment exhibited by Emmanuelle Maincent (2004), who reduced industrial policy to:
     ● the improvement of the regulatory framework;
     ● the harmonizing of European policies in order to cope with the competitiveness objective, whereas potential conflicts exist between the employment policies and productivity; between the environmental policy and the following constraints for firms; and between competition policy and the merger waves;
     ● take into account the sector specificity, even if the industrial policy is horizontal.

15. There is currently a team, including French and German industrialists, which examines the cooperation opportunities between firms of the two countries. Henrik Uterwedde (2004, p. 9) is only mildly optimistic about the results: 'If there is little to expect from industrial meccano between French and German firms as demonstrated by the Aventis Sanofi case or Alstom Siemens, the question of a real industrial Europe remains funda-mental. Fostering the merger movement between firms, improving the law framework in order to promote a European model of firms offer common fields to explore together. Therefore the Beffa–Cromme work team which has been charged to explore the pos-sibilities of co-operation between firms (from France and Germany) could be useful if it is not obsessed by a symbolic mammoth wedding.'

16. It is ironic to note that the welfare vindication of competitive markets is largely rooted in the Paretian French economist-engineers, whose heirs were to manage EDF and elaborate the second-best theory for imperfect markets. Marcel Boiteux, who gave his name to Ramsey–Boiteux pricing, complained about the privatization of EDF and defended the economic French model for electricity production and distribution (cf. Boiteux, 1997).

17. In the appendix we present the R&D and industrial policy implemented by the French defence ministry.

18. For example, the Quaero programme was supposed to provide an alternative to Google. But its implementation was very delayed and the divergences between the French and the Germans impeded its development, so the partnership was soon broken.

REFERENCES

Académie des Technologies, (2004), *Le système français de recherche et d'innovation*, June.
Agrawal, A. and I.M. Cockburn (2002), University research, industrial R&D and the anchor tenant hypothesis', NBER Working Paper 9212.
Airbus (2007), 'Power 8 prepares way for "New Airbus", press release, 28

February, available at: http://airbus.com/en/presscentre/pressreleases/press releases_items/07_02_28_Power8_Press_Conference_EN.html.

Alcouffe, A. (1999), 'Keynes and the French guardians of Say's Law before 1936', in L. Pasinetti and B. Schefold (eds), *The Impact of Keynes on Economics in the 20th Century*, Cheltenham, UK and Northampton, MA, Edward Elgar, pp. 53–72.

Allen, F. and D. Gale (1997), 'Financial markets, intermediaries and intertemporal smoothing', *Journal of Political Economy*, **105** (3), 523–46.

Beffa, J.-L. (2005), *Pour une nouvelle politique industrielle*, Paris: La Documentation française (Collection des rapports officiels).

Blanc, C. (2004), 'Pour un écosystème de la croissance', Report to the Prime Minister, May.

Boiteux, M. (1997), 'Concurrence et service public', *Sciences de la Société*, **42**, October, special issue edited by A. Alcouffe and M. Baslé, 9–10.

Boyer, R., M. Dehove and D. Plihon (2004), 'Les Crises financières', Report of the Conseil d'analyse économique, no. 50, Paris: La Documentation française.

Brière, L., Y. Duclos, C. Héricher and I. Raton (2004), 'Les services marchands en 2003', *Insee première*, no. 972, June.

Carayon, B. (2003), 'Intelligence économique, compétitivité et cohésion sociale', Report to the Prime Minister, June.

Carlberg, R. (2001), 'The persistence of the dirigiste model: wireless spectrum allocation in Europe, à la francaise', *Federal Communications Law Journal*, **1**, December, 129–64.

Chambolle, T. and F. Méaux (2004), 'Rapport nouvelles technologies de l'énergie', Paris: Ministère délégué à la recherche et aux nouvelles technologies, La Documentation française.

Chandler, A.D. Jr. (1990), *Scale and Scope: The Dynamics of Industrial Capitalism*, Cambridge, MA: Belknap Press (with the assistance of T. Hikino).

Cheminade, J. (2008), 'F.D.R. and Jean Monnet: the battle against British imperial methods can be won', available at: http://medaloffreedom.com/JeanMonnet. htm, accessed 9 December.

Clough, S.B. (1939), *France: A History of National Economics, 1789–1939*, New York and Chicago: Scribner.

Cohen, É. (1992), *Le colbertisme 'high-tech': économie des Telecom et du grand projet*, Paris: Hachette.

Cohen, É. (2003), 'French capitalism: new clevages', paper presented at the Conference 'The New Cleavages in France', jointly organized by Princeton University and Institut d'Etudes Politiques de Paris, Paris, 9–12 October.

Cohen, É., and J. Lorenzi (2000), *Politiques industrielles pour l'Europe*, Paris: La Documentation française.

Czarnitzki, D., T. Doherr, A. Fier, G. Licht and C. Rammer (2002) 'Öffentliche Förderung der Forschungs- und Innovationsaktivitäten von Unternehmen in Deutschland', Berlin: ZEW.

DATAR (2004), La France, puissance industrielle: une nouvelle politique industrielle par les territoires, réseaux d'entreprises, vallées technologiques, pôles de compétitivité', February, Paris: La Documentation française.

Deloitte Consulting LLP (2004), Report.

Dormois, J.P., (1999), 'France: the idiosyncrasies of volontarisme', in J. Foreman-Peck and G. Federico (eds), *European Industrial Policy: The Twentieth-Century Experience*, Oxford and New York: Oxford University Press, pp. 58–97.

Etats Généraux de la recherche (2005), 'Rapport final', Taillandier.

Etchegoyen, A. (n.d.), 'Regards prospectifs sur l'État stratège', http://www.plan.gouv.fr.

European Commission (2004), 'European Competitiveness Report 2004', Commission staff working document, SEC (2004)1397, Brussels.

Fontagné, L. (2004), 'Désindustrialisation-Délocalisations', Report of the CAE, October.

Fourastié, J. ([1949] 1979), *Le grand espoir du XXe siècle* (*The Great Hope of the Twentieth Century*), Paris: Gallimard.

Grignon, F. (2004), 'Rapport d'information fait au nom de la commission des Affaires économiques et du Plan par le groupe de travail sur la délocalisation des industries de main-d'oeuvre', No. 374, Sénat, Session ordinaire de 2003–04, Annexe au procès-verbal de la séance du 23 juin 2004, available at: http://www.senat.fr/rap/r03_374/r-03-3740.html.

Hackett, C.P. (1995), 'Introduction', in Clifford P. Hackett (ed.), *Monnet and the Americans: The Father of a United Europe and his U.S. Supporters*, Washington, DC: Jean Monnet Council, pp. 1–4.

Hall, P.A. (1986), *Governing the Economy: The Politics of State Intervention in Britain and France*, New York: Oxford University Press.

Housel, T.J. and W.H Davidson (1991), 'The development of information services in France: the case of Public Videotex', *International Journal of Information Management*, **11** (1), 35–54.

Kopp, P. (2003–04), 'Le secteur français des biotechnologies', France Biotech.

Krugman, P. and D. Obstfeld (1995), *International Economics: Theory and Policy*, 3rd edn, New York: Harper HarperCollins College Publishers.

Levet, J.L. (ed.) (2003), 'Les aides publiques aux entreprises: une gouvernance, une stratégie', Report, Paris: La Documentation française.

Lévy-Leboyer, M. (1991), 'La grande entreprise: un modèle français', in Maurice Lévy-Leboyer and Jean-Claude Casanova (eds), *Entre l'Etat et le marché: l'économie française des années 1880 à nos jours*, Collection Bibliothèque des Sciences Humaines, Paris: Editions Gallimard.

Maclean, M., C. Harvey and J. Press (2001), 'Elites, ownership and the internationalisation of French business', *Modern and Contemporary France*, **9** (3), 313–25.

Maddison, A. (2001), *The World Economy: A Millennial Perspective*, Paris: OECD.

Maincent, E. (2004), 'Quelle politique industrielle dans une Europe élargie?', Direction générale Entreprises, Commission européenne 10e séminaire annuel de la direction des statistiques d'entreprises de l'INSEE, 2 December.

Massé, P. (1965), *Le Plan ou L'anti-hasard*, Paris: Gallimard.

Meisel, N. (2004), *Governance Culture and Development: A Different Perspective on Corporate Governance*, e-book, Paris: OECD.

Monick, E. (1970), *Pour Mémoire*, Paris: Firmin-Didot.

Monnet, J. (1976), *Mémoires*, Paris: Fayard.

Moravcsik, A. (1998), 'De Gaulle and European integration: historical revision and social science theory', Center for European Studies Working Paper Series Program for the Study of Germany and Europe, Working Paper Series 8.5, May.

Nora, S. and A. Minc (1978), 'L'informatisation de la société', Paris: La Documentation française.

Postel-Vinay, G. (2000), 'La politique industrielle en France: évolutions et perspectives', in: *Politique industrielle*, Report of the CAE no. 26, Paris : La Documentation française.

Rincé, J.-Y. (1990), *Le Minitel*, Paris: Puf.

Rodrik, D. (2004), 'On the Efficacy of reforms: policy tinkering, institutional change and entrepreneurship', CEPR Working Paper, available at: http://www.cepr.org/pubs/new-dps/dplist.asp?dpno=4399.

Service des études et des statistiques industrielles (SESSI) (2003–04), 'L'industrie en quelques chiffres'.

Shleifer, A. (2000), *Inefficient Markets: An Introduction to Behavioural Finance*, Oxford: Oxford University Press.

Uterwedde, H. (2004), 'Une politique industrielle franco-allemande', *Regards sur l'économie allemande*, **69**, 6–10.

Weber, H. (2004), 'Introduction', in *Pour une mouvelle politique industrielle*, Actes du colloque, Paris-Assemblée nationale, 28 April, Paris: Parti Socialiste.

Websites

Airbus internal documents and communications

http://www.airbus.com/about/history
http://www.airbus.com/media/innovation
http://www.airbus.com/en/presscentre/pressreleases/
  pressreleases_items/07_02_28_Power8_Press_Conference_EN.html
GIFAS (Groupement des Industries Aéronautiques et Spatiales), http://www.gifas.asso.fr/

APPENDIX

Technologies, Industry and Research: The Law on Military Programming, 2003–08

Research and technology: increased effort to improve preparation for the future

A total of €3815 million will be devoted to research and purchasing technologies under the law on programming. This is a significant increase. The technological level of France's arms, associated with a reasonable army, is a factor that will allow France to keep its rank on the international scene and to remain an important player when military intervention is on the agenda. The part that France could play in a coalition will depend on these key factors. The planned effort will keep available technologies necessary for national independence (including deterrent power) and to develop others in a cooperative framework (especially in a European framework). Therefore France will remain acquainted with the latest technologies, but also, in accordance with the international agreements and the principles of its foreign policy, will be able to implement these technologies in relation to the weapons produced by the industry, alone or in cooperation. The 2003/8 period will be characterized by the beginning of several production programmes and consequently less intensity in industrial development. The effort devoted to research and technology will allow the industry to maintain its competencies in several fields and to prepare the conception and development of a future range of defence equipment.

A model of technological capacities

In order to improve its programming in research and technology, the Ministry has carried out a survey of technologies essential to military need until 2015 and the type of weapons required over 30 years. This survey has determined the technologies that will be necessary until 2015 and the financial resources required. Classed in 40 technological key groups, they are associated to different classes of weapons. In order to reduce uncertainty and risk, the development of prototypes has been planned, which will determine the launching of future programmes. This kind of programming should permit some research cooperation with European partners, which could facilitate cooperation in production.

Source: Projet de loi relatif à la programmation militaire pour les années 2003 à 2008, Assemblée nationale, onzième legislature, no. 3255, enregistré 31 juillet, available at: http://www.assemblee-nationale.fr/11/pdf/projets/pl3255.pdf.

Index